D0272736

From Conflict Resolution
to Reconciliation

From Conflict Resolution to Reconciliation

Edited by

YAACOV BAR-SIMAN-TOV

OXFORD
UNIVERSITY PRESS

2004

OXFORD
UNIVERSITY PRESS

Oxford   New York
Auckland   Bangkok   Buenos Aires   Cape Town   Chennai
Dar es Salaam   Delhi   Hong Kong   Istanbul   Karachi   Kolkata
Kuala Lumpur   Madrid   Melbourne   Mexico City   Mumbai   Nairobi
São Paulo   Shanghai   Taipei   Tokyo   Toronto

Published by Oxford University Press, Inc.
198 Madison Avenue, New York, New York 10016

www.oup.com

Oxford is a registered trademark of Oxford University Press

Library of Congress Cataloging-in-Publication Data

From conflict resolution to reconciliation / edited by Yaacov
Bar-Siman-Tov.
        p. cm.
Includes bibliographical references and index.
    ISBN 0-19-516643-4
    1. Conflict management.   2.   Pacific settlement of international
disputes.   3.   Reconciliation.   I.   Bar-Siman-Tov, Yaacov, 1946—
HM1126 .F76 2003
303.6'9—dc21   2003000753

9 8 7 6 5 4 3 2 1

Printed in the United States of America
on acid-free paper

Acknowledgments

I would first like to thank the ten contributors to this volume for participating in a truly intellectual effort to understand the theory, conditions, and prospects for reconciliation within and between nations. Owing to their spirit of collaboration and voluntarism, this complex research project became reality.

I would like also to express my gratitude to the Konrad Adenauer Foundation in Israel and especially to its director, Dr. h. c. Johannes Gerster, for recognizing the significance of the project on reconciliation and for his willingness to support generously both the international workshop and the international conference.

I am grateful to the Leonard Davis Institute staff—Laura Wharton, Sharon Yakin-Mazar, and Amira Weiss—for contributing their efforts in arranging the workshop and conference, as well as in bringing this manuscript to a book format. I would like also to thank David Hornik for editing and improving the manuscript. Finally, I would like to dedicate this book to the children of the Middle East, with the hope they will experience stable peace and reconciliation.

Contents

Contributors

Yehudith Auerbach is a senior lecturer in the Department of Political Science and head of the Division of Journalism and Communication Studies of Bar Ilan University. She has published articles about such Israeli leaders as David Ben-Gurion, Moshe Dayan, and Yigal Allon and their part in peacemaking, as well as most recently, about Yitzhak Rabin (with Charles Greenbaum, "Assessing Leader Credibility During a Peace Process: Rabin's Private Polls," *Journal of Peace Research*, 2000). Her current research interests are political leadership, reconciliation, and forgiveness processes.

David Bargal is professor at the Paul Baerwald School of Social Work of the Hebrew University of Jerusalem. He has published 80 articles in diverse professional journals and books, in addition to seven edited books and two books under his authorship, including *Living with Conflict: Encounters Between Jewish and Palestinian Youth*, with H. Bar (1995). He is currently involved in research on conflict management and reconciliation-transformation workshops for Arab and Jewish youth.

Dan Bar-On is professor of psychology in the Department of Behavioral Sciences at Ben-Gurion University. Together with Professor Sami Adwan from Bethlehem University he co-directs PRIME (Peace Research Institute in the Middle East). His book *Legacy of Silence: Encounters with Children of the Third Reich* has been translated and published in French, German, Japanese, and Hebrew; his two latest books are *The Indescribable and the Undiscussable* (1999) and *The Others Within Us: Changes in Israeli Collective Identity from a Psychosocial Perspective* (1999).

Yaacov Bar-Siman-Tov is Giancarlo Elia Valori Professor of International Relations at the Hebrew University of Jerusalem and director of the Leonard Davis Institute for International Relations and the Swiss Center for Conflict Research, Management, and Resolution. He is the author of many articles and five books, including *Israel and the Peace Process, 1977–1982: In Search of Legitimacy for Peace* (1994), and *The Shift from War to Peace: The Complexity of Decision-Making—The Israeli Case* (1996). His fields of expertise include conflict management, resolution, negotiations, and the Arab-Israeli conflict.

Daniel Bar-Tal is professor of psychology at the School of Education of Tel Aviv University and director of the Walter Lebach Institute for Jewish-Arab Coexistence Through Education. He also is coeditor of the *Palestine-Israel Journal*. He has authored and co-edited numerous books, the most recent of which are *How Children Understand War and Peace* (1999), *Shared Beliefs in a Society* (2000), and *Patriotism in Israel* (2003). In addition, he has published over 100 articles and chapters in major social and political psychological journals and books. His primary research interest is the psychological foundations of intractable conflicts and peacemaking.

Gemma Bennink currently works in Jakarta for UNICEF Indonesia, assisting in setting up projects for psychosocial support for children in emergencies and projects for building community resilience. She received a master's degree in social and intercultural psychology from the University of Utrecht in the Netherlands. Later she received an European master in humanitarian assistance at the University of Groningen in the Netherlands. While researching at the Tel Aviv University in Israel, she developed an interest in the psychological aspects of peace building and reconciliation.

Raymond Cohen is professor of international relations in the Department of International Relations at the Hebrew University of Jerusalem. Among his books are *Culture and Conflict in Egyptian-Israeli Relations: A Dialogue of the Deaf* (1990), *Negotiating Across Cultures* (1991 and 1997), and *Amarna Diplomacy: The Beginnings of International Relations* (with Ray Westbrook, 2000). He has written on diplomacy, intercultural communication, negotiation, and conflict resolution. Much of his work has been an attempt to understand the cultural and psychological dynamics underpinning the Arab-Israel conflict.

Tamar S. Hermann is a senior lecturer in the Political Science and Sociology Department of the Open University of Israel and director of the Tami Steinmetz Center for Peace Research at Tel Aviv University. Her most recent publications are "The Sour Taste of Success: The Israeli Peace Movement, 1967–1998" (in Gidron, Katz and Hasenfeld, eds., *Mobilizing for Peace—Conflict Resolution in Northern Ireland, Israel/Palestine, and South Africa*), and *Is the Israeli-Palestinian Conflict Solvable?* Her fields of interest are Israeli politics, extra-parliamentary politics and peace activism, as well as public opinion and foreign policymaking.

Herbert C. Kelman is Richard Clarke Cabot Research Professor of Social Ethics at Harvard University and director of the Program on International Conflict Analysis and Resolution (PICAR) at Harvard's Weatherhead Center for International Affairs. His books include *International Behavior: A Social-Psychological Analysis* and (with V. Lee Hamilton) *Crimes of Obedience: Toward a Social Psychology of Authority and Responsibility*. He has applied interactive problem solving—an unofficial, third-party approach to the resolution of international and ethnic conflicts—to the Israeli-Palestinian conflict for more than three decades.

Louis Kriesberg is Maxwell Professor Emeritus of Social Conflict Studies, Professor Emeritus of Sociology, and founding director of the Program on the Analysis and Resolution of Conflicts at Syracuse University. His most recent books include *Constructive Conflicts: From Escalation to Resolution* (first edition 1998, second edition 2003), and *International Conflict Resolution: The U.S.-USSR and Middle East Cases* (1992), as well as numerous articles and book chapters related to conflict resolution and peace studies. He is currently doing comparative research on reconciliation and changing accommodations between ethnic, religious, and other communal groups.

Ifat Maoz is an assistant professor in the Department of Communications and Journalism at the Hebrew University of Jerusalem and an evaluator of reconciliation-aimed encounters between groups in conflict. Her main research interests are patterns of communication and interaction between groups in conflict, and the effects of bias mechanisms on attitudes toward conflict and its resolution.

Marc Howard Ross is William R. Kenan, Jr. Professor of Political Science at Bryn Mawr College. He has written or edited six books, including *The Culture of Conflict* and *The Management of Conflict*, and has published over 50 articles.

His current work has two major themes: (1) social science theories of conflict and their implications for conflict management and (2) the role of culture in the escalation and de-escalation of ethnic conflict.

Emmanuel Sivan is professor of history at the Hebrew University of Jerusalem. His major books include *Radical Islam, Mythes Politiques Arabes, War and Remembrance in the Twentieth Century*, and, most recently, *Strong Religion* (2000). His specialties are Islamic Fundamentalism, political myths, and decolonization.

From Conflict Resolution
to Reconciliation

Introduction: Why Reconciliation?

Yaacov Bar-Siman-Tov

This book on reconciliation is the result of a multidisciplinary research project initiated by the Leonard Davis Institute for International Relations and the Swiss Center for Conflict Research, Management, and Resolution, both at the Hebrew University of Jerusalem. The project came in the wake of meetings, international workshops, and a conference convened in Jerusalem in 2000 and 2001. The basic assumption of the research project is that the subject of reconciliation is a multidisciplinary one and therefore requires the participation of researchers from a variety of fields. The research group included Israeli and American scholars from the following disciplines: history, international relations, philosophy, psychology, sociology, and political science.

The idea of focusing on reconciliation emerged naturally from our previous project on stable peace. That project, which was conducted only by scholars of international relations and was published as an edited volume (Kacowicz et al., 2000), explored the conditions for maintaining and consolidating peace. Although it ascribed considerable importance to structural, functional, and instrumental conditions for stable peace, it attributed less importance and paid only minimal attention to cognitive and emotional conditions. However, the conclusion of my own chapter in the volume, "Israel-Egypt Peace: Stable Peace?" asserts that we should reconsider the role of reconciliation in stable peace: "Reconciliation is probably the most important condition for shifting the current peace toward stable peace. Only reconciliation can build mutual trust and provide mutual assurances for maintaining peace in [the Middle East]." Nevertheless, "Reconciliation is probably the most difficult condition because it asks for a deep cognitive change, a real change of beliefs, ideology, and emotions not only among the ruling elites but also among most if not all sectors of both societies [that is, Israel and Egypt]" (Bar-Siman-Tov, 2000: 237). The importance of this point encouraged me not only to consider a new research project on reconciliation, but also to conduct it on a multidisciplinary basis.

Although the concept of reconciliation has long been familiar to researchers and practitioners, only in the last decade has it emerged as a specific area of interest in peace studies. It evolved from the understanding that there is a need to study the conditions for stabilizing peace after the resolution of domestic or international conflicts. Both scholars and practitioners realize that although conflict resolution terminates a conflict, it does not necessarily stabilize the peace or prevent the emergence of a new conflict in the future, which may even lead to renewed violence.

When the sides still encounter severe difficulty in overcoming the built-up bitterness and grievances of a protracted conflict, and in altering their hostile perceptions and mutual fears, they may fail to stabilize peace relations. Reconciliation is therefore a crucial factor in stabilizing peace after the resolution of an international conflict and in transforming the relations between former enemies. Reconciliation, then, goes beyond conflict resolution and addresses the cognitive and emotional barriers to normalization and stabilization of peace relations.

In its simplest form, reconciliation means restoring friendship and harmony between the rival sides after conflict resolution, or transforming relations of hostility and resentment to friendly and harmonious ones (Ackerman, 1994; Kriesberg, 1998a; Phillips, 1998; Arthur, 1999; Gardner-Feldman, 1999; Kelman, 1999a; Bar-Tal, 2000b; Bar-Tal and Bennink, this volume). Most of the literature on reconciliation does not refer to international conflicts but rather to conflicts ranging from family to intercommunal and ethnic ones and civil wars. Reconciliation may take place within divided societies or within one country after interethnic, interracial, or interreligious conflicts, which tend to be protracted, zero-sum conflicts, involve extensive violence, cost many casualties, and accumulate animosity and hatred (Lederach, 1997; Phillips, 1998; Bar-Tal and Bennink, this volume). Reconciliation is not necessary for ending all international conflicts but probably only for conflicts that are protracted and zero-sum, and thus similar to internal conflicts and civil wars. The historical record shows that reconciliation proved necessary for stabilizing peace relations between Germany and France, Germany and Poland, and Germany and the Czech Republic; probably it will also be required in the Arab-Israeli conflict, particularly the Israeli-Palestinian conflict.

Various studies suggest different conditions that the sides need to fulfill so as to facilitate the reconciliation process during the post-peace agreement period, in which reconciliation is urgently required. Whereas the liberal approach in international relations emphasizes the need to accelerate the security, economic, and political cooperation between the sides, thereby enabling the peace to spill over from the ruling elites to all sectors of the population (Adler and Barnett, 1998a; Kacowicz, 1998; Kacowicz et al., 2000), the social psychological approach stresses the cognitive and emotional aspects of reconciliation (Bar-Tal and Bennink, Kelman, Kriesberg, all in this volume).

According to the social psychological approach, the reconciliation process should openly address painful questions of past conflict so as to build a foundation for normal peace relations. This may require unilateral or mutual willingness to apologize for previous transgressions, unilateral or mutual forgiveness, an offer of appropriate compensation, a mutual perception of a just peace agreement (that is, one that is responsive to the needs and fears of both sides), mutual satisfaction with the peace agreement and with the development of the relations, mutual acceptance and respect for each other's national identity, internalization of the peace values, and a willingness to open a new chapter in the relationship (Tavuchis, 1991; Scheff, 1994; Shriver, 1995, 1999; Kelman, 1999a and this volume; Bar-Tal, 2000b; Kriesberg, this volume; Bar-Tal and Bennink, this volume).

Since reconciliation is a mutual and consensual process, it cannot be imposed by one side or even by an external side (that is, a mediator). The process is likely to develop naturally and slowly, with direction or intervention by the leadership, who must be accountable for its role if the process is to succeed. Both sides' leaders should act simultaneously and jointly in encouraging the internalization of the peace relations and their spillover to all domains of life and all sectors of the society.

In the course of our meetings, workshops, and conference, we mainly explored the theoretical and methodological aspects of reconciliation. We acknowledged that reconciliation is a multidimensional phenomenon that combines different disciplines and approaches. It has different connotations, and there is no consensus as to its role in stabilizing peace and the required conditions for it. Our aim was, accordingly, to extend the theoretical and methodological knowledge on reconciliation.

In the course of the book, we pose the following questions:

1. What is the meaning and nature of reconciliation? What are its main characteristics? How can we differentiate reconciliation from stable peace? What are its major dimensions?

2. Why is reconciliation so difficult for former enemies? What kinds of conflict require reconciliation? What is the role of reconciliation in domestic and international conflicts, respectively?

3. What are the differences between reconciliation as an outcome and as a process? What are the necessary, sufficient, and favorable conditions for reconciliation? What methods and techniques should be used in a reconciliation process?

4. What are the structural and psychological barriers to reconciliation? How can they be overcome?

5. What can theoretical and empirical knowledge about reconciliation contribute to peace studies?

6. In terms of policy implications, what lessons can be drawn from our theoretical discussions for current domestic and regional conflicts?

The Framework

In chapter 1, "The Nature of Reconciliation as an Outcome and as a Process," Daniel Bar-Tal and Gemma H. Bennink define the conceptual parameters and research boundaries of the subject. Relying much on recently published work, they examine the nature of reconciliation both as an outcome of peacemaking and as a long process in which parties in a postconflict resolution stage build stable peace. Specifically, they first describe and analyze the characteristics of conflicts that are relevant to reconciliation, then discuss reconciliation as an outcome, then elaborate on the process of reconciliation, suggesting the necessary conditions and facilitating factors. Bar-Tal and Bennink then look at the different methods of reconciliation and the factors that affect the reconciliation process.

In the second chapter, "Reconciliation: Reflections on the Theoretical and Practical Utility of the Term," Tamar Hermann introduces the theoretical and practical limitations of *reconciliation* as a term. She first considers the theoretical limitations by examining the meaning of reconciliation, its level or unit of analysis, as well as its essence, purpose, and timing. She then discusses the shortcomings of reconciliation as a method for stabilizing peace. The rest of her chapter, as she puts it, "is meant to demonstrate the rather 'heretical' idea of the potential perils of context-insensitive reconciliation attempts, based on the Israeli-Palestinian case."

Yaacov Bar-Siman-Tov, in chapter 3, "Dialectics Between Stable Peace and Reconciliation," argues that stable peace can be established when the sides to a peace agreement are satisfied with the agreement, and after the underlying structural-institutional, cognitive, and emotional conditions of a protracted conflict have been transformed to the sides' mutual satisfaction via a process of learning and reconciliation. He suggests that a better understanding of the issue of maintaining and consolidating peace requires a combination of international relations theories and social psychology theories, or, in other words, a combination of theories of stable peace and of reconciliation. He introduces a conceptual framework that links the following clusters of conditions and demonstrates their interrelatedness: mutual satisfaction, structural-institutional, learning, and reconciliation.

In chapter 4, "Comparing Reconciliation Actions Within and Between Countries," Louis Kriesberg explores the multifaceted nature of reconciliation. He first considers alternative explanations for how reconciliation actions promote conflict transformation and improve relations between the former foes. He then differentiates among four kinds of reconciliation acts pertaining to truth, justice, regard, and security, and examines their impact on domestic and international conflicts based on society contexts, which differ according to four criteria: the degree of integration in the society, the extent of shared identity and culture, the boundedness of entities, and the multiplicity of parties and identities.

In chapter 5, "Reconciliation as Identity Change: A Social-Psychological Perspective," Herbert C. Kelman focuses on reconciliation in the context of an emerging or recently completed process of conflict resolution. He argues that reconciliation goes beyond conflict resolution in representing a change in each party's identity. This change poses a major dilemma for both sides in terms of the amount and kind of identity change that is required. Specifically, the chapter begins by discussing the relations among reconciliation, resolution, and settlement; it then presents reconciliation as embedded in identity change. The final section looks at how the sides in a conflict can reach the difficult point of revising their identity so as to accommodate the identity of the other.

In the sixth chapter, "Leadership and Reconciliation," David Bargal and Emmanuel Sivan discuss the role of national political leadership in reconciliation. They begin by presenting three historical cases of reconciliation, two international and one domestic: Germany-France, Germany-Israel, and Spain. They then elaborate a theoretical framework derived from the social psychological literature, which serves as the theoretical basis for discussing the historical cases. The theoretical framework consists of a mapping sentence that includes the facets (content areas and conceptual domains) composing the process in which political leadership contributes to reconciliation. This framework introduces the following variables and their interrelations: transformational leadership, bases of social power, nature of the conflict, activity measures, target audiences, extent of legitimacy, phases of change or stagnation, and outcome.

Yehudit Auerbach, in chapter 7, "The Role of Forgiveness in Reconciliation," examines forgiveness as one of the methods or required conditions for reconciliation. She first discusses the differences between conflict resolution and forgiveness and their relation to reconciliation. She then considers the nature and components of forgiveness, and its role in advancing peace between nations. Next she explores the following necessary conditions for forgiveness to contribute to the reconciliation process: the religious-cultural context, national interests promoted through reconciliation and forgiveness, power asymmetry, status of leaders, authenticity of the request, time, and supportive international environment. Finally, Auerbach examines the case of Israel-West Germany as a special case that enabled interstate normalization without reconciliation.

In chapter 8, "Apology and Reconciliation in International Relations," Raymond Cohen focuses on the phenomenon of apology in international relations. He suggests a useful framework that is based on a comparative cross-cultural perspective grounded in the dispute-processing philosophy of the law and society movement. This approach can be applied to human behavior in many societies with different beliefs and customs. Cohen first introduces the dispute-processing approach, then discusses the role of apology in the disputing process across different cultures. He concludes by differentiating among three concepts of diplomatic apology: apology as moral restitution, apology for acknowledged injury, and nonapology.

In chapter 9, "Ritual and the Politics of Reconciliation," Marc Howard Ross explores the concept of reconciliation by raising the following questions: "(1) What is meant by reconciliation and who is to be reconciled? (2) Is reconciliation necessary for peacemaking and/or peace building? (3) If reconciliation makes a difference, what does it look like? How do we know it when we see it? (4) What are the techniques and mechanisms by which reconciliation works?" After answering these questions, he then considers a feature of reconciliation that is particularly important when large groups are concerned, namely, the emphasis on symbolic and ritual action in deescalating and redefining long-term ethnic conflict.

In the tenth chapter, "Social-Cognitive Mechanisms in Reconciliation," Ifat Maoz suggests that the way in which people subjectively construe events, actions, and behaviors related to conflict and to the transition from conflict to peace can significantly influence the reconciliation process. Accordingly, the paper's goals are "(1) to map major cognitive biases and subjective construals of information in conflict situations that can serve as barriers to reconciliation, and (2) to present cognitive 'debiasing' techniques that may help overcome these barriers and shift toward frames that are more conducive to forming a relationship of cooperation and reconciliation."

Finally, in Chapter 11, "Will the Parties Conciliate or Refuse? The Triangle of Jews, Germans, and Palestinians," Dan Bar-On notes that there are some conflicts in which the parties refuse to conciliate. He examines the reasons for this in the context of two cases: Jewish-German interactions after the Holocaust, and the Israeli-Palestinian conflict. Following this macrolevel discussion, Bar-On focuses on a microlevel case in which these parties (Palestinians, Israeli Jews, and Germans) tried to work through the obstacles to conciliation.

I

The Nature of Reconciliation as an Outcome and as a Process

Daniel Bar-Tal
Gemma H. Bennink

A true and lasting peace also requires a *culture for peace*, that is, a comprehensive, society-wide system of values, beliefs and attitudes, the interplay and impact of which in and on the civil society would lead citizens of the Middle East—Arabs, Israelis, Palestinians—in their daily lives, *on the ground*, to put a premium on peace, to desire peace, to seek peace and to stand for peace.

> —Proceedings of the United Nations Department
> of Public Information's International Encounter
> for European Journalists on the Question of
> Palestine, June 9–11, 1993, London

Although the concept of reconciliation has long been known and used in the social sciences, only over the past decade has the study of reconciliation emerged as a defined area of interest in political science and political psychology (for example, Krepon and Sevak, 1995; Asmal, Asmal, and Roberts, 1997; Lederach, 1997; Arnson, 1999a; Rothstein, 1999a). It evolved out of the recognition that there is a need to go beyond the traditional focus on conflict resolution, to expand the study of peacemaking to a macrosocietal perspective, which concerns reconciliation between society members. The study of conflict resolution reveals the mechanisms, methods, and conditions that the rival parties use in order to resolve their conflict peacefully. It refers mainly to the processes of negotiation, bargaining, mediation, and arbitration that sometimes result in an agreement on a mutually acceptable solution, signed by the parties. Such an agreement symbolizes the formal ending of the conflict (for example, Smith, 1971; Deutsch, 1973; Mitchell, 1981; Burton, 1987; Kriesberg, 1992; Ross, 1993a; Rubin, Pruitt, and Kim, 1994; Bercovitch, 1995).

However, in recent years it has become evident that formal peace agreements fall far short of establishing genuine peaceful relations between the former adversaries (for example, Lederach, 1997; Simpson, 1997; Lipschutz, 1998; Wilmer, 1998; Knox and Quirk, 2000). Formal conflict resolution sometimes involves only the leaders who negotiated the agreement or narrow strata around them or but a small part of the society. In these cases, the majority of society members may not accept the negotiated compromises, or even if they do they may still hold worldviews that have fueled the conflict. As a result, formal resolutions of conflicts may be unstable; they may collapse as in the case of Angola, or turn into cold peace as in the case of Israeli-Egyptian relations. In these and similar cases, hopes of turning the conflictive relations of the past into peaceful societal relations have not materialized because the reconciliation process either never actually started, was stalled, or has progressed very slowly.

We suggest that it is the process of reconciliation itself that builds stable and lasting peace. Reconciliation goes beyond the agenda of formal conflict resolution to changing the motivations, goals, beliefs, attitudes, and emotions of the great majority of the society members regarding the conflict, the nature of the relationship between the parties, and the parties themselves. These changes take shape via the reconciliation process, promote the peace as a new form of intergroup relations, and serve as stable foundations for cooperative and friendly acts that symbolize these relations.

In this chapter we will examine the nature of reconciliation as an outcome of peacemaking and as a process in which the parties in conflict embark on the long path of forming a genuine and stable peaceful relationship, relying much on recently published work in this area. We will first describe the characteristics of conflicts, which have bearing on the analysis of reconciliation. Second, we will discuss reconciliation as an outcome. Third, we will elaborate on the process of reconciliation, describing its different methods and facilitating factors. Finally, we will present several conclusions.

The Nature of Conflicts and Reconciliation

Intergroup conflicts are pervasive and permanent features of social life. They occur on every level of intergroup relations when the goals of one group contradict those of another (Mitchell, 1981; Brown, 1988; Fisher, 1990; Kriesberg, 1998a). In this chapter we focus mainly on large-scale societal conflicts involving nations and ethnic, religious, or ideological groups. Such conflicts differ with respect to causes, contradictory goals, intensity, involvement, actions, and other characteristics. Some last for a short period, involve mainly leaders, and are hardly noticed by society members. These conflicts, considered as tractable, are eventually resolved peacefully through negotiation. They do not require reconciliation, since they do not involve psychological investment on the part of society members, no societal beliefs about them are formed, and they do not penetrate the cultural infrastructure of the societies involved. In contrast, there are other types of conflict, labeled as deeply rooted, protracted, intractable, or of enduring rivalry, that last at least a few decades, concern existential issues for the rivaling parties, involve violence, extensively preoccupy members of the implicated societies, and are perceived as of zero-sum nature and irreconcilable (Azar, 1990; Goertz and Diehl, 1993; Bar-Tal, 1998; Kriesberg, 1998a). Resolution of this second type of conflict is a complex challenge, often requiring many years, and some of them remain unresolved. But even when these conflicts are resolved peacefully and formal, mutually accepted agreements are signed, they still require a reconciliation process for rebuilding the relations between the societies (for example, the Northern Ireland and Middle East conflicts). The distinction between the types of conflict points to the fact that not all of them require reconciliation. What kinds of conflict, then, call for reconciliation?

We propose that *reconciliation is required when the societies involved in a conflict evolve widely shared beliefs, attitudes, motivations, and emotions that support adherence to the conflictive goals, maintain the conflict, de-legitimize the opponent, and thus negate the possibility of peaceful resolution and prevent the development of peaceful relations.* Of special importance in this repertoire are widely shared beliefs (called societal beliefs),[1] which often foster the emergence of collective emotional orientations (for example, fear, anger, and hatred) and sometimes even become a central part of societal ethos. They are formed in the course of the conflict, disseminated to society members, maintained by societal institutions, and supported by collective memory. They fuel the continuation of the conflictive relations and constitute obstacles to the progress of peacemaking (Bar-Tal, 1998, 2001). These beliefs, attitudes, and emotions do not change overnight even when the groups' leaders resolve the conflict peacefully and sign a peace agreement. They continue to inhibit the development of peaceful relations until they change slowly via a reconciliation process, should one take place. The latter point implies that reconciliation is not a naturally occurring process, but one that requires active efforts to overcome obstacles.

Discussions of reconciliation require two important classifications of conflict. The first concerns the outcome of the conflict and the status of the groups after conflict resolution. That is, whereas in some conflicts the two groups will live in two separate political entities (that is, states) following the conflict resolution, as in the case of the German-French and Israeli-Egyptian conflicts, in other instances, despite the vicious conflict, the two rival groups will have to continue to live together in one entity (a state), as in the case of South Africa, Guatemala, El Salvador, or Spain. This classification is important for deciding on the type of reconciliation process that is needed, as well as what form the final outcome must take. In general, rival groups that will be living together as a single peaceful society will need to construct mechanisms that foster integration. In contrast, in the other cases, the rival societies will need to construct mechanisms of intergroup relations in two different systems, which involve different processes and outcomes. In both categories, however, both of the opposing sides must undergo a similar psychological change so as to form new motivations, goals, beliefs, attitudes, and emotions.

The second classification is more complicated. It refers to the attributed responsibility for the outbreak of the conflict and especially for the negative acts committed during the conflict (see Asmal et al., 1997; Kriesberg, 1998a). Although each party involved in a conflict usually perceives itself as the victim and the other side as being responsible for the outbreak of the conflict and the negative acts committed, the international community, according to defined international criteria of justice, sometimes blames one side more than the other (Asmal et al., 1997). Such international judgment can affect the reconciliation process. When one side is attributed more responsibility than the other for injustice (as in the interstate conflict between Japan and Korea or Germany and Poland, and in the intrastate conflict in South Africa or Chile), then this side is often required to take special steps in the of reconciliation process (for example, paying reparations, stating an apology).

Having made these clarifications, we can now begin to explore more deeply the notion of reconciliation as an outcome and as a process.

Reconciliation as an Outcome

All students of reconciliation in the present decade agree that it concerns the formation or restoration of a genuine peaceful relationship between societies that have been involved in an intractable conflict, after its formal resolution is achieved (Ackermann, 1994; Chadha, 1995; Asmal et al., 1997; Kopstein, 1997; Lederach, 1997; Kriesberg, 1998a; Lipschutz, 1998; Wilmer, 1998; Arthur,

1999; Gardner-Feldman, 1999; Kelman, 1999a; Murray and Greer, 1999; Norval, 1999; Bar-Tal, 2000b). The focus is on peaceful relations between societies, since reconciliation requires more than friendly relations between leaders, which sometimes develop in the course of the conflict resolution process. Reconciliation, then, requires the support of the entire society or at least the majority of it; only then can peace be stable and lasting. A peace that is not supported by society as a whole will always be at risk of breaking down.

The question, then, concerns the nature of stable and lasting peaceful relations subsequent to the reconciliation process (see Bar-Siman-Tov, this volume). Social scientists have offered different answers to this question, some consisting of brief definitions and others more detailed (see, for example, Kacowicz and Bar-Siman-Tov, 2000). In our view, *stable and lasting peace is characterized by mutual recognition and acceptance, invested interests and goals in developing peaceful relations, as well as fully normalized, cooperative political, economic, and cultural relations based on equality and justice, nonviolence, mutual trust, positive attitudes, and sensitivity and consideration for the other party's needs and interests.* These characteristics include both structural and psychological elements. We believe the psychological elements stem directly from the reconciliation process, since we see reconciliation as a psychological process and outcome that takes place between rival groups. We suggest, therefore, that reconciliation as an outcome consists of *mutual recognition and acceptance, invested interests and goals in developing peaceful relations, mutual trust, positive attitudes, as well as sensitivity and consideration for the other party's needs and interests.* All these elements of reconciliation apply to postconflict situations in which the two groups build peaceful relations in two separate political entities—their states, as well as to situations in which the two rival groups continue to live in a single political entity. However, there is a difference with respect to the normalization of political, economic, and cultural relations. Whereas in the former situation this requirement pertains to bilateral relations between two states, in the latter situation it involves the integration of past adversaries into a single political-economic-cultural system.

Peacemaking techniques have traditionally focused on the structural aspects of restoring or forging relations between former rivals (see Charif, 1994; Corm, 1994; Saidi, 1994; Lederach, 1997; Lipschutz, 1998; Wilmer, 1998; Murray and Greer, 1999). This focus was based on the assumption that equal interactions between the parties, together with economic and political restructuring, lead to new, cooperative links that stabilize peaceful relationships (Ackermann, 1994; Elhance and Ahmar, 1995; Weiwen and Deshingkar, 1995; Gardner-Feldman, 1999). The literature focused on such structural elements as exchanging representatives in various political, economic, and cultural spheres; maintaining formal and regular channels of communication and consultation between the leaders of the states; reducing threats and tensions by such acts as disarmament, demilitarization, reduction of military manpower, and minimization of military manpower close to the borders; developing joint institutions and organizations; developing free and open trade; developing cooperative economic ventures; exchanging information and developing cooperation in different areas; developing free and open tourism; and exchanging cultural products. These structural elements of stable and lasting peace pertain mainly to cases in which the rival parties live in two states.

When the rival groups must live together in one state, the formal acts involved in establishing stable and lasting peaceful relations are different. They aim at internal institutional reforms, mostly in the political and economic systems. The structural outcome of reconciliation requires political integration, meaning the inclusion of all groups in the power system, the establishment of structural equality and justice, and the observance of human and civil rights as well as democratic rules of political governance (Corm, 1994; Corr, 1995; Kriesberg, 1998a; Lederach, 1998; Arnson, 1999b; Murray and Greer, 1999; Zalaquett, 1999). In the economic domain, peacemaking requires the inclusion of all the society's groups in the economic system, the creation of equal opportunity for them, and often the redistribution of wealth (Corr, 1995; Lipschutz, 1998; Wilmer, 1998; Zalaquett, 1999).

All the political and economic acts described are assumed to foster interdependent relations and cooperation and thus to promote peace. Thus, it is of utmost importance to avoid violent acts by both sides. In conflicts between states, the international community provides an array of rules, institutions, and mechanisms to resolve them peacefully through bilateral negotiation, or mediation and arbitration by third parties. In the case of intrastate conflicts, the society has to restructure its institutions so as to provide the mechanisms for peaceful conflict resolution. In all the cases, however, what is essential is to treat the other side with respect, justice, equality, and sensitivity to its needs and goals.

It became clear, however, that creating economic and political mechanisms and institutions to foster interdependence and affinity does not guarantee lasting peaceful relations (Lederach, 1997, 1998; Simpson, 1997; Kriesberg, 1998a; Lipschutz, 1998; Wilmer, 1998; Arnson, 1999b; Arthur, 1999). As Wilmer points out, "[although] structural factors may contribute to precipitating a conflict or to constructing a framework for stable peace, structural factors alone neither cause nor resolve protracted and violent conflict" (1998: 93). Structural elements establish formal relations without necessarily spreading the new message of reconciliation among society members. Such elements are sometimes perceived as irrelevant to the personal lives of society members and often do not induce a deep change in the public's psychological repertoire. The case of Yugoslavia, in which Tito's communist regime imposed many structural acts of multicultural coexistence, demonstrates the weakness of such measures if they are not accompanied by complementary psychological changes (Wilmer, 1998). *The essence of reconciliation is a psychological process, which consists of changes of the motivations, goals, beliefs, attitudes, and emotions of the majority of society members* (Lederach, 1997; Shonholtz, 1998; Wilmer, 1998; De Soto, 1999; Kelman, 1999a). Psychological change is vital because without it the rival parties do not establish lasting peaceful relations (see Maoz, this volume). *Reconciliation is, then, the necessary condition for stable and lasting peace.* Structural measures alone may facilitate psychological change, but they cannot establish reconciliation. As Lipschutz remarks in regard to intrastate conflicts: "Relationships among people, among individuals, are the fundamental basis of the state; restoring only the institutions of the state (and the economy) will not restore those relationships rent by years of violence and war" (1998: 16).

Thus, the next section focuses on the psychological requirements for reconciliation.

The Outcome of Reconciliation

The outcome of reconciliation consists of motivations, goals, beliefs, attitudes, and emotions that support the objective of peace, the new nature of peaceful relations, and positive views of the partner. This psychological basis of reconciliation must be reflected in people's subjective experience. As Lederach notes: "To be at all germane to contemporary conflict, peacebuilding must be rooted in and responsive to the experiential and subjective realities shaping people's perspectives and needs" (1997: 21). The fundamental requirement is that the psychological dimension penetrate deep into the societal fabric, so as to be shared by the majority of society members (Asmal et al., 1997; Lederach, 1997; Kriesberg, 1998a; Bar-Tal, 2000b). Only such change can guarantee lasting peaceful relations between rival groups, because then stable foundations are formed that are rooted in the psyche of the people.

The psychological changes may not encompass all society members, since a small section of a society may continue to harbor the wish to maintain the conflict, despite its resolution and the new, peaceful climate. An example is the German irredentist groups, which do not accept the peace agreement and reconciliation between Germany and Poland or between Germany and the Czech Republic (Handl, 1997; Gardner-Feldman, 1999). But if such groups are small and marginal (as in the case of Germany) whereas the great majority of the society, including its dominant groups, has internalized the psychological basis of reconciliation, then reconciliation is not affected.

Reconciliation also requires a measure of complementarity between the psychological bases of the former rivals (Asmal et al., 1997; Lederach, 1997; Kriesberg, 1998a). That is, both parties must undergo a similar psychological change and a majority of both parties must support the peaceful relations. An imbalance in these changes will impair reconciliation and lead one of the parties to feel betrayed and cheated.

Although most of the researchers agree on the importance of the psychological component of reconciliation, they are vague or disagree about its nature. Most thinkers on reconciliation have recognized the importance of creating a common psychological framework to promote this process (Asmal et al., 1997; Kopstein, 1997; Lederach, 1997; Hayes, 1998; Kriesberg, 1998a, Volkan, 1998a; Hayner, 1999; Whittaker, 1999). They realize that during the conflict the rival parties had different views about the conflict itself, about each other, and about their relationship. To ensure reconciliation, these different views must undergo a dramatic adjustment. What, then, is the nature of the common psychological framework?

There is wide agreement that reconciliation requires forming a new, common outlook on the past. Once there is a shared and acknowledged perception of the past, the parties have taken a significant step toward reconciliation. As Hayner observes, "where fundamentally different versions or continued denials about such important and painful events still exist, reconciliation may be only superficial" (1999: 373). Reconciliation requires that both parties not just become aware of but truly acknowledge what happened in the past (Asmal et al., 1997; Chirwa, 1997; Hayes, 1998; Lederach, 1998; Norval, 1998, 1999; Gardner Feldman, 1999; Hayner, 1999). Acknowledgment of the past entails at least recognizing that there are two narratives of the conflict (Kopstein, 1997; Hayner, 1999; Norval, 1999). This is an important factor in reconciliation, since the parties' collective memories of their own past sustain the conflict and obstruct peacemaking (Bar-Tal, 2003). Reconciliation necessitates changing these societal beliefs (that is, collective memories) about the past by learning about the rival group's collective memory and admitting one's own past misdeeds and responsibility for the outbreak and maintenance of the conflict. Through the negotiation process, in which one's own past is critically revised and synchronized with that of the other group, a new narrative emerges (Asmal et al., 1997; Hayes, 1998; Norval, 1998). With time, this new historical account of events should come to replace the previous version.

Often, however, preoccupation with the past requires more than that. During the conflict, each party accumulates many grievances toward the other.

Years of violence leave deep scars of anger, grief, a sense of victimhood, a will to revenge, and so on. These grievances must not only be known, but also truly acknowledged by the rival society (Ross, 1995; Asmal et al., 1997; Kriesberg, 1998a; Lederach, 1998; Wilmer, 1998; Norval, 1999). Some researchers have gone a step further by asserting that collective acknowledgment of the past is not enough to promote a process of reconciliation. Instead, they argue, the process of reconciliation should ultimately lead to collective healing and forgiveness for the adversary's misdeeds (Shriver, 1995; Lederach, 1998; Arthur, 1999; Hayner, 1999; Staub, 2000). Lederach has referred to this element as the spiritual dimension: "Spiritual for me signifies moving beyond the issues and toward an encounter. It is a journey toward an encounter with self and the other. The purpose of the reconciliation journey is healing" (1998: 244).

The spiritual dimension signifies the importance of healing and forgiveness. Reconciliation, in this view, consists of restoration and healing. It allows the emergence of a common frame of reference that permits and encourages societies to acknowledge the past, confess former wrongs, relive the experiences under safe conditions, mourn the losses, validate the experienced pain and grief, receive empathy and support, and restore a broken relationship (Montville, 1993; Lederach, 1998; Minow, 1998; Staub, 1998, 2000). It creates a space where forgiveness can be offered and accepted. The element of forgiveness as an outcome of reconciliation is of special importance in cases of unequal responsibility, where one party is attributed responsibility either for the outbreak and maintenance of the conflict, or for misdeeds committed during the conflict (see also Auerbach, this volume) or both. It is forgiveness that then makes the reconciliation possible (Staub, 2000). It symbolizes psychologically departing from the past for new, peaceful relations (Lederach, 1998; Norval, 1999). As Montville puts it: "healing and reconciliation in violent ethnic and religious conflicts depend on a process of transactional contrition and forgiveness between aggressors and victims which is indispensable to the establishment of a new relationship based on mutual acceptance and reasonable trust" (1993: 112).

It should be noted, however, that not all the thinkers on the subject of reconciliation agree with this view. Some seriously question whether forgiveness and healing are possible, or even necessary (Horowitz, 1993; Hayes, 1998; Gardner-Feldman, 1999). They agree that a collective reconstruction of the past is a necessary element in any reconciliation process, but are skeptical as to whether this can lead to healing and forgiveness. Especially in severely divided societies, such as South Africa and Northern Ireland, this is a difficult if not impossible objective to obtain. Hayes, for example, argues that "reconciliation is not about the [individualism of] forgiveness of the dreadful and vile acts committed in the name of apartheid, but how all of us are going to act to build a new society" (1998: 33).

Returning to the general issue of reconciliation, a number of definitions have been proposed by different writers (see also the chapters by Kelman, Kriesberg, and Ross in this volume). Asmal et al. suggest that reconciliation is "the facing of unwelcome truths in order to harmonize incommensurable world views so that inevitable and continuing conflicts and differences stand at least within a single universe of comprehensibility" (1997: 46). Marrow proposes that reconciliation "is reestablishment of friendship that can inspire sufficient trust across the traditional split" (1999: 132). In emphasizing trust, he asserts that the basic thrust of reconciliation is to be sensitive to others' needs, the principal question being not what *they* have to do, but what *we* have to do to promote the reconciliation process. Lederach (1997) focuses mainly on intrasocietal reconciliation and posits four elements of it: *truth*, which requires open expression of the past; *mercy*, which requires forgiveness to enable building new relations; *justice*, which requires restitution and social restructuring; and *peace*, which entails a common future, wellbeing, and security for all the parties. Kelman (1999a) presents elaborated components of reconciliation in what he calls a "positive peace." In this view, reconciliation consists of the following components: (a) resolution of the conflict, which satisfies the parties' fundamental needs and fulfills their national aspirations; (b) mutual acceptance and respect for the other group's life and welfare; (c) development of a sense of security and dignity for each group; (d) establishment of patterns of cooperative interaction in different spheres; and (e) the institutionalization of conflict resolution mechanisms.

In a recent article Bar-Tal (2000b), focusing on the cognitive aspect, elaborates on the types of psychological change that are necessary for reconciliation. He proposes that achieving reconciliation requires changes in five themes of societal beliefs that were formed during the conflict: societal beliefs about the group's goals, about the rival group, about one's own group, about relations with the past opponent, and about peace.

SOCIETAL BELIEFS ABOUT THE GROUP'S GOALS. An important change concerns the societal beliefs about the justness of the goals that underlie the outbreak and maintenance of the conflict. Groups involved in conflict construct beliefs about their own goals that provide an epistemic basis for the conflict. They present these goals as supremely important and accord them justifications and rationale. Reconciliation requires changing these beliefs—in essence, abolishing them or at least indefinitely postponing the societal aspirations expressed in goals, which caused the intergroup conflict. Instead, new societal beliefs about goals must be formed. The new beliefs must present new goals for the society that have been shaped by the conflict resolution agreement, and that center on maintaining peaceful relations with the former enemy. In addition, these beliefs must provide rationalization and justification for the new goals, including new symbols and myths.

SOCIETAL BELIEFS ABOUT THE RIVAL GROUP. Another determining condition for reconciliation is a change of the images of the adversary group. In times of conflict, the opposing group is delegitimized in order to explain its aberrant behavior, the outbreak and continuation of the conflict, and to justify actions taken against the adversary (Bar-Tal and Teichman, in preparation). To promote a process of reconciliation, perceptions of the rival group need to be changed. It is important to legitimize and personalize its members; legitimization grants humanity to members of the adversary group, after years of its denial. It allows viewing the opponent as belonging to the category of acceptable groups, with which it is desired to maintain peaceful relations. Personalization enables seeing members of the rival group as human individuals who can be trusted and have legitimate needs and goals. The new beliefs should also contain a balanced stereotype consisting of positive and negative characteristics and a differentiating perception of the group that acknowledges its heterogeneous composition. Finally, the new beliefs should permit seeing the other group as a victim of the conflict as well, since its members also suffered in its course (Kelman, 1999a; Bar-Tal, 2000b).

SOCIETAL BELIEFS ABOUT ONE'S OWN GROUP. Reconciliation requires changing societal beliefs about one's own group. During the conflict, groups tend to view themselves in a one-sided way involving self-glorification and self-praise, ignoring and censoring any information that might shed negative light on the group. But in the reconciliation process, the group must take responsibility for its involvement in the outbreak of the conflict, if that was the case, as well as its contribution to the violence, including immoral acts, and refusal to engage in a peaceful resolution. Thus, the new societal beliefs present one's own group in a more "objective," critical light, especially regarding its past behavior.

SOCIETAL BELIEFS ABOUT THE RELATIONSHIP WITH THE PAST OPPONENT. Reconciliation requires the formation of new societal beliefs about the relations between the two groups that were engaged in conflict. During conflict, the societal beliefs support confrontation and animosity (Bar-Tal, 1998). To promote reconciliation, these beliefs need to change into beliefs that stress the importance of cooperation and friendly relations. Of special importance is the accent on equality of relations and mutual sensitivity to each other's needs, goals, and general well-being. These new beliefs about the relationship should also concern the past. As discussed earlier, the new beliefs should present the past relations within a new framework that revises the collective memory and forms an outlook on the past that is synchronized with that of the former rival.

SOCIETAL BELIEFS ABOUT PEACE. During the intractable conflict, the parties yearn for peace but view it in general, amorphous, and utopist terms, without specifying its concrete nature or realistic ways to achieve it. Reconciliation requires forming new societal beliefs that describe the multidimensional nature of peace, realistically outline the costs and benefits of achieving it, connote the meaning of living in peace, and specify the conditions and mechanisms for achieving (for example, negotiation with the rival and compromises) and especially maintaining it. Of special importance is the recognition that for lasting peace, the well-being of the two sides is in the interest of both parties and hence peace also requires ongoing sensitivity and attention to the needs and goals of the other group.

The above psychological framework focuses almost entirely on the change of beliefs and attitudes of both parties. Nevertheless, the outcome of reconciliation also requires positive emotions about the peaceful relations with the past opponent. Positive affects should accompany the described beliefs and indicate good feelings that the parties have toward each other and toward the new relations. The good feelings should be reflected in mutual acceptance, recognition, trust, and caring about the other side's well-being. This kind of caring does not develop out of altruistic considerations but as a response to interdependence and common goals. Reconciliation requires that past rivals develop and disseminate a psychology of cooperation among society members. In regard to emotions, reconciliation requires a change in the collective emotional orientations of fear, anger, and hatred, which often dominate societies in intractable conflict. Instead, societies in peace should develop an emotional orientation of hope, which reflects the desire to maintain peaceful, cooperative relations with the other party. This emotional orientation involves a positive outlook for the future and expectations of pleasant events, without violence and hostilities (Averill, Catlin, and Chon, 1990; Bar-Tal, 2001).

Reconciliation as a Process

The concept of reconciliation is not only used in reference to an outcome, but also to connote a process. Genuine and stable peaceful relations are achieved through a long process of reconciliation, lasting many years. It encompasses psychological changes of motivations, goals, beliefs, attitudes, and emotions, which are reflected in structural changes; these, in turn, facilitate the process of reconciliation. Although some of the structural changes can be decided and implemented relatively quickly, the psychological changes do not occur in the same way. They take place via the slow psychological processes of information processing, unfreezing, persuasion, learning, reframing, re-categorization, and formation of new psychological repertoire. These processes are slow because the psychological repertoire formed during the conflict is central and held with high confidence. Therefore its change, which must encompass the majority of society members, is a complex, arduous, prolonged, and many-faceted task that needs to overcome many inhibiting factors. First, however, we will note a few points regarding the process of structural change, which, on the one hand, facilitates the process of reconciliation and, on the other, often provides criteria about its success.

Structural Changes as Facilitators and Reflections of Reconciliation

The literature on the process of reconciliation specifies certain policies and acts that are considered necessary to this process. One important prerequisite is the cessation of violent acts. The parties in conflict must adopt the principle of peaceful conflict resolution and stop using violence. This requires, first of all, the establishment of mutually accepted structural mechanisms that can resolve any possible conflict and disagreement that may erupt after the documents of peaceful conflict resolution are signed. In the postconflict era, when both parties lack trust and are insensitive to each other's needs, establishing structural mechanisms to prevent violence represents a major challenge in their peace efforts. These may include not only the mechanisms to resolve conflicts but also many measures to reduce the perception of threat and feelings of fear that often underlie the eruptions of violence. Such measures may include demobilization of military forces, disarmament, demilitarization of territories, and so on. All these steps facilitate the development of trust and positive perceptions (Ball, 1996; Canas and Dada, 1999; Spalding, 1999). An example of such acts can be seen in the reconciliation process in Nicaragua, which involved disarmament and demobilization of the Contras military forces, successfully supervised by the International Commission for Support and Verification (CIAV) set up by the Organization of American States (Sereseres, 1996). Another example is the confidence-building measures to improve the Israeli-Egyptian relations, which consisted of restricting military movements close to the borders and creating a multinational force (MFO) to supervise the disengaged parties.

When the rival parties will have to live under the same political system (as, for example, in South Africa, El Salvador, Guatemala, Nicaragua, Chile, Argentina, or Northern Ireland), the focus is on long-term reconstruction, re-structuring, restabilization, and rehabilitation. The reconciliation process depends on the development of policies that aim to create linkages, which foster inclusion and integration of all the groups in the society. This can be achieved by setting superordinate goals that are agreed on by all the parties, constructing inclusive identities, and abolishing all forms of discrimination (Horowitz, 1993; Charif, 1994; Saidi, 1994; Corr, 1995; Kriesberg, 1998a; Murray and Greer, 1999).

Many analysts suggest that democratization is the first condition for reconciliation in situations of intrastate conflict (Charif, 1994; Corr, 1995; Arnson, 1999b; Zalaquett, 1999). Democratization consists of establishing democratic rules and realizing formal democratic procedures that include freedom of expression and the right to political organization and political activity (Charif, 1994; El-Hoss, 1994; Corr, 1995; Lipschutz, 1998; Arnson, 1999b; Azburu, 1999). The electoral system should be perceived by all parties as free and fair and should create incentives to moderation (Horowitz, 1993; Canas and Dada, 1999). Democratization should lead to new distribution of political power, restoration of civil and human rights, emergence of new democratic political institutions and organizations, enforcement of democratic principles and rules of governance, and wide political participation. Moreover, it should be possible to replace the political and military leaders who were associated with the abuses perpetrated during the conflict. In this regard, it is also important to establish a legal system that is independent of the political, economic, and military bases of power. This system should be managed according to the principles of justice, equality, and fairness (Azburu, 1999). In essence, the reconciliation process requires the evolvement of civil society, whose values, laws, and norms support peaceful and democratic life (Azburu, 1999; Spalding, 1999).

Political restructuring may require the creation of new structures of governance. An example is participatory governance, which means a reduction in state activity and increased responsibility at the local level. Participatory governance is a way of involving the civil society in the reconciliation process. This type of governance is promoted in some regions in Northern Ireland in the form of partnerships—local interest groups of elected community representatives and representatives of business, trade unions, and statutory agencies. The goal of these partnerships is to reinforce a peaceful and stable society and to encourage reconciliation by increasing economic development and employment, promoting urban and rural regeneration, developing cross-border co-operation, and extending social inclusion (Murray and Greer, 1999).

In addition to political processes, economic processes are an important condition for reconciliation. Economic processes are necessary to foster economic interdependence, to include all groups in economic development, and to remove past discrimination and inequalities (Charif, 1994; Corm, 1994; El-Hoss, 1994; Elhance and Ahmar, 1995; Weiwen and Deshingkar, 1995). They can include redistributing land, wealth, and economic power, allowing equal opportunity for economic participation, and providing compensation to groups that have suffered systematic discrimination.

If the rival groups are going to live in different political systems, the focus should be on creating economic and political linkages that foster cooperation (Ackerman, 1994; Barua, 1995; Elhance and Ahmar, 1995; Ganguly, 1995; Weiwen and Deshingkar, 1995; Gardner Feldman, 1999). This can be achieved by stimulating political and economic interdependence. There are numerous structural measures that both groups can take to foster the reconciliation process. Diplomatic relations, visits of leaders, exchanges of delegations, trade, joint economic projects, and cooperation in different areas of common interest are only a few examples from a long list of possibilities. All the structural measures must be implemented on the basis of equality and sensitivity to the parties' needs and goals. A successful example of a structural process was the development of peaceful relations between France and Germany. In 1951, the two countries established an economic union for coal and steel production as one of the first steps in the reconciliation process. In 1963 the Franco-German Treaty was signed, which institutionalized many of the structural measures so as to accelerate the process of reconciliation (for example, regular meetings between foreign, defense, and education ministers). In 1988 the Franco-German Cultural Council was established, and in 1995 even joint military units were formed (Ackermann, 1994). Another example of a structural process is the creation of the extensive economic and political linkages between Germany and Poland. Building on their 1991 treaty, the two states established various cooperative ventures to promote the reconciliation process such as the Fund for German-Polish Cooperation, the German-Polish Economic Promotion Agency, the Committee for Cross-Border Collaboration, and the Committee for Interregional Collaboration (Gardner-Feldman, 1999). On another continent, India and Pakistan have been trying to reconcile their differences for decades. In 1983 the two signed an agreement to establish a joint commission to strengthen relations and to promote cooperation in economics, health, science and technology, sports, travel, tourism, and consular matters (Elhance and Ahmar, 1995).

Whether the rival groups will live in one state or in two, the improvement of the economic situation of all members of the groups is always important (Rothstein, 1999b). Individuals in all the groups must feel that peaceful relations are worthwhile, and will contribute to the reconstruction of the economy after the conflict, the facilitation of economic growth and employment, and the improvement in individuals' standard of living. These economic benefits constitute powerful tools for peace because they mobilize group members to support peace and become an interest group for it. Therefore, special efforts are often made to encourage financial support, investments, and economic planning in the postconflict period by various national and international organizations and institutions. An example can be seen in Bosnia, where the World Bank, the European Bank for Reconstruction and Development, and the United Nations Development Program provided the money, plans, and personnel to reconstruct the country for all the groups that accepted and cooperated with the Dayton Agreement (Woodward, 1999).

Finally, one of the most important factors in fostering reconciliation processes in cases of interstate and intrastate conflict is the establishment of policies, institutions, and mechanisms to ensure justice (Shriver, 1999). Conflicts by their nature violate principles of justice, and the reconciliation process requires specific structural acts that signal to the groups involved that justice has been restored (Deutsch, 2000). The restoration of justice depends much on the nature of the particular conflict and the nature of the transgressions perpetrated during it. Examples of such transgressions include systematic and institutionalized discrimination, institutionalized violation of human rights, ethnic cleansing, mass killing, and even genocide. In some conflicts one side is clearly responsible for unjust acts, but in others the sides share the blame. In both situations, however, the structural acts of justice restoration are an inseparable part of the reconciliation process. For example, in the Balkans, the Dayton agreement gave each Bosnian family the right to return to their prewar home if they so desired, or alternatively to receive compensation for their lost property (Woodward, 1999).

The Reconciliation Process

According to the present conception, the reconciliation process begins when psychological changes begin to take place. That is, reconciliation begins when the parties in conflict start to change their beliefs, attitudes, goals, motivations, and emotions about the conflict, each other, and future relations—all in the direction of reconciliation. Such changes usually begin before the conflict is resolved peacefully and in fact can pave the way to its peaceful resolution. In

turn, the peaceful resolution of the conflict, with the initiation of various measures to establish formal relations, serves as a crucial catalyst for the psychological changes. The reconciliation process is by its nature an informal one
that lasts for a very long time and, therefore, does not have a formal beginning
or ending. It is not a linear process of continuous change in the direction of
peaceful relations, but one of regressions and advances.

The process of psychological change almost never begins with a large-scale
change by the majority of society members. Instead, the slow process of unfreezing and changing the beliefs and attitudes toward the societal goals, the
conflict, the adversary, one's own group, or the resolution of the conflict always
begins with a small minority. This minority is often at first perceived by the
majority as traitorous, and a long process of persuasion has to occur before
psychological change encompasses the majority of society members. Social
psychology has devoted much study to this process, which goes beyond the
scope of the present chapter (see, for example, Moscovici, Mugny, and Van
Avermaet, 1985; Levine and Russo, 1987; De Vries, De Dreu, Gordijn, and
Schuurman, 1996).

For our purposes, it is important to recognize that although the reconciliation process may begin either with the leaders or the grass roots, to be effective it must always proceed top-down and bottom-up simultaneously. This
means that whereas, on the one hand, the psychological change among leaders,
especially mainstream ones, greatly influences the society members, on the
other hand, the evolvement of a mass movement that embraces the psychological change has an effect on the leaders. In the long process of reconciliation,
both phenomena usually take place. Eventually, however, the leaders are of
crucial importance, since it is they who negotiate the peaceful resolution of the
conflict and are in a position to lead the reconciliation process (for example,
Begin and Sadat in the Israeli-Egyptian case, or Mandela and de Klerk in South
Africa; see Bargal and Sivan, this volume). But it should be noted that in all
the cases there was significant mass support for conflict resolution and eventual reconciliation, without which it would be very difficult to accomplish. The
success of the reconciliation process depends on the dissemination of the ideas
associated with it among the grass roots. This is essential to convincing the
masses to change their psychological repertoire from supporting the conflict
to favoring the emergence of peaceful relations.

In general, then, the reconciliation process requires policies that aim at
changing the psychological repertoire of society members (Ackermann, 1994;
Shonholtz, 1998; Volpe, 1998; Gardner-Feldman, 1999; Kelman, 1999a).
These policies cannot merely be relayed in statements and speeches, but must
be reflected in formal acts that symbolically communicate to society the change

in the relationship with the past rival. The formal acts occur in various spheres, beginning with formal meetings between the representatives of the rival groups, later between the leaders, then the establishment of formal relations, followed by political, economic, and cultural acts. These acts must be institutionalized and widened to encompass many society members, institutions, and organizations (Chadha, 1995; Kriesberg, 1998a; Lederach, 1998; Kelman, 1999a; Norval, 1999).

The mobilization of the masses for the psychological change is also performed by middle-level leaders—that is, prominent figures in ethnic, religious, economic, academic, intellectual, and humanitarian circles (Khalaf, 1994; Lederach, 1997, Thompson, 1997; Lipschutz, 1998). In this process elites play a very important role. The elites include those individuals who hold authoritative positions in powerful public and private organizations and influential movements (Kotzé and Du Toit, 1996). Such individuals can take an important part in initiating and implementing policies of reconciliation and reconstruction (Ackermann, 1994; Chadha, 1995; Lederach, 1998). At the grassroots level, local leaders, businessmen, community developers, local health officials, and educators can also play an important role in initiating and implementing such policies (Chetkow-Yanoov, 1986; Thompson, 1997; Lederach, 1998).

The challenge of reconciliation calls for different methods to facilitate the psychological change. We now turn to some of these.

Methods of Reconciliation

A variety of methods to facilitate reconciliation have been proposed in the literature. Some are part of the formal policies and some are carried out voluntarily and informally. All, however, serve as mechanisms to change society members' motivations, goals, beliefs, attitudes, and emotions in the direction of reconciliation. We will describe several of these methods, especially those that can be used for interstate as well as intrastate reconciliation.

APOLOGY. As most analysts have pointed out, reconciliation requires confrontation with the past, especially when transgressions were performed by one or both parties in the conflict (Bronkhorst, 1995). In these cases, the victims of the transgressions harbor strong negative feelings toward the perpetrators, which stand as major obstacles to reconciliation. Such negative feelings must be reduced to enable the psychological change required for reconciliation. Here, one method is formal apology offered by the side(s) that committed the misdeeds (Scheff, 1994). Through apology, the past injustices and grievances are acknowledged and addressed. Apology is a formal acceptance of responsibility for the misdeeds carried out during the conflict and an appeal to the victims for forgiveness. It implies a commitment to pursuing justice and truth (Asmal et al., 1997; Kriesberg, 1998a; Gardner-Feldman, 1999; Norval, 1999). Apology allows the victims to forgive and be healed so that eventually their negative feelings toward the past enemy will change. An example of apology can be seen in the case of South Africa's former president, F. W. de Klerk, who in August 1996, after Nelson Mandela was elected president, publicly apologized for the pain and suffering caused by the past policies of the National Party. He acknowledged that the National Party governments had approved unconventional measures that had created an environment in which abuses and gross human rights violations occurred (Kriesberg, 1998a). The Czech-German Declaration on Mutual Relations and Their Future Development, signed in January 1997, is an example of mutual apology. Germany accepted responsibility for the events of World War II and expressed regret for the sufferings and wrongs wrought against the Czech people; the Czech Republic expressed remorse for the sufferings and wrongs perpetrated against innocent Germans expelled from the Sudetenland after the war (Handl, 1997).

TRUTH AND RECONCILIATION COMMISSIONS. These commissions are a way of dealing extensively with the past. Their purpose is to reveal the truth about the past and to serve as a mechanism for establishing justice. They are of special importance in light of the fact that in most cases individual compensation is not possible. They expose acts of violence, violations of human and civil rights, discrimination, and other misdeeds perpetrated by the formal institutions of the state or by groups and individuals (Asmal et al., 1997; Barnes, 1997; Kaye, 1997; Kriesberg, 1998a; Liebenberg and Zegeye, 1998). In this process, the revelation of the past allows the groups to construct their new collective memory and thereby facilitates recovery (Asmal et al., 1997; Chirwa, 1997; Hayner, 1999; Norval, 1999; Zalaquett, 1999).

In recent years, variants of such commissions have been undertaken in South Africa, Chile, Argentina, El Salvador, Honduras, Uruguay, and Rwanda. Among these, the South African Truth and Reconciliation Commission (TRC) has received the most attention (Asmal et al., 1997; Chirwa, 1997; De la Rey and Owens, 1998; Hayes, 1998; Hamber, 1998; Liebenberg & Zegeye, 1998; Norval, 1998). It was established in 1995 with the principal objective of promoting "national unity and reconciliation in a spirit of understanding which transcends the conflict and divisions of the past." To this end, the TRC was supposed to (a) establish a comprehensive record of the causes, nature, and extent of gross human rights violations that occurred from March 1, 1960, to May 10, 1994; (b) decide on granting amnesty to individuals who made full disclosure of the transgressions they had committed in a political context; (c) restore the dignity of the victims by giving them an opportunity to recount their experiences; and (d) recommend measures for reparation and rehabilitation, as well as for preventing future human rights violations.

PUBLIC TRIALS. Public trials of particular individuals, charged for human rights violations and crimes against humanity, constitute another method that is regarded as facilitating the reconciliation process (Kritz, 1996). First, such trials provide an opportunity to reveal the misdeeds and thus acknowledge the victims' suffering. Second, when the criminals are found guilty and punished, the trials fulfill the deep-seated desire for retribution and give the victims the sense that justice has been carried out. In addition, the trials place the responsibility for crimes on particular individuals, thereby reducing the responsibility of the group to which they belong. Finally, these trials serve as warnings by showing that those who commit such crimes can be found, tried, and punished (Kriesberg, 1998a; Lederach, 1998; Liebenberg and Zegeye, 1998). In essence they enable catharsis, foster a sense that grievances have been addressed, and thus allow progress toward reconciliation by satisfying the basic needs of the victims. Examples of such trials are taking place at the War Crimes Tribunal in the Hague, where perpetrators from the Balkan conflict and the Rwandan genocide are being judged.

REPARATIONS PAYMENTS. This method is used when one or both sides accept responsibility for the misdeeds performed during the conflict and are willing to compensate the victims. This method goes beyond apology and facilitates changes of the psychological repertoire (see Shriver, 1995). On the one hand, the reparations offer indicates an admission of guilt and regret by the perpetrator; on the other, the victims' acceptance of the reparations signals a readiness to forgive. These elements are important for reconciliation when transgressions were perpetrated. An example is the compensation paid to the Czech victims by the German government for their sufferings under German occupation during 1939–1945 (Handl, 1997; Kopstein, 1997).

WRITING A COMMON HISTORY. This method involves recreating a past that can be agreed on by groups that have been in conflict. It usually involves a joint committee of historians who work together to collect and select materials, and finally negotiate to establish an agreed account of the past events. Such work requires exposure to the untold past of one's own group, which often includes misdeeds, and to the unheard past of the other group. Moreover, this method requires adhering to agreed facts and rejecting myths and unfounded accusations. The product of this joint work should allow the construction of a well-founded and agreed narrative that sheds new light on the past of both groups. This narrative provides a basis for the eventual evolvement of a new collective memory that is compatible with reconciliation.

The jointly published document not only has a symbolic value but should also have practical applications. It should serve as a basis for rewriting history textbooks, which can affect the beliefs and attitudes of new generations. These textbooks can also influence many other important cultural and educational products, such as books, films, television programs, and so on.

An example of this method is the Franco-German commission of historians, which by the 1950s had already critically scrutinized the myths of hereditary enmity between the French and German peoples and revised the existing history textbooks. As a final product the commission provided new accounts of the history of both nations, based on facts agreed to by the historians of both groups (Willis, 1965). Another example is the German-Czech committee of historians, which produced a document that presented an agreed account of their common history (Kopstein, 1997). It is not always necessary, however, to revise the entire history between nations; sometimes reconciliation may require rewriting only the history of a significant and symbolic event. Thus, in the case of the Polish-Russian reconciliation, a joint commission of historians investigated the murder of 15,000 Polish officers by the Soviets in Katyn in 1939. For years the Soviets had claimed that the Germans had performed the atrocity, whereas many Poles blamed the Russians. This bitter controversy formed one of the major obstacles to reconstructing Polish-Russian relations. The commission, which investigated the Soviet state archives, provided unequivocal evidence of Soviet responsibility. The commission's work led to a formal Russian acknowledgment of responsibility and apology to the Polish people.

EDUCATION. Education constitutes one of the most important methods for promoting reconciliation (Chetkow-Yanoov, 1986; Calleja, 1994; Gordon, 1994; Chadha, 1995; Asmal et al., 1997; Kriesberg, 1998a). This mostly involves using the school system for peace education, since this system is often the only institution of which the society can make formal, intentional, and extensive use to change the psychological repertoire of society members. Peace education aims at constructing the students' worldview (that is, their values, beliefs, attitudes, motivations, skills, and behavior patterns) in a way that reflects the reality of the peace process and prepares them to live in an era of peace and reconciliation (Bar-Tal, in press). This means the school system must provide students with knowledge that is consonant with the principles of reconciliation (for example, about the other group, the course of the conflict, future peaceful relations, the nature of peace, and conflict resolution). In addition, peace education should aim at developing new attitudes and skills among students (for example, tolerance, self-control, sensitivity to others' needs, empathy, critical thinking, and openness). This is a large-scale endeavor that requires setting educational objectives, preparing curriculum, specifying textbook contents, developing instructional material, training teachers, constructing a climate in the schools that is conducive to peace education, and so on (Bjerstedt, 1988, 1993; Harris, 1988; Hicks, 1988; Reardon, 1988; Burns and Aspeslagh, 1996).

Examples of peace education that have advanced reconciliation can be found in Japan, where, among other subjects, it has had to deal with the atrocities perpetrated by the Japanese during War World II, the meaning of apology, and the nature of peaceful relations in postwar Japan (Murakami, 1992). In conflict-ridden South American societies, peace education aims at teaching the young generation about human rights, and how to prevent structural violence and economic inequality (Garcia, 1984). In Northern Ireland, peace education seeks to foster Mutual Understanding programs (EMU), whose goal is to create a genuine culture of peace in the Protestant and Catholic school systems (Duffy, 2000).

MASS MEDIA. The mass media can be a very powerful tool for promoting reconciliation (Bruck and Roach, 1993; Calleja, 1994; Chadha, 1995; Elhance and Ahmar, 1995; Barnes, 1997; Kopstein, 1997; Kriesberg, 1998a; Norval, 1999). It can be used to transmit information to a wide public about the new peaceful goals, the formerly rival group, one's own group, the developing relations, and so on. However, first and foremost the media serves as a channel to communicate leaders' messages about peace and reconciliation. The media in itself constructs public reality by framing the news and commentaries. Its support for the reconciliation process is often crucial. In democratic states, however, the media cannot be mobilized via decrees and orders; instead, it too must be persuaded of the importance of peace.

PUBLICIZED MEETINGS BETWEEN REPRESENTATIVES OF THE GROUPS. Much has been written about various types of meetings between members of rival groups (for example, Burton, 1969; Kelman, 1996). These encounters, which often are secret, are aimed at gaining greater understanding of the psychological dynamics of the conflict and may even contribute to conflict resolution if the participants have influence over decision making. To promote reconciliation, however, these meetings must be well publicized. If so, and especially when carried out between the epistemic authorities of both sides, such meetings influence the attitudes and beliefs of society members. They indicate that members of the other group are human beings, that it is possible to talk with them, treat them as partners to agreements, trust them, and even consider their needs. For example, the meetings, symbolic handshakes, negotiations, and signed agreements between Israeli Prime Minister Binyamin Netanyahu and Palestinian Authority (PA) Chairman Yassir Arafat had a significant positive influence on Israeli supporters of the hawkish parties. Montville (1993) offers two other examples of the positive influence of such meetings on public opinion: one, in Northern Ireland, included representatives of rival political parties; the other, in the Middle East, included respected theologians and scholars representing Christians, Muslims, and Jews of the region.

THE WORK OF NGOS. Nongovernmental organizations, either from the societies involved in conflict or from the international community, can contribute to the reconciliation process (for example, Chetkow-Yanoov, 1986; Aall, 1996). They can help spread the message about the importance of constructing peaceful relations, help establish cooperative and friendly relations with the past adversary, or provide economic assistance to the society members and thereby show that peaceful relations have important benefits. NGOs often have direct contacts with the grassroots level and therefore can play the role of facilitator and mediator (Voutira and Whishaw Brown, 1995). They can even facilitate a healing process by providing professional help (for example, Staub and Pearlman, 2001). In societies involved in conflict, NGOs can serve as peace movements; examples include the Peace People Movement in Northern Ireland, organized by the Protestant Betty Williams and the Catholic Mairead Corrigan, and the Peace Now movement in Israel (Beeman and Mahony, 1993).

JOINT PROJECTS. Joint projects of different kinds are an additional method of facilitating psychological reconciliation. Joint projects in different areas can foster links between members of the two groups at different levels of society, such as elites, professionals, as well as the grass roots. These projects provide opportunities for personal encounters in which past opponents can form personal relations (Chetkow-Yanoov, 1986; Brown, 1988; Chadha, 1995; Kriesberg, 1998a; Volpe, 1998), which, in turn, can help legitimize and personalize members of both groups. Joint projects may also create interdependence, common goals, and benefits for society members. Thus, members of both groups learn about each other and about the importance of peaceful relations.

Joint projects can take various forms. In the French-German reconciliation process, a project of town twinning during 1950–1962 created 125 partnerships between French and German towns. By 1989 this project had expanded to include over 1,300 towns and went beyond towns to establish twin relations between secondary schools as well as universities (Ackermann, 1994). In the Czech-German reconciliation process, with the aim of facilitating changes in the psychological repertoire, a number of joint projects were initiated that included meetings between young people of the two nations, tending to monuments and graves and so on (Handl, 1997).

TOURISM. Tourism is another very important method for facilitating psychological reconciliation in cases of interstate conflict. First it is built on trust, since people do not visit places where they encounter inconvenience, danger, or rejection. If the members of the formerly rival groups visit each other, it indicates that some of the psychological barriers to social relations have successfully been removed. Second, tourism provides an opportunity to learn about the past rival's readiness to form peaceful relations. Finally, tourism allows learning about the other group—its culture, history, economy, and so on. Social psychologists have long recognized the importance of tourism for improving intergroup relations (for example, Allport, 1954; Amir, 1969; Hewstone, 1996). Some years ago, Ben-Ari and Amir (1988) demonstrated the positive influence of Israeli tourism to Egypt on changing the Israeli tourists' attitudes and beliefs.

CULTURAL EXCHANGES. Another method that is especially effective in interstate reconciliation is that of various cultural exchanges, such as translations of books, visits of artists, or exchanges of films, television programs, or exhibitions. These events provide the opportunity to learn about the past opponent in human and cultural perspective. Chadha (1995) notes that performances by Indian and Pakistani artists across the border of each state contributed to changing the two nations' negative images of each other.

There are, then, different methods to promote the process of psychological reconciliation, and they can involve different sectors and layers of society. No single method is best; what is required is a combination of methods. The use of particular methods depends on many different factors, such as the nature of the conflict, the types of misdeeds perpetrated during it, the extent to which one or both sides were responsible for the outbreak of the conflict and the misdeeds committed, the history of relations between the groups, the culture of the groups, the availability of economic resources, the involvement of the international community, and so on. It is important, however, to note that the reconciliation process requires establishing well-defined and unequivocal policies that are supported by the institutions and leadership of the state(s). These policies must be executed in a well-planned manner with the objective of involving as many society members as possible in the reconciliation process.

Nevertheless, the success of the reconciliation process is never assured; many different factors influence its outcome (see also discussions by Kriesberg, 1998a; Gardner-Feldman, 1999; Bar-Tal, 2000b). The next section outlines some major factors in determining the success of such processes.

Factors Affecting the Reconciliation Process

First of all, the reconciliation process depends on the peaceful resolution of the conflict. Moreover, the resolution has to be satisfactory to both parties, who must perceive that it has fulfilled their basic needs and addressed their fundamental aspirations (Kelman, 1999a). These are decisive requirements in any conflict resolution; if they are not upheld, the process is doomed to fail eventually. This does not mean groups cannot relinquish their visions, alter their goals, or reframe their concerns. Every group, however, has existential needs and a raison d'être, and if these are compromised under pressure or weakness, the result will not only hamper the reconciliation process but also plant the seeds for future conflict.

Second, the reconciliation process depends on conciliatory acts, both formal and informal, by both parties (Hayner, 1999; Zalaquett, 1999). After years of mistrust, hatred, and hostility, both parties must exhibit much goodwill in order to change these feelings. Reconciliation depends on overcoming deep suspicion, and this requires performing many different, often small and symbolic, acts that signal good intentions, the wish to build peaceful relations, adherence to aspirations of peace, and sensitivity to the other group's needs and goals. Such acts create and disseminate a new climate of relations among the masses. They set the tone for reciprocity, positive spirals of behavior, or even the initiation of unilateral, positive gestures.

Third, reconciliation depends on the determination of the leaders involved in the peacemaking and also on the good and trustful relations that they build with each other. Their moves are often met with opposition among their own group in the form of pressure, public mobilization, and sometimes even smear campaigns or violence, all aimed at obstructing the peace process. Leaders must overcome these obstacles and show great resolve and devotion to the peace process. They must signal to group members that they are determined to advance the reconciliation successfully despite the opposition. Nelson Mandela and F. W. de Klerk in South Africa, or Helmut Kohl and Vaclav Havel in the Czech-German case, were crucial players whose resolute stance provided the necessary catalyst for the progress of the reconciliation (Handl, 1997; Rothstein, 1999b).

Fourth, the reconciliation process depends on the activism and strength of those who support it (Elhance and Ahmar, 1995; Kriesberg, 1998a; Gardner-Feldman, 1999; Bar-Tal, 2000b). It requires the involvement of individuals, groups, and organizations in persuading hesitant or opposing group members of the importance of reconciliation. Reconciliation also requires an active approach to cementing the peaceful relations between the past enemies. That is, it is important to convey both to one's own and the other group that reconciliation is the goal.

Fifth, the success of reconciliation depends on mobilizing society's institutions to support the process (Gardner-Feldman, 1999; Bar-Tal, 2000b;). This pertains to political, military, social, cultural, as well as educational institutions (Asmal et al., 1997; Thompson, 1997; Zalaquett, 1999).

Sixth, the reconciliation process depends on the international context—specifically, the extent to which the international community shows interest in the particular reconciliation, facilitates it, encourages the parties to carry it out, and provides concrete assistance for pursuing it in the form of both involvement and economic assistance (Hume, 1993; Elhance and Ahmar, 1995; Lederach, 1997, 1998; Kriesberg, 1998a; Gardner-Feldman, 1999; Bar-Tal, 2000b). There is no doubt that the international community has played a crucial role in facilitating conflict resolution and reconciliation in most cases of intractable conflict over the past decade (for example, Northern Ireland, El Salvador, Nicaragua, Bosnia). In recent years, with the end of the Cold War, the international community, through such organizations as the United Nations, the European Union, or the Organization of American States, has had a great interest in promoting the peaceful resolution of conflicts followed by reconciliation.

Conclusion

Over the past decade, the discussion on peace processes has focused a good deal on the issue of reconciliation. Years of study of conflict resolution have shown that peaceful resolution of a conflict does not guarantee lasting peaceful relations. Parties may negotiate an agreement on conflict resolution, but often it concerns only the leaders and is not relevant to the group members. In such cases, conflict can erupt again. To cement peaceful relations between the rival sides to an intractable conflict, reconciliation is necessary. It is reconciliation that includes group members in the peace process, since it requires a change of their psychological repertoire. The essence of reconciliation is the construction of lasting peaceful relations between former rivals based on genuine support by the majority of the group members. Reconciliation, then, requires the formation of new beliefs, attitudes, motivations, goals, and emotions that support the peaceful relations. This new psychological repertoire includes the evolvement of mutual respect, trust, positive attitudes, and sensitivity to the other group's needs, fostering friendly and cooperative relations marked by equality and justice. Reconciliation, then, is essentially a psychological endeavor achieved through a psychological process. Structural measures both contribute to its evolvement and are among its consequences.

This psychological change is a very arduous process. It requires changing beliefs, attitudes, motivations, goals, emotions, and behavior patterns that have been part of society members' repertoire for many years, sometimes decades and even centuries. This repertoire was functional during the intractable conflict, allowing adaptation and successful coping with the enemy. It was based on the ongoing experiences both of individual society members and the collective. In addition, this repertoire was propagated by all the groups' channels of communication and institutions, transmitted to new generations via the educational system, and grounded in the groups' collective memory.

Reconciliation requires changing this repertoire, abolishing old fears, mistrust, hatred, and delegitimization of the enemy, and often also adjusting the group's longstanding dreams and aspirations. Such change is very long and complex, marked by both progress and setbacks. It requires new experiences that can induce the change of the psychological repertoire by transmitting a new message of peace and a new image of the former enemy. However, such experiences do not come about by themselves. People have to create them, act on them, and disseminate their meaning. That is, people must perform acts that provide the new experiences, such as peaceful gestures, meetings, ceremonies, and so on. Such acts supply the information that enables group members to look at the world differently. But changing group members' worldview requires a large accumulation of new experiences that support peacemaking. There is a need to form a supportive climate that indicates to all society members that the new reality can evolve free of threats, dangers, and fears. Such a reality is not always easy to form, since in societies engaged in a process of peace and reconciliation there is always a potent opposition to the process, and small groups may even resort to violence to put a halt to it.

As noted earlier, the evolvement of the new reality is an active process, requiring the involvement of leaders, elites, professionals, the grass roots, organizations, and institutions. This is a major undertaking for a society. Just as during the conflict the society was mobilized to wage the violent struggle with greater resolution and sacrifice, the reconciliation process, too, requires determination and efforts to persuade the opposition of its benefits.

Moreover, the reconciliation process requires not only persuading the members of one's own group but also convincing the other side of one's sincere desire to build peaceful relations. To do so, groups need to focus on their own shortcomings, misdeeds, and inhibitions and ask what they can do to facilitate reconciliation. This is a very challenging requirement, since groups are conditioned to focus on the other group's shortcomings and demand that it demonstrate its good intentions, while overlooking their own failings and negative intentions. Thus, groups usually tend to blame others for failures in the reconciliation process.

The reconciliation process requires forming a new ethos embedded in a culture of peace. This entails a major societal transformation. New norms, values, opinions, symbols, and collective memory have to emerge. Groups have been able to undergo such transformations successfully, as the Franco-German case of reconciliation demonstrates. That process, however, took almost four decades to complete. Individuals and groups always rally more easily to the banner of fear and hate than to the banner of trust and respect. But it is only trust and respect that provide hope for a better life, and it is the duty of humanity to enable groups to follow the path of the reconciliation process. We, as social scientists, can contribute to a better understanding of this process and the factors that influence it. That is our mission for the well-being of human society and for preventing future bloodshed and suffering.

ACKNOWLEDGMENT   The research for this chapter was supported by a grant from the Leonard Davis Institute for International Relations, the Hebrew University of Jerusalem. The final draft was written by the first author when he was a fellow at the Netherlands Institute for Advanced Study in the Humanities and Social Sciences. Correspondence about this chapter should be directed to Daniel Bar-Tal, School of Education, Tel Aviv University, Tel Aviv 69978, Israel; daniel@ccsg.tau.ac.il.

NOTE

1. *Societal beliefs* are defined as the society members' shared cognitions on issues that are of special concern to society and contribute to its unique characteristics. They are organized around themes and consist of such contents as collective memories, ideologies, goals, and myths. *Ethos* combines central societal beliefs into a particular configuration and gives meaning to societal identity. During intractable conflict, the involved societies tend to form conflictive ethos composed of eight themes: societal beliefs about the justness of one's own goals, security, positive self-image, one's own victimization, de-legitimization of the opponent, patriotism, unity, and peace (Bar-Tal, 1998, 2000a).

2

Reconciliation: Reflections on the Theoretical and Practical Utility of the Term

Tamar Hermann

War and peace, peace and war: this duality has always been of major interest to students of human collective behavior (historians, social scientists, and philosophers), as well as to practitioners (politicians, military professionals, or, alternatively, peace activists). Unlike many other matters of debate in the sociopolitical area, these two basic existential situations have also been a focus of the general public's attention, since their ultimate relevance to people's well-being has almost no equivalent. Still, the question of the transition process from a violent conflict to coexistence, or the opposite, in the relations between two or more national, ethnic, or religious communities has become of particular theoretical and practical interest in our days. This growing salience reflects developments that sometimes seem to show startling contradictions. On the one hand, it can be attributed to the shockingly violent outbreak or dramatic aggravation of bloody conflicts, such as the ethnic strife in former Yugoslavia or the genocide in Rwanda. On the other, the last decades have also seen the launching of peace negotiations and sometimes even the signing of formal agreements in cases of highly visible and protracted conflict, such as those in South Africa, Northern Ireland, the Basque country, Sri Lanka, or Israel-Palestine. Nevertheless, efforts to solve the puzzle of the transition to or away from war, and to find better conceptual and practical tools to deal with it, have been affected by the partial or even total and rapid collapse of several of these recent peace processes. Thus, conflicts that seemed to have been resolved, or close to it, have erupted again, often leaving the sides in a situation worse than before the peace process began, since they now, on top of the renewed bloodshed, must deal with disillusionment and disappointment, as the shining prospect of peace that had risen over the horizon sinks, again, out of sight (for example, Giliomee and Gagiano, 1990).

Hence, whereas not long ago there was a focus on notions such as "getting to yes," which emphasized the negotiating process (for example, Fisher and Ury, 1986), today inquiry centers on the stabilization of such achievements and the prevention of the resurgence of deadly conflicts. It has become clear that the signing of formal documents is hardly sufficient to make a fundamental change in intergroup, intercommunal, or interstate relations, and that settling conflicts "is not simply a matter of finding a clever interest-based constitutional formula or a way to split a limited pie" (Ross, this volume).

The 1980s and 1990s witnessed several hampered, ailing, or failing peace processes that were dealt with intensively by leaders. At the same time, the general public has shown a growing involvement in the political arena, including in matters of foreign and security policy that formerly were the domain of experts. This suggests that the roots of the difficulties in preventing wars and reaching stable peace should be sought not only on the elite level or in the formal procedures and documents but to no less an extent on the informal, people-to-people plane. As Saunders observes, "conflict is not just a clash among institutions, as it has often been depicted traditionally, nor is peace made by governments alone. The critical element is human beings in relationship—citizens in government and citizens outside government in the associations they create to do the work they need to do. . . . Profound change in our world—the beginning of a new era—compels us to go beyond traditional approaches to focus on this human dimension" (Saunders, 1999: 4–5). Thus a number of new notions have arisen, such as "peace spoilers" (Darby and MacGinty, 2000) or "peace dividends," referring to the general public's motivations in supporting or questioning peace processes launched by leaders. Perhaps the most salient term that conflict-resolution experts have recently elaborated (though not, of course, invented) against this background is that of "reconciliation," sometimes presented by both theoreticians and politicians as the panacea that can rescue us from the shortcomings of the theories and practical blueprints for getting from war to peace.

I maintain here, however, that at least for now the notion of reconciliation cannot serve as the key concept for cracking the enigma of peacemaking and peace stabilizing. Indeed, a careful examination of the literature reveals that on the theoretical level this notion is still a rather crude analytical tool. The lack of a widely accepted definition of reconciliation and its components—

apart perhaps from the very basic understanding that "until relationships are changed, deep-rooted human conflicts are not likely to be resolved" (Saunders, 1999: 31)—makes reconciliation little more than a buzzword, an amenable but loose framework for different contents, depending on the user's disciplinary affiliation, cultural background, or the particularities of the cases at hand. Reconciliation, then, is still an embryonic concept, needing much further refinement, beyond the understandable yet insufficient desire of conflict-resolution theoreticians to make a difference, and much greater rigor, as we insist on when not so heavily captivated by the subject matter.

I also argue that this theoretical fluidity is strongly manifested on the practical level. Thus, reconciliation as an operational method for bolstering processes of conflict resolution is also deficient. As we shall see, the course of action, timing, phases, and context limitations have not yet been sufficiently specified. Thus reconciliation mechanisms, such as "truth telling" commissions, can probably help promote peace processes that in any event have a high potential for success. In cases with a low success potential and a high risk of collapse and resumed violence, however, such as the Israeli-Palestinian case, which will be considered below, the ambiguity of the notion of reconciliation may be quite troublesome insofar as it raises expectations that it is often unable to fulfill.

Reconciliation: What Does It Mean?

Academic writing differs from most other kinds of literary work insofar as its communicative function is only secondary to its intellectual contribution. Complexity is not regarded as a flaw, nor semantic transparency as a requisite. Together with the use of highly abstract concepts and paradigms, this means academic writings are often nearly unintelligible to the vast majority of the readers who are not part of the professional milieu. Nevertheless—and despite the fact that by its nature academic discourse is characterized by the ongoing, dialectical elaboration of paradigms—such highly abstract notions as, for example, human rights or citizenship have been developed to the point that their essence is widely agreed upon and they have become operative in daily life. This is still not the case, however, with reconciliation. To demonstrate this notion's theoretical volatility at present,[1] the different views of its origin and locus, relevant level or unit of analysis, essence, purpose and timing, will be briefly discussed here with special reference to the chapters presented by the participants in the first workshop of this project.

Origin and Locus

When not used simply as a synonym for negotiating peace in the context of a protracted conflict (for example, M. Maoz, 1999), the common point of departure for elaborating the notion of reconciliation—beyond which little consensus has been reached thus far—is that to make the transition from war to peace possible, a fundamental change must occur in the sides' relations with each other. The use of the quite disturbingly neutral verb "occur" reflects the first point of theoretical disagreement: is reconciliation a natural, spontaneous process or, alternatively, a planned sociopolitical strategy? Thus, whereas certain scholars see reconciliation as a spontaneous, "bottom-up process of psychological reconciliation between populations . . . usually differentiated from instrumental, top-down peace making processes" (M. Bar-On, 1996: 1), other analysts place more emphasis on the strategic, "top-down" aspect of the process, highlighting the role of leaders in launching it: "The political leader is a major actor in initiating reconciliation processes in society. He accomplishes this through the use of his personality resources (charisma) as well as his formal high position (legitimate power)" (Bargal and Sivan, this volume). A similar perception is implicit in the "problem-solving" workshop models, which bring together public opinion leaders of the opposing sides so as to develop greater mutual familiarity and perhaps even understanding of the other side's attitudes and claims.[2]

Level or Unit of Analysis

The locus of the reconciliation initiative is closely related to the question, also rather complicated, of the unit of analysis—that is, who is to reconcile or be reconciled? Clearly the conflicts considered here are of a collective nature, but at what level is reconciliation to take place? Political scientists relate to the state as the basic relevant unit or actor so far as resolving international conflicts is concerned. Therefore, they understand reconciliation as a secondary process that occurs after the conflict has already been practically resolved at the state level: "If you ask most political scientists and international relations scholars what role reconciliation should have in peace, you are apt to receive a dazed look and perhaps an uneasy silence as well. The reason for this reaction is that political scientists think about peace making among large collective entities and see reconciliation as concerning personal relations or religious experiences for individuals and small face to face groups" (Ross, this volume). There are, of course, exceptions among international relations scholars to this emphasis on the state rather than the society ("A stable peace will be maintained only if it is supported by most of the people. . . . A societal reconciliation is the only process that may bring the people to internalize the meaning of peace and then support it" (Bar-Siman-Tov, this volume). Yet as this is still the prevalent view, one is bound to ask: how can states, as abstract entities, reconcile?

Often the symbolic act of reconciliation between states is performed by their heads, usually presidents or prime ministers. Although these individuals are indeed authorized to act on behalf of their nations when it comes to launching war or signing formal documents such as peace agreements, are they authorized to repent or forgive for the body politic they represent? Furthermore, to what extent does their asking forgiveness actually reflect genuine collective repentance? There is not a single case of a symbolic act of repentance—for example, when German Chancellor Willy Brandt apologized for the evils inflicted by the Nazis, or when the Japanese prime minister asked the forgiveness of the Korean women forced to serve as sex slaves for Japanese soldiers during World War II—in which a referendum was first held to find out to what extent the nation actually condoned its leader's act. Later political developments often suggest that such acts mainly reflected the individual leader's worldview or policy, and this, in turn, suggests that at least symbolic acts of reconciliation may well be investigated and understood on the individual level, not necessarily the societal one, with all the theoretical and of course practical implications of such a focus.

The question of level is even more complicated by the fact that those who adjoin reconciliation to ethics and religion also tend to focus on the individual level. They see the collective that is supposed to undergo the reconciliation process as composed of individuals, who are expected individually, in this context, "to let bygones be bygones. [Even] If your grandfather's bones turned to ashes at Auschwitz, if you threw your child into the river for a better death than one at the edge of a Hutu machete, if your mother was raped on order from a Serbian officer, if your brother hobbles on crutches to this day from the effects of an Irish Republican Army" (Shriver, 1999: 207–208). The question is then, again, the delegation of the power of reconciliation from the individual to the collective. In fact, in the South African case the Truth and Reconciliation Commission (TRC)[3] granted amnesty on an individual basis only, although in the hope that the accumulation would lead to reconciliation on the ethnic-group level.

Nevertheless, most social psychologists and sociologists tend to downplay both individual and state inputs (for example, D. Bar-On, this volume) when exploring the meaning of reconciliation, concentrating mainly on the society and social groups as the most appropriate units of analysis: "Processes of reconciliation between estranged romantic partners may be similar, but are not identical to processes of reconciliation between groups that have emerged from years of protracted and bloody conflict. This theoretical void calls for a development of research and theory on psychological processes of reconciliation and peace building between adversarial groups" (Nadler, 2001: 4). Yet here again there seem to be some dilemmas concerning the relevant unit of analysis, arising from empirical evidence that different sociopolitical and sociodemographic groups of the same society react differently to a process of rapprochement with the former enemy and may even clash with each other over this issue. Furthermore, "intragroup competition determines who represents the group in intergroup situations in ways that can have significant constraints on intergroup peacemaking and reconciliation" (Ross, this volume). Hence, the relevant unit of analysis may in fact be smaller than the "society" at large. Indeed, many of the observations on reconciliation processes have been based on meetings between youth of the opposing groups: Catholics and Protestants in Northern Ireland, or Israelis and Palestinians in the Middle East. This, however, brings in its wake another problem: how far "down" should one go, considering that the smaller the relevant unit, the smaller its significance for the overall process?

Essence

Another unresolved basic issue concerns the essence of the reconciliation process. What does reconciliation actually mean—or, better, how does one know if what one sees is reconciliation or, perhaps, something else, such as normalization? The way out of this empiricist dilemma is often to offer extremely general definitions of the notion, for instance: "Reconciliation is best understood as a continuum, meaning that there can be degrees of reconciliation." Thus the author differentiates between strong and weak versions of reconciliation, the strong one constituting a total transformation in the relations between former opponents, while the weak one involves sufficient change that the interactions between the groups are increasingly constructive and violence comes to an end" (Ross, this volume). Another such general definition sees reconciliation as "the process of developing conciliatory accommodation between formerly antagonistic groups" (Kriesberg, 1998c), and a more minimalist one reflecting a similar approach makes do with "a readiness for transition to more peaceful relations based on cooperation" (I. Maoz, this volume).

In the more specific definitions, however, three major kinds of emphasis can be discerned: cognitive, emotional-spiritual, and procedural, which are not mutually exclusive.[4] Thus, those who stress the cognitive aspect believe that "reconciliation goes beyond the agenda of formal conflict resolution to changing the motivations, goals, beliefs, attitudes and emotions by the great majority of the society's members regarding the conflict, the nature of the relationship between the parties, and the parties themselves" (Bar-Tal and Bennink, this volume). In other words, here reconciliation refers to the gradual, bottom-up reconstructing of one's own and mutual perceptions in a different, nonconflictual cognitive framework.

Those who emphasize the emotional-spiritual component go beyond the attitudinal change that is the focus of the cognitive approach and call for repentance and forgiveness: "forgiveness is perceived as an integral part of reconciliation and adds the spiritual-moral flavor to it" (Auerbach, this volume). Particularly in Christian contexts, forgiveness is a very familiar idea, since it constitutes a necessary stage in the religious sequence of confession, repentance, forgiveness, and reconciliation. The transformability issue arises here as well, though in a different sense, since religion and politics are not necessarily the same. Thus, for instance, Archbishop Desmond Tutu often found it necessary to emphasize in his speeches that these concepts were not only applicable to the realm of religion and spiritual affairs but equally so to the domain of political practice (Du Toit, 2001: 32–33). However, as many have already observed, whereas in the Christian tradition forgiveness is a necessary and sufficient act for reconciliation, in other religio-cultures, such as Judaism and Islam, forgiveness is not a central religious theme. In such contexts, therefore, it would be unreasonable to expect it to become an integral part or necessary condition for reconciliation. This is also the case where both sides feel victimized and hence expect the other to repent, while not feeling obligated to do so themselves because of the harms inflicted on them.

Other definitions, as mentioned, focus more on the practical-procedural aspect of reconciliation. Reconciliation procedures vary from holding sustained dialogue groups on the grassroots level to semilegal procedures, as in South Africa with the TRC. The latter is, in fact, the example most adduced today for a workable process, despite the deep disagreements about its real contribution.[5] But it is worth noting that the similar technique of well-structured, public "story/truth telling," intended to establish a legal means of exchanging "admission of guilt" for "forgiveness," has also been used over the past two decades or so in about thirty other countries, mostly Latin American, that have undergone intergroup conflict resolution processes.

Somewhere in between these perceptions of the meaning of reconciliation there is also the inclusive idea of reconciliation as a "locus," a place where truth (acknowledgment, transparency, revelation, and clarity) meets mercy (acceptance, forgiveness, support, compassion, and healing), justice (equality, right relationships, rectification, and restitution), and peace (harmony, unity, well-being, security, and respect). Reconciliation, then, is "the point of encounter where concerns about both the past and the future can meet. Reconciliation as encounter suggests that space for the acknowledging of the past and envisioning of the future is the necessary ingredient for reframing the present" (Lederach, 1998: 27).

These differences in how reconciliation is conceptualized point to another, as yet unresolved dilemma: is reconciliation a process or an outcome, or perhaps both? (Bar-Tal and Bennink, this volume). Although such an identification is somewhat problematic from the philosophical point of view, things are somewhat easier for those who maintain in practice that reconciliation is both the process and the outcome. However, those who separate the former from the latter should, but often do not, tell us what to call the process if reconciliation is its outcome, or, alternatively, what the outcome is if reconciliation is the process.

Purpose and Timing

The process-outcome dilemma brings us, in turn, to the two very central and intertwined issues of purpose and timing, on which there also seems to be no consensus at present. Is reconciliation the ultimate aim, or is it perhaps only a means of getting to the normalization of relations between the former foes? When should or does it take place?

Some theories, particularly those that look at the reconciliation process from an instrumental standpoint, suggest that it is best to think in terms of different interim goals of reconciliation at different stages of the conflict-resolution process. Thus, in the preagreement stage the purpose of reconciliation is to bring the parties to the negotiating table (Kelman, 2000). The assumption here is that without some degree of reconciliation, the former enemies will never get to the table: "presettlement reconciliation begins the transformation of an enemy into a future neighbor by helping the parties imagine that coexistence is possible" (Ross, this volume). In the postsettlement phase, the task of reconciliation, according to this analytical framework, is different: to help establish institutions and practices of regularized interaction, or the normalization of relations.

Particularly among political scientists and international relations scholars, however, reconciliation is perceived as a (preliminary) mechanism for stabilizing peace: that is, reconciliation is the precondition for maintaining and consolidating peace relations, and a stable peace is possible only after concluding a mutual reconciliation. In other words, things go in this order: first the signing of a formal peace agreement, then reconciliation, then the stabilization of peace. Others, however, maintain that reconciliation can be used interchangeably with "stable peace," and regard it as "the long term goal of any process of conflict resolution" (Rothstein, 1999c: 237)

Indeed, most researchers put reconciliation as the end product and final phase of the peacemaking process. This is particularly true for those who see reconciliation as a socio-emotional phenomenon. When reconciliation is regarded as a means of achieving societal healing and establishing justice, then it is the end product, a perception that underlay the South African endeavor of the TRC: "we were looking for healing, and it's probably an African concept of our understanding of penology. What's the purpose of justice? The purpose is ultimately the restoration of harmony" (Tutu, 2000: 105).

Thus far we have looked briefly at the theoretical ambiguities and incongruities relating to the core issues of locus, level of analysis, essence, purpose, and timing of the reconciliation process/product. It is also important to point to several major lacunae in the literature that must be filled in the future if the notion is to be analytically functional. To start with, both the direction and criteria of measuring success or failure are almost a terra incognita. Is reconciliation linear or nonlinear, that is, reversible or irreversible? Furthermore, how long must the relations between the relevant collectives remain amicable for us to know that reconciliation has genuinely taken place? If full-scale hostilities resume a short time after the signing of the peace agreement, then clearly reconciliation has failed or did not occur: But what if only a few violent clashes of a limited scale occur here and there while in general the two formerly hostile populations interact peacefully? Is the absence of violence indeed the only litmus test of reconciliation? Against the background of a protracted conflict, does a prolonged "cold peace" signify practical reconciliation? What about cases in which there never was amity in the past—what is "reconciliation" or "normalization" then, since the very notion implies the return to a previous situation of harmony? Last but not least, the question of transferability from the small-group level to the larger ones, up to the level of the nation, is yet to be thoroughly investigated. To what extent are all findings and sophisticated analyses regarding the motivations and interactions that take place in reconciliation workshops or in other, similar small-scale activities, conducted in well-controlled and highly constructed environments, at all relevant to our understanding of reconciliation processes in the very different, much larger, and almost uncontrollable contexts of which the "real world" is composed?

Reconciliation: A Workable Notion?

Once the notion of reconciliation is translated into practice, the theoretical-paradigmatic dilemmas discussed above are reflected and even magnified. This is of critical importance since, after all, conflict-resolution theories are inevitably prescriptive.[6] Following are just a few examples of this problematic spillover from the theoretical to the practical level.

If the locus and origin of the process—top-down or bottom-up—are not clear, those who plan reconciliation strategies are practically in limbo as to where to direct their efforts and offer their services. One alternative consists of the politicians and other public opinion leaders, so that they in turn will influence and unify their constituencies; however, it may be more effective to concentrate on grassroots-level programs, for example, organizing citizens' dialogue groups so as to create a public atmosphere that will eventually influence the leaders to pursue peace.

A similar dilemma involves the theoretical ambiguity on the question of whether reconciliation is a spontaneous process or needs to be introduced and encouraged so as to gain momentum. If the first hypothesis is correct, then those seeking to promote peace by reconciliation should not do much, since it is just a matter of time until the formal situation of peace percolates down to the people-to-people level and the confidence-building measures start to take effect so that normalization and thus reconciliation begin to evolve. Yet if reconciliation does not automatically develop under peace conditions, then not doing anything to encourage it may lead sooner or later to the collapse of the formal peace agreement because of a lack of solid societal foundations.

The variety of views on the essentials of reconciliation, its purpose and therefore timing, is also problematic when one gets to the practical stage. In seeking models to follow, the practitioners who aim to promote peacemaking on a large scale—that of ethnic groups or even whole nations—must choose between either techniques developed in "laboratory" contexts and with the participation of small groups of people, most of whom had a preliminary commitment to the idea of conflict resolution (for example, I. Maoz, this volume; Ross, this volume), or reconciliation techniques used in national contexts that often are quite different in terms of history, culture, human composition, resources, and the like. Thus, the applicability question is acute. For example, on the issue of Northern Ireland there was a heated debate on the extent to which the seemingly successful South African TRC approach could be used to bridge between the Republicans and the Loyalists in Ulster, with some experts objecting that this method was unsuitable to the case at hand (McGarry, 1998).

The problem of contexts also arose in a meeting of the Nobel peace laureates in which peacemaking and reconciliation were discussed. Archbishop Desmond Tutu argued for the universal advantages of the TRC method and its applicability to no-win situations, which are the point of departure for many conflict-resolution processes: "[it] didn't happen because South Africans were particularly smart—it was forced on them because of the realities of our situation: no one won. The Apartheid government didn't win, the liberation movements didn't win. Stalemate. . . . And they struck on this compromise. . . ." (Tutu, 2000: 104). Another participant, Harn Yawngwhe of Burma, challenged him by stressing the difficulty of transposing a successful method into a different cultural environment: "Will this work in a situation like Burma where, really, we don't have a concept of forgiveness? We have compassion, we may excuse people, but the concept of forgiveness is something quite different." (Tutu, 2000: 109).[7] This clearly points to the need for "culturally dependent" notions of reconciliation, for "Although some of the theories and techniques are universal . . . particular cultural, social and historical elements are of major importance in conflict resolution processes" (Steinberg, 2001: 4).

The remainder of this chapter is meant to demonstrate the rather "heretical" idea of the potential perils of context-insensitive reconciliation attempts, based on the Israeli-Palestinian case.

The Israeli-Palestinian Case

In this section I will examine two efforts to introduce certain aspects of reconciliation into Israeli-Palestinian relations. This conflict has often been characterized as particularly resistant to resolution (for example, Rouhana and Bar-Tal, 1998). Indeed, in the early 1990s a prominent Israeli political analyst made an observation that today, almost eight years down the road from the signing of the first Oslo agreement, seems unfortunately to have lost none of its relevance: "nothing seems to change and no resolution is in sight. Issues raised twenty, forty years ago seem valid forever. So one does not have to alter one's messages as they seem perennially relevant; nor should one suggest new remedies. The problem, once defined, remains unaltered and the paradigm durable. After all, we are no closer to resolving the conundrum, so why bother to redefine it?" (Benvenisti, 1990: 117). The reason for this resistance to change, he asserts, is that "The struggle goes beyond the apparent physical survival of the people involved and encompasses basic issues of identity and integrity. The core-issue is therefore non-negotiable, for issues of identity are a zero-sum game" (Benvenisti, 1990: 121). However, it is exactly in this sort of conflict that reconciliation is most needed; hence it is against such a background that the utility of the notion can be tested.

The first reconciliation effort to be discussed here is the ongoing activity of the various peace groups, such as Gush Shalom, Rapprochement, or Bat Shalom, which have been engaged for many years now in organizing "sustained dialogue" between Israelis and Palestinians (for example, Golan and Kamal, 1999; Schnell, Awerbuch, and Manor, 2000). Compared to the emotional and material resources that have been invested in it, this noninstitutional, grassroots endeavor has borne only few fruits in terms of changing societal beliefs about the Palestinians on the Israeli side (Hermann: 2001). The second, institutional effort at reconciliation consisted practically, although not explicitly, of the peace plan presented by Prime Minister Ehud Barak at the Camp David II summit in the summer of 2000. This plan marked an unprecedented attempt by the top-level Israeli decision makers to address directly the core issues of the conflict—including the refugee problem and Jerusalem— while also considering acts of restorative justice (for example, admitting a number of Palestinian refugees into Israel), a conceptual breakthrough of the kind recommended by the reconciliation models mentioned above. However, for reasons to be discussed below, this move, which was carried out (and failed) at the decision makers' level, backfired even more severely at the grassroots level, so that the two sides reverted to their "traditional," highly antagonistic, diametrically opposed postures.

The Efforts of the Peace Groups

The peace groups sustained dialogue throughout their long years of activity, which began decades before any formal Israeli-Palestinian peace negotiations were launched (for example, M. Bar-On, 1996; Sharoni, 1995). Thus the peace activists were the first in Israel to challenge the prevalent belief that the conflict's final outcome would be determined by military means; to point to the fact that the David versus Goliath myth was inexact, at least so far as the Israeli-Palestinian balance of power was concerned; and to emphasize the fact that the same international norms on whose basis the Zionist movement had claimed the Jews' right to a state justified the Palestinians' demand for an independent state of their own. Furthermore, the peace groups were the first to maintain that even if one accepts the notion that all or most of the wars had been forced on Israel and were therefore defensive ones, much suffering, not all of it unavoidable, had been inflicted on the Palestinian people as well. Israel, the peace activists asserted, should therefore end the occupation by withdrawing completely from the territories conquered in 1967, and recognize its own part in the responsibility for the Palestinians' suffering as well as compensate them for it materially and symbolically.

These noninstitutional, propeace activities fell into three categories, according to their respective audiences: (a) the Israeli authorities, via protest activities against certain state measures and policies; (b) the Israeli public, via consciousness-raising activities aimed, as mentioned earlier, at pressuring policymakers from below to come up with a peace plan and at creating a solid base of grassroots support for such a peace plan once launched; and (c) the Palestinians, via dialogue meetings, so as to persuade them that the Israeli people were interested in resolving the conflict even if their government's policies did not necessarily indicate such interest.[8]

The protest activity was the most instrumental and least complicated of these three: it took only mobilizing some hundreds or thousands of people to demonstrate against the government's policies or share the costs of newspaper ads. This hardly necessitated a change of the other side's image, or direct interaction with members of the "enemy" collective. To a large extent this was a domestic matter—a dispute between Israelis and their leaders on how to promote Israel's national interest. The appeals to the Israeli and Palestinian publics, however, involved some soul-searching, including the overcoming of stereotypes and a confrontation with the origins of the conflict. It also meant surmounting the natural tendency to self-indulgence, and seeking means of redress for those on the other side who had been individually and collectively victimized, while at the same time not denying the basic need for both national and personal security. Indeed, it proved much easier to recruit participants for the protest activities than for the other two types.

The organizers of the Israeli-Palestinian dialogue meetings aimed first and foremost at changing the mutual images of the participants. The details of a workable peace plan were of only minor importance in that context, perhaps because of the participants' lack of relevant information and experience but even more so because dealing with the practical aspects of conflict resolution would have hindered the creation of an amicable social climate. The underlying idea was that if the Israeli and Palestinian participants got the opportunity to know each other personally and on an equal footing, they would discover the many things they had in common, and begin to exert pressure from below on their respective political leaders to start negotiating a resolution of the conflict.

As of the late 1980s these dialogue meetings mushroomed, with women and youth participating even more than men. On the Israeli side the participants were mostly Ashkenazi, secular, urban, middle-class, and highly educated, and many were immigrants from English-speaking countries. The Palestinian participants showed a similar sociodemographic and socioeconomic profile, with a salient presence of Christians. Efforts to widen the circle of participants were unsuccessful. Some of the forums were held on an ongoing weekly or monthly basis; others were of a more ad hoc kind. Mainly for technical reasons, most of these meetings were held in the occupied territories, so that the Israeli participants got some firsthand experience of what life under occupation feels like—a factor that heavily influenced the discourse that developed in these sessions.

Nevertheless, despite the good intentions of the organizers and the considerable material resources that were invested (part of which came from private, NGO, or government-foundation sources outside of the region), a sober accounting of this endeavor must acknowledge that it came to very little. By and large, the Israeli Jewish public has rejected the reconciliatory message that the peace activists tried to disseminate.[9] A variety of factors curtailed the popularity and credibility of the dialogue program; among these, the above-mentioned sociodemographic profile of the participants alienated large segments of the Israeli Jewish public. The heavy involvement of women also acted as an impediment by projecting a "soft" image.

However, the main thing that prevented the peace movement from mobilizing large-scale support for its reconciliation efforts was that these could not possibly conform with the deeply rooted zero-sum definition of the conflict, a pillar of the mainstream Israeli ethos. This definition highlights the existential threat inherent in Israel's geopolitical position as a Jewish state in a mostly Muslim-Arab Middle East—a situation often likened to that of a tiny island in a vast, stormy, hostile ocean. Thus, the conflict with the Arabs in general and the Palestinians in particular has for decades been regarded as irreconcilable, total, and focal, with the other side having a vested interest in its continuation (Bar-Tal and Oren, 2000: 4). During the stressful, costly, and prolonged years of war, this ethos proved functional, since it enabled Israel to cope successfully with the conflict's painful consequences. But when the peace negotiations were launched in the early 1990s it needed to be modified, and indeed it was albeit only to a limited extent. In the late 1990s, for example, public opinion surveys indicated that the principle of exchanging land for peace had become widely accepted (Arian, 1999: 17). A significant transformation could also be discerned regarding the Palestinians' right to an independent state. Whereas the establishment of such a state had in the past been considered taboo by almost all Israeli Jews, a short while before the second Intifada erupted a majority of them (about 70 percent) were convinced that a Palestinian state was at least a fait accompli, and a somewhat smaller majority of about 55 percent also believed that its establishment was morally justified (Peace Index Survey, June 2000).

This growing readiness by the Israeli public to make territorial concessions should not, however, mislead us. At the same time, national and personal security have remained Israel's principal concerns, and Arabs in general and the Palestinians in particular still remain negatively stereotyped for the most part. For instance, when asked in a public opinion survey in late 2000 about the ultimate Palestinian intentions toward the state of Israel, over 70 percent of Israeli Jewish respondents answered that if they had the capability, the Palestinians would destroy Israel. Even in the mid-1990s when the peace negotiations were moving ahead, the number of those agreeing with this statement was not much smaller.[10] In other words, today, despite all the numerous dialogue activities, the majority of Israelis still perceive the Palestinians—with whom they have been negotiating peace for almost a decade now—as basically hostile. Hence they favor the "fence option," that is, complete physical separation between the two peoples even if and after a formal peace agreement is finally reached.[11]

As noted earlier, many theorists believe that one of the main components of reconciliation is the readiness of the protagonists in a conflict to acknowledge their responsibility for each other's suffering. No such readiness seems to be evident in Israel today. When asked back in 1999, during Barak's term, when it seemed the peace process was advancing, "who is responsible for the creation of the refugee problem in 1948—Israel or the Arabs," only 9.5 percent of Israeli Jews said Israel was to blame, almost half (47.5 percent) said the Arab side was responsible, 25 percent put equal blame on both sides, and the rest had no clear opinion (Peace Index Survey, December 1999).

It is not surprising, then, that the peace movement's admonitions to try and look at the situation through the Palestinians' eyes as well have not resonated. The universalistic, liberal approach that underlies the reconciliation endeavor has been rejected in particular by the Orthodox and ultra-Orthodox sectors, as well as by the vast majority of Israelis of Mizrahi (Middle Eastern) origin, the younger age cohorts, and by those of low income and education. The peace activists (and particularly the women) were blamed for being unpatriotic ("Arab lovers"), for neglecting Israel's national security, and for over-identifying with the enemy by accepting its historical narrative as legitimate.[12] Their insistence on maintaining their contacts with the other side against the background of waves of terrorism was often characterized as psychologically "unnatural" or "twisted," reflecting a loss of healthy survival instincts. As noted by two prominent peace activists, an Israeli and a Palestinian, who organized many dialogue meetings: "In both societies, dialogue was viewed as fraternizing with the enemy. By entering into dialogue, you were according the enemy legitimacy and, possibly, dulling your own spirit, perhaps crippling your own ability to fight. . . . Both societies and most of their political bodies feared the possible effects of dialogue: How can you kill if you are friends?" (Golan and Kamal, 1999). This, in its turn, has facilitated the efforts of right-wing politicians and even some in the center to delegitimize the movement and its agenda.

The efforts of the Israeli peace movement to join forces with the Palestinians in developing reconciliation programs also proved quite problematic.[13] The dynamics that evolved in the dialogue meetings—whether academic symposia, small-scale encounters in private homes, or political gatherings designed for planning joint activities, whether in meetings aimed at fostering social dialogue or in those aimed at creating a confrontation so as to get at the origins of the conflict—were almost always similar: the "objective" power relations between the two sides were practically reversed. The Israeli participants, rejected and sometimes even ostracized by the majority on their own side because of their association with the "enemy," showed a defensive and apologetic posture. This reflected their sense of standing on a shaky moral ground belonging, at least formally, to the "evil" side that had inflicted so much pain on their dialogue partners, to the occupier who was militarily, economically, and in certain respects politically so much stronger. This feeling clashed with the Israeli Jewish historical narrative of David versus Goliath. The Palestinians, for their part, were energized by their sense that they were always the victims and the underdogs and hence owed no compassion to the Israeli side, and they often took a militant posture in these meetings and saw the Israeli participants' *mea culpa* attitude as a sign of weakness. Thus, the Palestinians accused their interlocutors of serving as the fig leaf of the Israeli occupation system, and demanded that they prove their "innocence" by publicly repudiating their own people and leaders as war criminals in the worst case or peace resisters in the better one. This, of course, put the Israeli peace activists in a very difficult cognitive situation, leading many of them to quit the joint activities sooner or later. The minimal effect of these "sustained dialogue" events is made plain by the following analysis of the present crisis in Israeli-Palestinian relations:

> Today one can state with considerable certainty that never before—
> since the sprouting of the first buds of the desire for coexistence be-
> tween Israelis and Palestinians—have the disengagement, hostility,
> and estrangement between them been so high, and in particular be-
> tween those who devoted their energy and talents to promoting rec-
> onciliation between their respective peoples. The optimistic view
> that the peace process is unavoidably a linear one led to the shatter-
> ing of the perception of peace in the face of reality. In place of the

shattered hopes came great frustration, which led to despair. The
sense that a war is going on is, of course, nourished by the high
level of Palestinian violence, by the acts of suicide terrorism, but to
no less an extent by the overt hostility expressed by people who had
participated in dozens of meetings and dialogues. (Benvenisti, 2001:
B1)

The Barak Peace Proposal

The second, very different and much more controversial example of an effort
to introduce components of reconciliation into the Israeli-Palestinian conflict-
resolution process was that involving Prime Minister Ehud Barak in the summer of 2000. The severe criticism of his peace policy at the time, which came
both from the right (for allegedly making excessive practical and symbolic concessions and being overeager to appease the Palestinians at the expense of
Israel's national interests and most cherished values) and the left (for suppos-
edly pushing Arafat too aggressively into participating in the Camp David II
summit and offering him too little while asking for too much), suggests that
Barak's move indeed marked a real turning point in the Arab-Israeli peace
negotiations. The political difficulties inherent in his move and the risk of
opening a dangerous attitudinal gap between the decision makers and the
public were clear to him, as is evident from a press interview he gave as far
back as late 1999: "There is an urgent need for peace between governments;
peace between peoples, genuine reconciliation, could take three to four generations."[14] If Camp David had been fruitful, that is, if a permanent status
agreement had emerged from it, then no doubt it would have met the three
criteria for reconciliation events: (1) direct physical contact or proximity between opponents, usually senior representatives of the respective factions, (2)
a public ceremony accompanied by substantial publicity, and (3) ritualistic behavior indicating that the parties regard the dispute as having been resolved.
Yet the fact that it failed to produce such an agreement can hardly, I maintain,
nullify its character as a planned reconciliation event.

It was in Camp David II that, for the first time, the most sensitive issues
standing at the heart of the conflict were openly put on the table, whereas the
practical-technical aspects that had deliberately been given centrality in the
previous negotiation phases were now made secondary. It was commonly felt
in Israel that the sides were indeed getting to the core matters, and that such
a confrontation of truths and narratives might weaken the firm bargaining
positions of Israel's negotiators, who would fear missing this opportunity—
perhaps the last for a long time—to arrive at a permanent peace agreement.

It was to alleviate these apprehensions that Barak, before leaving Israel for this summit, set forth his "red lines," which did not seem to reflect a reconciliatory posture at all. He promised to deny any Israeli responsibility for the refugee problem, to resist all pressures to divide Jerusalem, to insist that any agreement not undermine Israel's national security, and to ensure that the large settlement blocs would remain intact.[15] Yet in the context of the American-mediated, two-week-long summit, these "nos" were apparently transformed into a far-reaching, reconciliatory peace plan. The Palestinian right of return was indeed addressed, as well as the issue of sovereignty over Jerusalem in general and over the holy places in particular. The future of the settlements—the main thorn in the flesh for the Palestinians—seemed to be much less guaranteed than in Barak's pre-takeoff speech. Although it was never officially confirmed, the media reported a highly forthcoming Israeli offer to the Palestinians that was meant to cut the Gordian knot: it was said to have included withdrawal from almost all of the occupied territories (thereby terminating the relations of occupier and occupied), a practical division of Jerusalem giving the Palestinians control over large parts of the city and de facto recognition of their hold over the Temple Mount (thereby satisfying a major Muslim religious claim), and, no less controversial from the Israeli standpoint, the admission of 100,000 Palestinian refugees into pre-1967 Israel[16] and as many as wanted into the areas controlled by the Palestinian Authority (PA), soon to become the independent Palestinian state (thereby practically acknowledging the Palestinians' attachment to the land and also, in fact, at least some Israeli responsibility for creating the refugee problem). In return, the major demand presented by the Israeli representatives was that Arafat, on behalf of the Palestinian people, declare that the conflict had ended.

This peace plan, then, albeit indirectly, related to the past and the future as well as the restoration-of-justice issue and the issue of "let bygones be bygones"—all necessary steps in the direction of genuine, longstanding conflict resolution and reconciliation. Yet this endeavor collapsed; the summit ended with no final agreement and, worse, with much mutual anger and disappointment that rapidly turned into sheer violence with the breakout of a second Palestinian Intifada. In keeping with a point noted in the theoretical discussion above, the peace move that had been made at the leadership level raised the important question of authority. Was the PA authorized to sign a final status agreement with Israel that included compensation for the vast majority of the refugees who would not be allowed to return, and, even more so, to call an end to the conflict on behalf of the entire Palestinian people, thereby actually taking a major step toward forgiveness? Was the Israeli prime minister authorized to relinquish large parts of Jerusalem, including holy places, without obtaining in advance the consent of the Knesset or even the public, not to mention the Jewish people in the Diaspora or the Jewish people of past and future generations?

The Palestinians rejected Barak's plan on the basis that neither their demand for sovereignty in Jerusalem, including the Temple Mount, nor their claim for the full right of return for the refugees had been fulfilled. They rejected the Israeli demand to declare that the conflict had ended, calling it unacceptable and asserting that even if Israel were to fulfill all of its obligations to the last detail and even if they had to come to terms with Israel's existence out of political realism, they could not, in consideration of past and future generations, recognize Israeli ownership over any segment of the land. Thus they totally repudiated the notion of forgiveness.

The backlash on the Israeli side was not much gentler. Barak, stung both by disappointment at the Palestinian rejection of what he saw as a most generous offer and by the severe domestic opposition to his peace policy, pronounced all his proposals to be null and void. He also declared that the last opportunity to make peace for the foreseeable future had been squandered because of Palestinian stubbornness.[17] Public opinion, which had been quite reserved about Barak's peace plan to begin with, now reacted sharply to the Palestinians' unwillingness to accept it. When asked: "Do you feel that the positions presented by Barak at Camp David for the final stage of the peace process were too tough, too conciliatory, or appropriate, meaning not too harsh and not too yielding?" the majority, 44 percent, replied that they were too conciliatory; only 9 percent deemed Barak's positions too tough, and 35 percent felt they were appropriate. Moreover, 48.5 percent of Israelis felt it was the Palestinians who had more wisely looked out for their own interests at Camp David, whereas only 26 percent believed it was Israel (the rest responded that there was no difference, or had no opinion) that had done so. At the same time, a decisive majority (65 percent) held the Palestinians responsible for the failure of the talks whereas only 13 percent put the blame only or mostly on Israel's shoulders. In October 2000, only 20 percent of the respondents thought the Palestinians were genuinely interested in peace with Israel (compared, for example, to June of that year, when about 50 percent believed so). The November survey indicated that the Jewish public was generally not empathetic toward Palestinian motives regarding the Intifada: it not only considered the Palestinians to be wholly responsible for its outbreak, but viewed them as indifferent to the value of human life and therefore as maintaining their violence despite the large numbers of dead and wounded that they themselves had sustained. Moreover, the Jewish public agreed that since the Palestinians realized the high value that the Jewish people placed on human life, they exploited this fact so as to erode Israel's morale. Rightly or wrongly, then, most Israeli Jews perceived the Barak initiative as an act of reconciliation that was not appreciated or equivalently reciprocated. Instead, they believed, the Palestinians had interpreted his initiative as a sign of political weakness, thus raising their expectations and demands. Therefore, as often occurs in such situations (Kriesberg, this volume), Israelis felt shortchanged and sought to regain what they had lost.

What Is to Be Done?

Notwithstanding the theoretical and practical problems raised in this chapter, few would question that the discussion of reconciliation has contributed considerably to our understanding of the causes, components, and dynamics of various sorts of conflict, as well as the conditions for their resolution. The need to open channels, or space, for direct and candid communication between the protagonists, the role of rapprochement on the grassroots (and not only leadership) level in translating formal peace agreements into reality, the importance of the perpetrators' admitting the wrongs done and injuries inflicted and being pardoned by the victims, the importance of symbolic and practical reparations, the difficulty of resolving a conflict when the power relations are heavily imbalanced, the need to satisfy not only practical demands but also emotional needs when addressing the origins of the conflict—all these have been elaborated in an unprecedented manner in the academic discussion of reconciliation.

At the same time, this chapter indicates that much analytical work still needs to be done and creative modes of action need to be worked out. It appears that when and where conflicts are already ripe for resolution, reconciliation processes, though likely to gain momentum, have only a limited role and the effect of the problems raised above is relatively minor.[18] But when the conflict is deeply rooted and resolution-resistant like the Israeli-Palestinian one, practical rapprochement endeavors based on vague, unrefined notions of reconciliation are often nonproductive and possibly even detrimental if they induce strong negative reactions on the grassroots level.

There is a need to elaborate precise yet context-related conceptual and operative definitions of reconciliation, which on the one hand will distinguish it from conflict resolution, peacemaking, and normalization while on the other hand clarifying the essential linkages and chronological sequence between them. Last, but most important, it seems that what we desperately need is not a universal model of reconciliation, as sophisticated as it may be, but culture-related models that will "emerge from the resources present in a particular setting and respond to needs in this context" (Lederach, 1988: 55). We would then have reconciliation models suitable for "demotic cultures"—that is, political cultures in which power emanates from the bottom up and in which the elite pays close attention to the attitudes of its grassroots constituency—and models suitable for more elitist or autocratic political cultures where the direction of political initiatives is always from the top down. We would have models for cultures that are familiar with the sequence of repentance-forgiveness, and for societies that interpret the readiness to ask for forgiveness as manifesting collective weakness—and so on. Only in this way can we avoid or at least minimize the frustration stemming from low-effectiveness reconciliation efforts such as the one made by the Israeli peace movement, as well as backlashes like the one that followed the failure of the Barak peace initiative.

NOTES

1. This observation is by no means original, and in fact occurs in almost every chapter presented in this workshop ("the term tends to be fuzzy, its meaning largely determined by the context in which it appears" [I. Maoz, 1999: 2]).

2. For a comparative analysis of the various workshop models, see Avruch (1998).

3. An official Commission of Inquiry established in 1995 to describe and analyze public violence from 1965 to 1994, make recommendations about preventing future human rights violations, propose measures aimed at restoring the dignity of victims as well as making reparations to them, and recommend the granting of amnesty to perpetrators of violence (Du Toit, 2001: 32).

4. Gardner-Feldman (1999) uses a somewhat different categorization, maintaining that reconciliation has both philosophical-emotional and practical-material aspects. Nadler (2001) distinguishes between socio-emotional and instrumental reconciliation.

5. Du Toit, 2001: 32–33.

6. For the contribution of academic research to the resolution of concrete conflicts, see for example, Lederach (1995) and Kelman (2000).

7. Harn Yawngwhe was present at this discussion because the Noble laureate herself, Aung San Suu Kye, could not attend, since if she left Burma the authorities would not allow her to return.

8. The political establishment was well aware of the potential influence of direct dialogue at the noninstitutional level; hence in 1986 the Knesset enacted a law prohibiting meetings between Israeli citizens and PLO officials. In fact, some peace activists were sentenced to short prison terms for disobeying it. The law was overturned in 1993, soon after Labor returned to power.

9. In a recent public opinion survey, only 15 percent of the respondents in a representative sample of Israeli Jews said that they had ever taken part in any meeting with Palestinians (Peace Index Survey, April 2001).

10. For the exact numbers, see Peace Index surveys results at http://www.tau.ac .il/peace/Peace_Index/.

11. For the figures on Israeli support for total separation, see Peace Index Surveys, March 1995, January 1996, November 1997, February 1999, August 2000.

12. For a vivid, firsthand description of bypassers' reactions of this kind to women participating in a Women in Black vigil, see Helman and Rapoport (1997).

13. For a very recent account of the various dialogue activities and the obstacles they face, see Rotem (2001).

14. Makovsky, D., and D. Herman, "MERIA Israelist: Interview with Barak," Sept. 27, 1999, *Meria* (online journal); mail to: besa@mail.bui.ac.il.

15. The full texts of his speeches when departing and returning can be found on the home page of the Israel Ministry for Foreign Affairs (www.mfa.gov .il), under Peace Process/Documents.

16. Over 76 percent of the Israeli Jews opposed admitting these 100,000 Palestinian refugees (out of an estimated total of four million refugees and their descendants) based on family reunion or other humanitarian reasons, as suggested by Barak (Peace Index Survey, July 2000).

17. See Barak's statement on his return from Camp David—July 26, 2000, www .mfa.gov.il/mfa/go.asp.

18. For the concept of ripeness, see Zartman (1995).

3

Dialectics between Stable Peace and Reconciliation

Yaacov Bar-Siman-Tov

Most studies of conflict resolution and peacemaking concentrate more on the causes of and conditions for shifting from war to peace and less on the conditions necessary for maintenance and consolidation of peace after conflict resolution. Although conflict resolution leads to a formal termination of a conflict when a peace agreement has been reached and signed by the parties, it does not necessarily stabilize, normalize, or consolidate the new peace relations or even prevent the development of a new conflict in the future that may bring about renewed violence (Burton, 1990; Fisher, 1990, Kriesberg, 1992; Bar-Tal, 2000b).

Even when the sides to a protracted conflict succeed in resolving their conflict of interests, and especially those regarding territory, boundaries, resources, or sovereignty, they sometimes fail to satisfy one or both sides or overcome the bitterness and grievances inherent in a protracted conflict, nor their hostile perceptions and mutual fears. As a result, they may find it hard if not impossible to normalize and warm the peace relations, which remain minimal, cold, and limited to the political and security cooperation necessary for maintaining the peace. Reaching a political formula for resolving the conflict of interest is necessary but insufficient for surmounting the political and psychological barriers that may foil the normalization and stabilization of peace relations (Kriesberg, 1998a; Kelman, 1999a; Rothstein, 1999b, 1999c; Bar-Tal, 2000b).

Once peace is obtained, the main questions are

1. Can peace be maintained and stabilized?
2. What are the necessary, sufficient, and favorable conditions for maintenance and consolidation of peace?

Various studies in international relations and social psychology suggest various conditions that the sides should meet in order to facilitate stable peace and reach reconciliation.

The literature in international relations suggests two main clusters of conditions: structural-institutional and learning conditions. The structural-institutional cluster includes the following conditions: common characteristics of the states involved, extensive and intensive transactions and interactions between the nations, and a network of international organizations and institutions. The learning cluster includes strategic or complex learning and social learning. However, this literature neglects or minimizes the role of reconciliation in maintaining and consolidating of peace between and within nations mainly because it perceives reconciliation as concerning only intergroup, internal, or ethnic conflicts (Boulding, 1978; Russett and Starr, 1992; Adler & Barnett, 1998a, 1998b; Kacowicz, 1998, Brecke and Long, 1999; Kacowicz & Bar-Siman-Tov, 2000; Ross, this volume).

The social psychology literature stresses the need for reconciliation that combines cognitive and emotional factors in stabilizing peace following conflict resolution; however, it neglects or minimizes the role of structural-institutional and learning conditions. The reason for this is probably the concentration of most of this literature on internal conflict, which tends to deal more with social or political conflict and less with international conflict (Kriesberg, 1998a; Kelman, 1999a; Brecke and Long, 1999; Bar-Tal, 2000b).

In this chapter, I would like to argue that a better understanding of the question of maintenance and consolidation of peace requires a combination of the theories of international relations and social psychology—in other words, the combined notions of stable peace and reconciliation. This study suggests a conceptual framework that includes the following clusters of conditions as well as their interrelationship: mutual satisfaction, structural-institutional conditions, learning, and reconciliation.

A stable peace can be established only when the sides to a peace agreement are satisfied with the peace agreement and after the underlying of structural-institutional, cognitive, and emotional conditions of a protracted conflict have been transformed to the mutual satisfaction of the sides involved via a process of learning and reconciliation.

This chapter is organized in the following way. The first section begins with a discussion of the term *stable peace*. The second section deals with conditions for stable peace, including mutual satisfaction conditions, structural-institutional conditions, and learning conditions. The third section deals with the role of reconciliation in maintenance and consolidation of peace relations. The fourth section examines the interrelationship among the various types of conditions.

Stable Peace

Boulding, who was the first to present the idea of stable peace, defines it as "a situation in which the probability of war is so small that it does not really enter into the calculations of any of the people involved" (1978: 13). Stable peace, according to Boulding is the "object of policy" and a "deliberate decision" of the participants (1978: xi). George defines stable peace as a relationship between two sides in which neither side considers the use of military force or even the threat of it in any dispute between them (1992). Russet and Starr define stable peace (among the Organization for Economic Cooperation and Development—OECD—states) as "the absence of preparation for war or the serious expectation of war with each other" (1992: 376).

According to these definitions, stable peace, on the one hand, is an outcome, a situation, or a kind of relationship between states whereby the sides exclude the use of military force and even the threat of use of it in any dispute between them. On the other hand, stable peace is a long, gradual, and slow process whereby the sides follow different requirements in various stages in order to accomplish the peace. Stable peace does not exclude competitive behavior or even a conflict between the parties; however, it requires that every conflict be resolved only by peaceful means. These definitions imply that the actors involved in this relationship develop a common understanding and dependable and stable expectations regarding the continuation of peaceful relations without a concern of resorting to force (Deutsch et al., 1957: 5; Adler and Barnett, 1998b: 34–35). Since it is a deliberate decision of the actors to be in this kind of relationship, they also share the same interests, norms, and values regarding maintenance and consolidation of peace and develop institutions and mechanisms for management and regulation of their relations.

Although these definitions do not stipulate that the relations should necessarily be positive, warm, and harmonious, the common assumption accepted by scholars is that stable peace tends to be positive (Boulding, 1978), warm (Miller, 2000), and even the "distinctive feature" of a security community (Adler and Barnett, 1998b: 30–31). Boulding maintains that a relationship of stable peace "is not the same thing as having a common language, a common religion, a common culture, or even common interests" (1978: 17). Nevertheless, stable peace "is a condition of good management, orderly resolution of conflict, harmony associated with mature relationship, gentleness and love" (1978: 3). Although we do not expect love between nations, the degree of harmony of interests and cooperation may influence not only the nature of peace but also the prospects of its maintenance. This discussion leads to the questions, How does stable peace emerge and what are the conditions for it?

Conditions for Stable Peace

Stable peace requires some basic conditions. We can identify three clusters of necessary conditions: mutual satisfaction, structural-institutional conditions, and learning. Mutual satisfaction is the first and immediate precondition in the long process of stable peace and is necessary for development of the two others. Without mutual satisfaction with the peace agreement, both sides probably will fail to maintain the peace. Yet mutual satisfaction is not sufficient for developing structural-institutional and learning conditions. Without the emergence of these two other conditions, the sides will remain with no stable peace. In this section I shall discuss the individual conditions necessary for stable peace and their interrelationships.

Mutual Satisfaction

Mutual satisfaction with a peace agreement is a crucial condition required for stabilizing peace and a precondition for the transition toward stable peace. Satisfaction with the agreement is a crucial factor for preservation of the peace or, in other words, for the prevention of violation or revision of the agreement that may lead to a new conflict and violence.

Mutual satisfaction emerges when the peace agreement fulfills the basic needs and national aspirations of the sides involved. The sides should be satisfied, first, with the new territorial arrangements or with the new territorial status quo and, second, with other terms of the agreement, such as the distribution of other scarce resources and other benefits (Kacowicz, 1998; Kelman, 1999a; Kacowicz and Bar-Siman-Tov, 2000). Kacowicz even suggests the need for active satisfaction with the new status quo, which implies a disposition "not only to accept the existing order but also to uphold and defend it" (Kacowicz, 1998: 49). An active satisfaction with the new status quo means also a normative acceptance of the new borders and the lack of territorial ambitions toward other states. Therefore, mutual satisfaction constitutes an important generalization about maintenance of peace, especially following resolution of a regional conflict for which the question of borders is probably the main cause (although not the only one) and whose resolution to the satisfaction of the sides involved may eliminate the danger of a new conflict.

Aron defines this condition as *peace by satisfaction*. The conditions of peace by satisfaction are (1) the political actors should not look for territory external to that under their sovereignty, and no alien population; (2) they should not extend themselves, increase their material or human resources, and disseminate their institutions. "The satisfaction derived from respect of one principle of legitimacy must be supplemented by the suspension of rivalry for land and men, force and idea, and even for pride.... Satisfaction will be lasting and assured only on condition that is general" (Aron, 1966: 144).

Nevertheless, mutual satisfaction does not necessarily require equal or symmetrical outcomes, especially where individual and joint outcomes are evaluated separately. Each side may perceive satisfaction based on its earlier expectations and on the discrepancy between earlier expectations and the negotiation's outcomes.

Both sides should be aware that the degree of mutual satisfaction influences the prospects for stable peace relations; thus, any agreement that satisfies only one side may foil the process of implementation of the agreement. Satisfaction should not be limited only to the decision makers' echelon or to the ruling political or military elites, but should also include most of the political, economic, and social elites, as well as other sectors of the population. Wide satisfaction with the agreement will legitimize the peace agreement and minimize the influence of those who are less or not satisfied with the agreement (Kacowicz, 1998: 50–55; Rothstein, 1999b, 1999c).

Satisfaction may be accomplished when both sides see the negotiation process and the peace agreement as fair and just. It is reasonable for concerns about fairness and justice to be included in the negotiation of the peace agreement: "Such concerns provide the lenses through which information is evaluated and preferences determined" (Bazerman and Neale, 1995: 106). However, since fairness and justice are not self-defining and objective terms, it may be difficult for the parties to agree on what is fair and just. The assessments of what is fair and just are often biased by self-interest. The resulting conflict in perceptions of what constitutes fair and just agreement may create barriers to implementation of peace and relations.

Negotiation experts warn that concerns about justice and fairness can promote irrationality in the way that peacemakers make decisions in implementating and deepening the peace process. Such concerns can also lead to inefficiency, such that both parties are worse off as a result of fairness considerations (Bazerman and Neale, 1995). The sides may also remain uncertain as to the probability of maintaining the peace relations, and this uncertainty may limit the utility of the peace itself (Kahenman et al., 1986). Since there is no ideal solution to the satisfaction question, and since satisfaction is also perceptual and socially constructed, much depends on how decision makers politically and socially frame the peace negotiations and agreement. Framing the peace negotiations and agreement as a mutually beneficial trade-off between the parties, and developing commitment to the agreement as the most reasonable alternative for both sides, can influence the balance of satisfaction in the direction of stable peace and reconciliation (Bazerman, Magliozzi and Neale, 1985).

Structural-Institutional Conditions

Based on the experience of stable peace in Western Europe, the literature in international relations suggests that structural-institutional conditions may explain the emergence, maintenance, and consolidation of stable peace between and among nations. These conditions combine three dimensions: (1) common characteristics of the states involved, (2) high level of interaction and cooperation, and (3) joint institutions and organizations, including the formation of pluralist security community.

COMMON CHARACTERISTICS. A common assumption is that common characteristics are necessary for the emergence and consolidation of stable peace: "Cultural, political, social, and ideological homogeneity can lead to greater interaction and association, and the development of new organizations and institutions" (Adler and Barnett, 1998b: 51). Common characteristics not only enable better communication but also encourage trust and dependable expectations of peaceful change, which are necessary for stable peace. The literature suggests the following common characteristics of the states involved as necessary for stable peace: liberal-democratic regimes, a common cultural framework and normative consensus, shared knowledge or cognitive structures, and a high level of economic development and prosperity of each actor.

The link between liberal-democratic regimes and stable peace is quite evident. Democratic peace propositions maintain that democratic states do not fight each other and do not expect to do so. Mutual, stable expectations of nonviolence are at the core of the liberal-democratic peace (Doyle, 1983; Russett, 1993; Z. Maoz and Russett, 1993; Owen, 1994, 1997). Sharing a liberal-democratic governance, which also means sharing similar domestic institutions, ideas, values, and norms, is a causal mechanism for the emergence of stable peace and for its consolidation.

States who share liberal-democratic regimes tend to identify with one another and thus develop common interests, a shared knowledge, and stable expectations as to managing their relations. Compatibility of values is more prone to create shared meaning and understanding, a common cultural framework and normative consensus, as well as the networks of organized institutions and processes (Deutsch et al., 1957: 46–47, 123–129; Adler and Barnett, 1998b: 40–41).

The presence of democracies is therefore sufficient, although not necessary, for the emergence of stable peace. Stable peace may develop also between sides that are not democracies, such as among several of the states of the Association of Southeast Asian Nations (ASEAN), or between states only one of which is democracy; for example, the relationship between the United States and Mexico up to the 1990s (Acharya, 1998; Gonzales and Haggard, 1998).

In addition to sharing democratic regimes, norms, and knowledge, a high level of economic development and prosperity of each actor is another favorable condition for the emergence and consolidation of stable peace. The assumption is that peace is the result of the achievement and continued expectation of substantial economic benefits to all the parties involved, and this is possible only if all the actors involved have a high level of economic development and prosperity. This condition is necessary because it may enable economic cooperation, interdependence, and a greater interaction between and among actors, as well as development of joint organizations and institutions, including transnational relations. This of course does not mean that all actors should be equal in their economic wealth or development, but the fact that all actors have a high level of economic prosperity makes economic interaction beneficial for the participating sides (Deutsch et al., 1957: 139–148, 157–158).

In sum, shared characteristics of the actors create favorable conditions for the emergence and consolidation of stable peace. However, this does not mean necessarily that states without common characteristics are unable to arrive at a stable peace. Yet states with more characteristics in common have better prospects to enjoy peace. Indeed, Western Europe, Scandinavia, the United States, and Canada demonstrate the importance and the salience of these common characteristics.

HIGH LEVEL OF INTERACTION AND COOPERATION. Three main approaches in international relations—liberal, neo-liberal, and constructivism—emphasize the significance of intensive and extensive economic and social ties as significant factors for the emergence and consolidation of stable peace. These are the sources for the collective and the individual benefits that make peace beneficial for the sides involved. Stable peace is a result of the achievement and continued expectations of substantial economic and social benefits to all members.

The common assumption is that extensive economic interaction and transaction not only make the peace more beneficial for the sides involved but are also the main sources for generating reciprocity, building vested interests on peace, encouraging new forms of trust, developing joint interests, transforming security politics, creating new identifications, and even building up of a pluralistic security community (Deutsch et al., 1957: 141–148, 157–158; Adler and Barnett, 1998a, 1998b; Barnett and Adler, 1998). Through extensive exchange of trade, migration, tourism, cultural, and educational interactions, the sides learn the value of peace relations and deepen the trust between them. The spillover of cooperation across a range of domains, on the one hand, and from the elite to many sectors of the population, on the other hand, makes the peace even more beneficial for the sides, and guarantees its maintenance (Deutsch et al., 1957; Haas, 1964).

JOINT INSTITUTIONS AND ORGANIZATIONS. Intensive and extensive international interactions and transactions are the main cause for the development of international organizations and institutions. International organizations and institutions are not only the major sites of interaction for the states involved, but also the mechanisms for regulating the interactions between states. They provide states the means to manage their cooperation and to institutionalize it with more certainty and order. By monitoring the agreements of cooperation, establishing norms of behavior, and enacting confidence-building measures, the organizations and institutions minimize the risks involved in cooperation, especially those of defection or violation of agreements. In this regard they may play the role of trust builders or trust agents for the states involved. Organizations and institutions are also the sites for international socialization and learning, because they provide the forums in which the states can interact, and in time may even shape the identities of the states (Krasner, 1983; Adler and Barnett, 1998b: 41–43; Barnett and Adler, 1998: 418–421, Feldman, 1999).

In summarizing this section, it seems that stable peace may develop when the sides share some common characteristics, but there is a need also for intensive and extensive interactions and transactions among the sides involved, as well as establishment of international organizations and institutions for regulating and managing those interactions and transactions. Although common characteristics are necessary, it seems that without intensive and extensive interactions that are backed by a network of joint organizations and institutions, the states involved will not advance into a stable peace environment.

Learning

Learning is a crucial condition for peaceful change, as Deutsch maintains: "'peaceful change' does not seem assured without a continuous learning process, together with a continuous process of keeping in touch to prevent unlearning" (Deutsch et al., 1957: 130). Boulding also suggests that an increase in the strength of the system of relations depends on a "political learning process" (Boulding, 1978: 4). Russett and Starr look for leaders of vision who are able to conceive and carry out common plans, as well as a learning process at the levels of governmental bureaucracies and mass society (Russett and Starr, 1992: 339).

For the purposes of this study I use Levy's definition of learning: "a change of beliefs (or the degree of confidence in one's beliefs) or the development of new beliefs, skills or procedures as a result of the observation and interpretation of experience" (Levy, 1994: 283). Learning according to this definition is restricted mainly to a cognitive change (beliefs) at the individual level (decision maker), not necessarily change in policy or behavior, but based on different understanding of the reality. Learning generally involves a basic transformation in mode of thinking based on a thorough reassessment of fundamental beliefs and values (Tetlock, 1991: 45).

Learning may occur for the following reasons: (1) a negative experience because of repeated failures, unexpected failures, disappointments, or drastic disaster, (2) repeated failures to solve a crucial problem, (3) a new understanding of how to solve a crucial problem, (4) an arrival of a new information that may call into a question current beliefs and policies, or (5) past policy successes that confirm the rightness and the effectiveness of that policy (Tetlock, 1991: 28–31; Nye, 1987: 378–380; Levy, 1994: 286). These possible developments may bring people to two kinds of learning: causal and diagnostic. In causal learning people change their beliefs about "cause and effect, the consequences of actions, and the optimal strategies under various conditions." In diagnostic learning people change their beliefs "about the definition of the situation or the preferences, intentions, or relative capabilities of others" (Levy, 1994: 285).

Learning has great potential to change behavior or policy; however, personal, political, and institutional barriers may prevent achievement of a policy change. Learning may lead to a policy change in a four-stage causal chain: (1)

observation and interpretation of experience may lead to a change in the decision maker's attitudes and beliefs, (2) the change in attitude and belief may lead to a consideration of a policy change when the decision maker acknowledges the need to do so to reach his objectives, and (3) the adoption and implementation of a policy change depends not only on the decision maker's willingness to do so but also on his effective coping with the potential barriers to the required policy change, (4) which in turn depends on mobilization of institutional and political support as well as wide public support (Levy, 1994: 291; Stein, 1994: 180).

Learning is necessary (but not sufficient) for a stabilizing peace only when it is translated into a policy or behavior change, without which learning will remain only as a potential for that possibility. Learning takes place at different levels and at different stages in the process of peacebuilding.

This study suggests that it is necessary to differentiate between two types of learning in the process of stabilizing peace and in arriving at a consolidated stable peace. Whereas stabilization of peace immediately after resolution of a protracted conflict is not possible without complex or strategic learning, the shift to a consolidated stable peace requires broader social learning. Complex or strategic learning is limited to decision makers and requires a change of attitudes and beliefs. Social learning takes place simultaneously among decision makers and other political, economic, and intellectual elites, as well as the public, and requires basic and wide changes of beliefs and values.

Strategic or complex learning is a new stage in the prolonged learning process that was needed for conflict resolution. It is an active process of redefinition and reevaluation of the parties' beliefs about peacemaking and stabilization of peace. In particular, the actors must thoroughly redefine and reevaluate their beliefs about the basic causation of peace and security, or diagnostically examine the conditions under which peace relations can be maintained. Complex or strategic learning fosters changes in a leader's schemata that shape, in turn, a new policy direction for the peace relations (Nye, 1987; Bar-Siman-Tov, 1994; Levy 1994).

As decision makers realize the significance of their peace relations and the need to stabilize them, so that each leader perceives a mutual interest of stabilizing peace between them as the most important factor in assuring each other's security and even existence, they may enter the process of complex or strategic learning. In other words, each party learns that it is dependent upon peace relations to assure its security.

The change in the perception of the national interest means that decision makers not only regard war and violence as illegitimate means of attaining national objectives, they also internalize the norm that every conflict should be resolved only by peaceful means. Differences of interpretation about key provisions of the agreement, as well as major unresolved issues and new problems that might emerge in the future, should be accommodated within the framework of the agreement, and only by negotiations or other peaceful means accepted by the sides. This type of mutual learning is necessary for deepening and extending the initial mutual trust between the parties that enables the development of a substantial commitment to the peace agreement and its maintenance.

Complex or strategic learning may not be sufficient for stabilization of the peace unless it is institutionalized. The sides should develop mechanisms and institutions for management of their security and political relations. There should be also a certain degree of information exchange and a variety of communication channels in order to secure a high degree of certainty and confidence, if not mutual trust, which develops in stages.

Complex or strategic learning of decision makers enables the stabilization of peace and is a precondition for the emergence of social learning, which is required for stable peace. Social learning is "an active process of redefinition or reinterpretation of reality—what people consider real, possible and desirable—on the basis of new causal and normative knowledge" (Adler and Barnett, 1998b: 43).

Social learning is facilitated by the transactions, social exchanges, transnational communication, and the organizational and institutional networks that enable mutual changing of beliefs and values and encourage development of mutual trust and shared definitions of security. Social learning occurs when decision makers first, and political, economic, and intellectual elites later, internalize the idea that each state's overall condition will be improved tremendously only by a development of stable peace or even a pluralistic security community. In other words, when decision makers and other elites and even the public itself in each state change their basic beliefs and values to accept common norms, values, and shared definitions of security and prosperity, they are involved in a process of social learning. Social learning is therefore the most significant change in the long process of peaceful change in international relations, which normalize and warm peace relations among states. Social learning can promote mutual trust, shape the identities of actors, promote new definitions of security, develop of collective identity, and even redefine the region itself (Adler and Barnett, 1998b: 43–45; Barnett and Adler, 1998: 421–423).

Reconciliation

Most of the research on reconciliation does not refer to international conflicts but rather to other conflicts ranging from family to intercommunal and ethnic conflicts and civil wars. Reconciliation takes place within a divided society or within one country because of interethnic, interracial, or interreligious conflicts, which tend to be protracted zero-sum conflicts that endure many years, involve extensive violence, cost many casualties, and accumulate animosity and hatred (Lederach, 1997; Phillips, 1998; Bar-Tal, 2000b; Bar-Tal and Bennink, this volume).

Reconciliation is not a requirement to end every international conflict, probably only those conflicts that are characterized as protracted and zero-sum and similar to internal conflicts and civil wars. Although the common assumption is that conflict resolution is a precondition for reconciliation and only formal termination of a conflict enables the beginning of a reconciliation process, reconciliation may also begin before conflict resolution as a precondition for negotiations.

In its simplest form, reconciliation means restoring friendship and harmony between rival sides after resolution of a conflict, or transforming the relations between rival sides from hostility and resentment to friendly and harmonious relations (Ackermann, 1994; Phillips, 1998; Arthur, 1999; Gardner-Feldman, 1999; Kelman, 1999a; Kriesberg, 1998a). Like stable peace, reconciliation requires a long process through which the parties "form new relations of peaceful coexistence based on mutual trust and acceptance, cooperation, and consideration of each other's needs" (Bar-Tal, 2000b: 355).

Although stable peace and reconciliation aim to arrive to the same objective, namely consolidating of peace relations, it seems that they differ in the conditions required for reaching it. Whereas most of the scholars of stable peace emphasize the importance of the structural-institutional conditions and learning, most of the scholars of reconciliation argue that structural-institutional conditions are necessary but not sufficient for a stable peace. Political and economic cooperation and interdependence are significant for reconciliation but not sufficient for truly changing of the relations between former enemies. As Wilmer maintains: "Structural factors may contribute to precipitating a conflict or to constructing a framework for stable peace, structural factors alone neither cause nor resolve protracted and violent conflict" (1998: 93). Structural factors formalize peace relations without necessarily spreading the message of reconciliation among society members, and they often do not trigger a deep change in the public's psychological repertoire (Bar-Tal and Bennink, this volume).

For a stable and lasting peace there is a need for a reconciliation, which requires basic cognitive and emotional changes of both sides. The crucial aspect of reconciliation is psychological, requiring changes of goals, beliefs, attitudes, and emotions by the majority of society members. The basic requirement is that the psychological changes will penetrate deep into the societal fabric and will not be limited to the political leadership alone. Maintaining and consolidating peace relations cannot be reached only on the political level or between political elites or even by political reconciliation, but requires societal reconciliation, involving the whole society or at least a majority in the reconciliation process. A stable peace will be maintained only if it is supported by most of the people. The intensity with which the collectivity as a whole expresses support and commitment to the reconciliation is most significant because a high intensity minimizes the importance of those who oppose the reconciliation and act to hamper it. A societal reconciliation is the only process that may bring the people to internalize the meaning of peace and then support it (Lederach, 1997, 1998; Lipschutz, 1998; Wilmer, 1998; Arthur, 1999; Gardner-Feldman, 1999; Kelman, 1999a).

Cognitive Conditions for Reconciliation

As an informal societal-cultural process that encompasses the majority of society members, reconciliation requires mutual fundamental understanding, recognition, and legitimization. It also requires mutual repudiation of emotions of resentment. Reconciliation, therefore, asks for a mutual change of conflicting ethos or conflicting societal beliefs and the emergence of new societal beliefs that enable building of peaceful relations between former enemies (Lederach, 1997; Simpson, 1997; Lipschutz, 1998; Wilmer, 1998; Bar-Tal, 2000b; Bar-Tal and Bennink, this volume).

Societal beliefs in conflict determine how each side perceives itself and its rival in the conflict, as well as the sides' conflictual relations. Societal beliefs provide the psychological and social rationale to cope with a conflict and contribute to the solidification of the social and national identity in conflict situation. Societal beliefs are reflected in the society's attitudes, images, myths, and collective memories (Bar-Tal, 1998, 2000b).

Bar-Tal suggest that a process of reconciliation requires a change of the following societal beliefs: beliefs about one's goals, the rival side, oneself, relations with the rival, and peace. Among these beliefs, three are "key obstacles" to reconciliation: those concerning the justice of one's own goals, positive self-image, and de-legitimizing of the opponent.

The reconciliation process requires a change in each side's societal beliefs about the justice of one's own goals in the conflict. Contradictory beliefs that were involved in the outbreak of the conflict provide the rationale and the justification of the conflict for both sides. Only a mutual change of these beliefs, which are the cognitive foundations of the conflict, may enable the forming of new goals and beliefs, which may in turn justify and rationalize the need of maintaining and consolidating of peaceful relations with the former enemy.

Another crucial condition for reconciliation requires a change of societal beliefs that refer to one's positive self-image. The new beliefs should refer to the conflict with more objective attitudes, and even with self-criticism that includes recognition also of one's responsibility for the misdeeds throughout the conflict, and acceptance that both sides are victims of the conflict.

The shift from delegitimization and dehumanization of the other to legitimization and humanization is another crucial condition needed for reconciliation. Acceptance of the other side as a legitimate actor enables consideration of its national and human needs in positive terms and perception of it as a potential partner. New beliefs about the relations between the two sides must also be developed, including beliefs about the nature of the relations in the present, future, and past. With regard to the present, there is a need of developing beliefs about the significance of peace relations for each side and the need of normalizing them. As to future relations, the new beliefs should emphasize the need of establishing cooperative and friendly relations as the only basis for stabilizing peace.

These new beliefs should also refer to the past, the period of the protracted conflict. The reconstruction of the past is a crucial part of reconciliation, because the collective memory of each side underlines each side's version. The new beliefs formed in the reconciliation process should present the past in a balanced and objective way. This process requires a critical examination of the history of the conflict.

Reconciliation also requires the emergence of new beliefs regarding the nature of peace and the conditions necessary for living in peace. Living in peaceful coexistence and constructing cooperative relations are necessary for stabilizing peace. In addition, both sides should internalize the idea that new conflicts and disagreements must be resolved only by peaceful means accepted by both sides (Bar-Tal, 2000b: 357–359).

A change of societal beliefs in a conflict is a complicated, painful, and threatening process, for reasons that relate to special characteristics of conflicting societal beliefs during a protracted conflict. Throughout the protracted conflict that tends to endure at least a generation, societal beliefs provide the rationale and ideological basis for remaining in conflict, and they contribute to the shaping of the national and social identity. Any change of them may threaten the basis for consensus and solidarity that motivate the members of the society, as well as their collective identity. Reconciliation requires developing a sense of new collective identity with the past enemy that counters the old beliefs and ethos (Kriesberg, 1998a: 188–190; Bar-Tal, 2000b: 360).

Policies Fostering Reconciliation

Despite the psychological and social difficulties of changing societal beliefs, reconciliation is impossible without change. Such change requires mutual awareness not only of the significant contribution of reconciliation to stable peace but also the barriers to peace, and both sides must take measures to promote it.

Scholars suggest the following requirements for reconciliation: (1) successful conflict resolution that terminates the conflict formally; (2) mutual satisfaction with the peace agreement; (3) initiation of cooperation and joint ventures in political, economic, cultural, academic, and educational domains; (4) fostering of superordinate goals and identities through international institutions that promise mutual benefits; (5) sharing of important identities with a high level of integration; (6) a favorable international climate, such as peaceful international climate or changes in external conflicts, concerns, and interests of external forces that provide settings that encourage reconciliation; (7) leaders' accountability for peace and reconciliation and their willingness to mobilize wide domestic support; (8) a domestic coalition for peace and reconciliation that weakens opposition via mobilization of internal institutions and organizations; (9) education for developing new beliefs and values that can support reconciliation; (10) organization of public events such as ceremonies and parades that may help in forming shared emotions, commitments, and identities (Ackermann, 1994; Sparks, 1995; Kopstein, 1997; Handl, 1997; Kriesberg, 1998a; Arthur, 1999, Gardner-Feldman, 1999; Bar-Tal, 2000b).

Dialectics between Stable Peace and Reconciliation

Scholars of both stable peace and reconciliation discuss the possibility of maintaining and consolidating peace relations. Stable peace and reconciliation are defined as either specific outcomes, situations, or long processes aimed at arriving at situations that require definitive conditions. Both approaches accept that conflict resolution and mutual satisfaction with the peace agreement are necessary preconditions for stable peace and reconciliation. Although both approaches desire the same objective, they differ as to the necessary conditions for reaching it.

The conditions required for stable peace and reconciliation are clearly complementary, especially the structural-institutional conditions. Therefore, a common framework that combines structural-institutional conditions—especially a high level of interaction and cooperation, joint institutions and organizations, and social learning with basic cognitive-emotional changes—is clearly needed. Maintenance and consolidation of peace require both types of conditions. Only their interrelationship may secure a long and positive peace. Nevertheless, two questions are important in this regard: Is it possible to promote and advance simultaneously both sets of conditions? Alternatively, if this is not possible, what set of conditions is prerequisite for promoting and advancing the other set of conditions?

Neither approach discusses these questions in depth. Simultaneous development of both sets of conditions is probably the ideal process for advancing peace. Each set of conditions feeds the other and fosters realization of the benefits of peace, thus helping adjust cognitively and emotionally to the peace relations. Each side realizes that it is dependent on peaceful relations with the other for improving its security and wealth. Each side should internalize the fact that only peace relations that combine extensive cooperation and psychological change may maintain and consolidate the peace.

If a simultaneous development of both conditions is impossible because one or both sides are not ripe for it, the question becomes what set of conditions should come first. The common assumption in both approaches is that structural-institutional conditions probably are easier to accomplish following a protracted conflict than basic changes of societal beliefs, because the sides have to adjust to the new peace relations before accepting a painful and costly change of basic societal beliefs and values. Thus, reconciliation needs time and may take years, if not generations.

Therefore, it is easier first to maintain and consolidate initial interaction and cooperation and establish joint institutions and organizations. Implementation of some structural-institutional measures may encourage the parties to support the peace and to begin subsequent psychological change. One may conclude that structural-institutional conditions may serve as necessary preconditions for reconciliation. The political and security benefits of peace are prerequisite for the evolvement of stable peace and reconciliation. Establishing mutually accepted structural-institutional mechanisms for prevention of violence and peaceful management of potential conflicts, as well as developing other confidence- and security-building measures, may reduce the perception of threat and feelings of fear. The economic benefits of peace relations are powerful tools in fostering social investment in peace-building because society members see that it is in their own self-interest to support the peace process by maintaining and consolidating the peace. Only when the sides realize that peace relations are, indeed, beneficial because they provide not only security needs but also economic benefits do they internalize the value of peace to their security and wealth and thereby become ripe for reconciliation.

This common assumption may fit the development of stable peace and pluralistic security community in Western Europe after 1945, and it is generally accepted by scholars of international relations. Adler and Barnett (1998b) argue in this regard that initial accomplishment of some structural-institutional conditions is required for advancing the idea of security community. They distinguish among three phases in a development of a security community: nascent, ascendant, and mature. In the nascent phase, the sides are not ripe yet for establishing a security community but they are interested in stabilizing their security relations, lowering the transaction costs involved with their exchanges, and encouraging further exchanges and interactions. In the absence of trust, the sides will establish organizations and institutions to observe and verify the peace agreement in order to prevent its violation.

The ascendant phase is characterized by an increase in the number of new institutions and organizations, tightened military coordination and cooperation, deepening of mutual trust, extending and intensifying of interactions and transactions, and an emergence of collective identities that begin to encourage dependable expectations of peaceful change. These developments are driven by social learning, which increases the knowledge that each side's overall condition will be tremendously improved only by development of a security community. The inclusion of social learning in the second phase is interesting because it comes only after and as a result of the first steps of interaction and transaction, as well as after the creation of the first joint institutions and organizations. Hence the sides realize that peace relations are beneficial and only by deepening the cooperation and establishment of a collective identity may they improve their overall situation, but this realization requires a basic change of societal belief. Only such a change indicates that social learning has taken place. Social learning in turn deepens the mutual trust and advances the momentum toward a security community.

During the mature phase, the dependable expectations are institutionalized in both domestic and supranational settings. At this stage regional actors share an identity, and a security community emerges (Adler and Barnett, 1998b: 50–57).

The assumption that interaction and cooperation come first and may serve as preconditions for reconciliation seems logical. However, there is an alternative assumption that the process for stable peace or reconciliation should begin by changing attitudes and beliefs and that cooperation follows. The rationale for this assumption is that extensive interaction and cooperation, as well as establishment of joint institutions and organizations, are expressions of warm and normal peace, and these may be possible only after reconciliation. Without mutual cognitive and emotional changes, one or both sides will refuse to warm and normalize the peace relations. In other words, psychological change is a precondition for maintaining and consolidating of peace relations, and stable peace is possible only after concluding a mutual reconciliation. This kind of argument has been raised by Egypt since the signing of the peace agreement with Israel in 1979. Egypt argues that without true reconciliation, it would not warm and normalize the peace relations with Israel. Indeed, with the absence of true reconciliation, the Israeli-Egyptian peace relations remain cold and have failed to shift to a stable peace (Bar-Siman-Tov, 2000).

The Israeli-Egyptian peace introduces an alternative model for reconciliation as a prerequisite for stable peace. Probably the absence of common characteristics (political regime, norms, culture) in the Israeli-Egyptian case, in contrast to what we find in the Western-European case, as well as the difficulties of moving toward a comprehensive peace that could enable establishment of a regional community, foil the possibility of moving toward stable peace and reconciliation. The Egyptian insistence on reconciliation as a precondition for extensive cooperation prevents, therefore, an extensive economic cooperation and establishment of joint institutions and organizations that were proved necessary in Western Europe not only for stable peace but also for reconciliation.

One way to combine the structural-institutional and psychological conditions suggested by theories of stable peace and reconciliation is by linking learning and cognitive change. Although theories of international relations emphasize the significance of a learning process for maintaining and consolidating peace relations, theories of reconciliation stress the change of societal beliefs as the most important factor for transforming relations between former enemies. Since learning is required for cognitive change, the question is therefore what kind of learning process is necessary for reconciliation? Since reconciliation requires a mutual change of societal beliefs, this may occur only when most members of the population on each side internalize the significance of peace to the security and wealth of their respective societies and are ready for a change. Social learning is therefore the only means to achieve reconciliation, as well as stable peace.

Since scholars of reconciliation agree that the process toward reconciliation is slow, gradual, and long, usually begins with leaders, and only in time may expand to include most of the population, there is in the process of reconciliation, as in the process of stable peace, a need for strategic or complex learning. This kind of learning is necessary in order to enable leaders and elites to change their attitudes, beliefs, goals, motivations, and emotions about the conflict and about future peace relations. This psychological change in leaders enables them to start a process of limited cooperation with each other, and its enlargement may lead to a "ripening" of peace relations, which in turn may result in providing the fruits of peace. Peace benefits and dividends will help the leaders mobilize more support for the peace relations, thereby beginning a social learning process that will culminate in the societal belief change that is required for reconciliation.

Conclusions

Stable peace or reconciliation is the highest development of peace relations between international actors. One may conclude that there is not much difference between the two terms and that they are actually interchangeable. However, it seems that whereas stable peace may characterize a special type of peace relations between nations, reconciliation is more typical in stabilizing peace relations in internal conflicts. Both schools, international relations and social psychology, while ignoring each other arrive almost at the same conclusions as to the nature of this type of peace. Both approaches agree that stable peace or reconciliation is an outcome of a long, gradual, and slow process that requires various preconditions. Although scholars of stable peace emphasize the requirement of structural-institutional and learning conditions for stable peace, scholars of reconciliation stress the need for psychological change and structural-institutional conditions.

An examination of the two sets of conditions indicates that a combination of structural-institutional conditions and cognitive change best explains how to develop a stable peace. Social learning is probably a necessary means for a societal belief change; however, strategic or complex learning among decision makers is necessary for initial stabilization of peace relations, mainly because decision makers are the agents that trigger the emergence of the social learning process. It is commonly assumed that a psychological change or societal belief change is a more difficult requirement than an initial structural-institutional change, but it seems that the process toward stable peace or reconciliation generally begins with some structural-institutional change. Extensive communication, cooperation, and interaction among the parties produces the peace benefits or dividends that are necessary for emerging a social learning process.

4

Comparing Reconciliation
Actions within and
between Countries

Louis Kriesberg

Conflicts have always existed in human societies, but so have recon-
ciliations. People usually make up after a fight, whether the fight is
between spouses, neighbors, clans, or peoples. In every society, particular ways of settling fights have been developed and they often include processes for reconciling the antagonists and restoring social
relations. These developments persist as cultural traditions and often include rituals to overcome the recurrent ruptures in relationships (Gulliver, 1979; Lederach, 1995).

Particularly in traditional and relatively undifferentiated societies, chiefs, elders, or other leading figures play mediating or judicial
roles in bringing injured parties and their kin back into normal civility. For example, in traditional Hawaiian culture, this process is
known as *ho'oponopono* (Shook and Kwan, 1991; Wall and Callister,
1995). In Arab societies, too, there are rituals of *sulha* (settlement)
and of *musalaha* (reconciliation) (Irani, 1999).

Recently, even in countries with elaborated judicial and political
institutions, reconciliation actions are increasingly evident (Kritz,
1995; Weiner, 1998). These include formal truth commissions, explicit apologies, and affirmative action policies. The Truth and Reconciliation Commission (TRC) in South Africa is a well-known
example of a complex set of reconciliation actions, agreed upon in
negotiating the end of white domination.

Reconciliation in conflicts between members of antagonistic
countries, however, is different. Shared traditions for reconciliation

are largely absent, as is particularly evident in the aftermath of wars between countries. States have official diplomatic relations during peacetime, guided by shared rules about appropriate behavior. However, when those are disrupted, as by war, no general rules are held in common about restoring normal relations. Typically, peace treaties ending a war are imposed in an ad hoc manner, settling issues that had been contested in the war. A variety of peace-building actions may be taken, but they tend to be idiosyncratic or at the official level, such as prisoner-of-war exchanges or officials visiting each other's country.

In recent decades, nevertheless, reconciliation actions have become increasingly evident in international relations, as they have in domestic relations. Such actions include promoting justice by conducting war crimes trials and by providing compensation to victims, demonstrating regard for the other side by cooperating in finding and returning the remains of those killed, promoting security by devising confidence-building measures, and advancing truth by exchanging information about each side's point of view.

The current attention to reconciliation, within and between societies, is generally premised on the idea that it will help ensure an equitable and stable peace (Kacowicz et al., 2000). Yet it may be the coerced transformation of a conflict resulting in its termination that generates reconciliation practices, which simply confirm that the transformation has occurred. In this chapter, I try to explain how different kinds of reconciliation actions may help transform conflicts and so foster equitable and enduring relations between former antagonists. Reconciliation actions and their impacts are affected by many conditions, and I focus here on comparing the conditions within and between societies

To do so, I first discuss the multifaceted nature of reconciliation. Second, I consider the social conflict approach to explaining how reconciliation actions may affect conflict transformation and resolution. Third, I note how the context for reconciliation actions differs within and between countries. Finally, I examine how various reconciliation actions affect conflict transformation and social accommodations within and between countries.

The Dimensions of Reconciliation

Reconciliation can refer to actions that sometimes help transform a destructive conflict or relationship, the processes by which that transformation occurs, or the outcome of such processes. This range of meanings is discussed in this volume by Bar-Tal and Bennink. In this chapter, I focus on the mechanisms that may, or may not, contribute to the process of reconciliation. I examine actions affecting four primary dimensions of reconciliation—truth, justice, regard, and security—and the actions that move antagonistic parties toward their reconciliation along these dimensions (Lederach, 1997; Kriesberg, 1999). Reconciliation actions are actions undertaken by one or more parties that have been engaged in a destructive conflict or oppressive relationship. Other parties may facilitate, encourage, or otherwise support such actions.

Truth

Truths are an important part of reconciliation, since people on different sides of a conflict or an oppressive relationship have different experiences and understandings. Many people on each side generally hold beliefs that attribute blame to members of the opposing side for the injuries they have suffered; their partial truths typically justify anger, hostility, and vengeance. Furthermore, the truth about misdeeds is often known among the victims' side but is hidden and denied by members of the perpetrators' side. This discrepancy produces resentments that fuel new eruptions of conflict.

Consequently, truths, as they relate to reconciliation, refer especially to the development of shared beliefs about what happened in the past and what is happening currently in the relations between different sides. The comprehensiveness of the truths tends to vary in different stages and contexts of conflict transformation. In addition, the truth is often more evident about one side's misdeeds than about another side's offenses.

The truths also vary in how widely they are shared within and between adversary parties. Only some groups within the opposing sides may know certain truths. For the truths to be widely shared, official statements do not suffice. Novels, songs, films, textbooks, sermons, and many other media of popular communication must convey the information about what injuries were inflicted by whom and against whom.

Justice

Some people stress the attainment of justice as the primary component of reconciliation. Indeed, the sense that they are suffering injustices is often what drives the parties in a conflict. Reducing the sense of injustice is essential, then, to removing the basis for many conflicts. But justice is not an easily agreed-upon matter; sides are likely to disagree about who is acting unjustly toward whom.

Justice varies in several significant ways. It may be understood to mean punishment of those who had previously inflicted injuries; and the punishment may refer to individuals or to the collectivities they are considered to represent. Justice may also mean correcting the prior unjust conditions, which might include ending discriminatory and other oppressive practices. However, this can result in collective punishment or discrimination against the previously oppressive social strata or collectivities, and hence can become the basis for a new conflict.

Whatever the variety of justice being considered, it can be more or less comprehensively enacted. Thus, prosecutions of human rights violators may be quite limited in number or quite extensive. Redress for past injuries may be limited to the immediate survivors or may be extended to the category of people who were affected and their descendants. Consequently, what suffices for one generation may not suffice for subsequent generations.

Regard

I use the broad term *regard* to include expressions that recognize the humanity and identity of the other people.[1] Such recognition is a minimal, but significant, component of reconciliation. This was the case for the mutual recognition between the Palestine Liberation Organization and Israel manifested by the Declaration of Principles, signed on September 13, 1993, and the handshake between Yitzhak Rabin and Yasser Arafat (Jamal, 2000).

More profound expressions of regard are often emphasized in discussions of reconciliation. They may extend as far as making apologies and expressing forgiveness. Thus, members of one side, feeling remorse about the harms done to members of another side, acknowledge the wrongs they or their people committed. Members of the other side, to lessen their anger, hatred, or resentment, may forgive at least some members of the injury-inflicting side. Such actions may be coordinated or may be undertaken unilaterally by individuals or representatives of the sides. These sentiments of regard are varyingly manifested in speech, acts of compensation, or other ways. Forgiveness is relatively prominent in Christianity and related worldviews (Henderson, 1996).

Whatever the quality of the regard, it also tends to vary in the extent to which it is shared. The sense of remorse for injuries inflicted and the readiness of the injured to offer forgiveness may characterize only a few people or almost everyone. The few people may be leaders acting as representatives of their constituencies, or they may be persons acting on their own sentiments.

Security

Again I choose a broad and minimalist term, *security*, to refer to the fourth major dimension of reconciliation. At one end of the continuum, members of the formerly antagonistic entities believe only that they are now safe from physical injury by the other side. This is similar to the concept of negative peace (Galtung, 1980; Stephenson, 1999). More enhanced security would entail the absence of structural violence and the attainment of positive peace. Even greater security would involve an improved level of well-being, both for individuals and collectivities. This kind of security may be assured by constitutional provisions and by changes in the policies and composition of government agencies, such as police and security forces. At the relatively maximal level of security, gross disparities in economic well-being are minimized, and members of the formerly antagonistic parties can live in cooperation and a considerable degree of harmony.

Combining Dimensions

Truth, justice, regard, and security are each quite broad phenomena and none is wholly encompassed in any strategy of promoting reconciliation. At any given time, reconciliation efforts will tend to emphasize some dimensions more than others. For example, in figure 4.1, the reconciliation depicted is weighted toward truth and justice. The relative primacy of various dimensions tends to vary over time as reconciliation evolves during the transformation and resolution of a particular conflict.

Figure 4.1 also indicates that truth, justice, regard, and security can be manifested in ways that are not generally regarded as reconciliation actions. These actions are conducted by parties not directly engaged in the destructive conflicts and relationships, or by one of the engaged parties in a unilateral manner. Thus, the actions of the International Criminal Tribunal for former Yugoslavia may contribute to truth, justice, and security in the view of the international community. They may even contribute to the sense that justice has been done in the eyes of some groups in one ethnic community but not to most members of another community. Thus, too, one party may propagate the truths about its victimization by another group, but if this is done wholly unilaterally it would not generally be regarded as a reconciliation action. Such actions generally must involve some degree of mutuality, except for acts of contrition by people who feel they have wronged others.

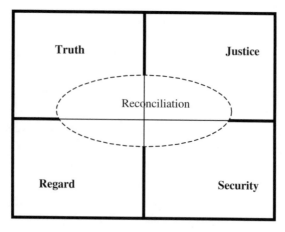

FIGURE 4.1. Dimensions of Reconciliation, Weighted Toward Truth and Justice

Reconciliation actions pertaining to each of the four dimensions sometimes reinforce each other, but at other times are contradictory (Minow, 1998). Striking the appropriate balance among the various dimensions is important, and pursuing any one unduly can hamper progress along another dimension.[2] Emphasizing different elements in sequence, however, is a way to make progress along several dimensions, but not all at once.

Alternative Explanations

Many approaches may be used to explain the escalation and deescalation of international and domestic conflicts and therefore help explain the role of reconciliation actions in the transformation of a destructive conflict into a constructive relationship.[3] Some approaches were developed to account for international relations and some for domestic relations and therefore may differ in their applicability to the other context. Six orientations warrant attention here. I briefly describe five of them and note their possible relevance to explaining the role of reconciliation in conflict transformations;[4] I then emphasize the last, a social conflict approach, which synthesizes the other approaches.

Realist Approach

Realism is a widely held view about international conflict and international relations generally, but it may also be adapted to domestic relations. According to the realist approach, power differences and the use of coercion by each group to maximize its domination and control of the other are extremely important in explaining the outbreak of an intense conflict and its termination. The wish of each group to dominate the other, or at least to avoid being dominated by the other, is taken for granted. Change in the accommodation that the groups have reached with each other largely depends on shifts in their relative power.

Some who espouse this approach stress coercive power, particularly as manifested in violence and the threat of violence. Other analysts using this approach, however, recognize the relevance of a wide variety of coercive power. They may stress demography and relative numbers, control of information, or economic resources. Furthermore, the contending actors rationally calculate their interests and how to advance them. The actors are generally regarded as unitary and possessing stable interests.

The accommodation that is reached between peoples, then, reflects the relative power of the different groups. A stable accommodation is largely a matter of an unchanging power balance and of people reconciling themselves to what they cannot change and justifying the existing relationship. Reconciliation actions, as discussed here, would play little independent role.

Of course, realism has many other elements when applied to international relations (Waltz, 1979). Notably, it assumes a system of sovereign states in an anarchic world. This may be questioned in an increasingly globalized world, and is certainly not the case within societies where cultural norms, political institutions, and many crosscutting social relations provide bonds that are not present in the world as a whole.

Calculated Self-Interest Approach

Adherents of the second kind of explanation stress the inevitable striving for advantage among individuals. They emphasize self-interested behavior and rational choice (Hardin, 1995). Individuals rally around symbols that give them a sense of collective identity that they can use to gain economic and political power. Thus, they may act collectively to impose a system of discrimination against others for economic advantage or may develop military capability to attain political advantage. As identities and capabilities change, so do the kinds of accommodation that different peoples try to make, more or less unilaterally.

Many analysts using this approach emphasize economic relations to explain international and domestic conflicts. Internationally, wars may arise from economic rivalry and attempts to exploit resources and peoples. Within societies, conflicts arise from class differences, and even racial and ethnic conflicts are associated with labor and other arenas of market competition. Some analysts of intercommunal conflicts tend to use a rational actor approach, but others stress prejudice and other sentiments that drive or channel discriminatory conduct (Hechter, 1975; Nagle and Olzak, 1982; Olzak, 1992).

This approach also does not seem to explain any independent role of reconciliation actions in transforming or sustaining intercommunal accommodations. However, insofar as prejudice and other sentiments related to communal differences are viewed as important sources of social conflict, reconciliation that alters such sentiments may contribute significantly to constructive accommodations.

Human Needs Approach

The third approach stresses the importance of satisfying basic human needs (Burton, 1990). These needs are universal, and if social, political, and economic institutions do not satisfy them, conflicts ensue and persist. According to a similar view, but one that is not based on assumptions about a particular set of basic needs, one-sided domination and grossly unequal life chances constitute structural and cultural violence (Galtung, 1996). Unless such conditions are transformed, a stable, equitable peace cannot be achieved.

According to this view, then, the justice dimension of reconciliation is crucial to the transformative role that reconciliation might play. To be effective, for example, reconciliation would have to provide compensation for past injuries or equitable access to future benefits.

Constructivism Approach

Explanations may emphasize the changing ways of thinking about intergroup and international relations. The world that is experienced is one that is socially constructed by humans trying to understand and act in their world (Wendt, 1992). Thus, ideas about self-determination, human rights, and racial differences vary greatly over time. For example, prevailing views at one historical period may be more or less racist. Changes in the discourse result in changes in what people regard as acceptable and produce changes in the relationship so that it seems more (or less) fair (Shapiro and Alker, 1996).

Social norms guide conduct. For example, norms about slavery, economic discrimination, and political rights have changed drastically over the years. As norms become established, they often are embodied in domestic laws. In recent years some norms, for example, about human rights, have gained such general international acceptance that they provide a basis for intervention within sovereign countries.

Intercommunal relations between and within every country are affected by the prevailing ways of thinking about such relationships. Ideologies of racism or ethnonationalism, on the one hand, or of pluralism or civil nationalism, on the other, have different implications for the evolution of intercommunal relations (Smith, 1991). Religious views about the nature of humans and their relationship to God have also had profound effects on either sustaining or ending racial segregation and subordination, as was the case for South African whites and their changing views about the morality of apartheid. Prevailing ways of thinking can also affect a sense of grievance by affecting the comparisons people make about their conditions, and thus shape their relative deprivation (Gurr, 1970).

According to this approach, insofar as reconciliation entails members of one communal group coming to believe that members of another communal group share important qualities with them, it contributes to equitable accommodations. Such beliefs are fostered by national laws about the universality of citizenship rights or by religious convictions that all humans are made in the image of God.[5]

Religious views may also foster particular approaches to transforming conflict relations. This may be the case for forgiveness. For example, in South Africa, Archbishop Desmond Tutu and Nelson Mandela exhibited and urged forgiveness, supported by Christian religious convictions that they shared with whites (Frost, 1998).

Institutionalism Approach

Some analysts give great weight to institutional arrangements, especially political institutions (McGarry and O'Leary, 1993). Constitutional provisions, political party systems, legal protection of individual and collective human rights, and other institutionalized democratic procedures serve to protect members of all communal groups in a society. They also provide mechanisms for constructive rather than destructive ways of altering unsatisfactory accommodations.

The relative weakness of global institutions tends to limit the contribution that this approach might make in accounting for constructive changes in international conflicts and equitable accommodations. Adherents of this approach deem the existence of such institutional arrangements to be crucial. Consequently, they tend to believe that overt reconciliation actions are not essential for equitable and enduring intercommunal accommodations.

Social Conflict Approach

Each of the previously discussed approaches has some value, but none is wholly adequate to explain the role of reconciliation actions in establishing stable and equitable relations after destructive conflicts. Consequently, I emphasize the explanation that draws from these approaches and synthesizes them: an analytical approach to social conflicts. After all, social conflicts are a basic way in which accommodations between peoples are sustained and changed. Although conflicts do not fully explain all changes in accommodations, they play an important role in them. They also often escalate in terribly destructive ways. Such destructive escalations and their constructive transformations are of primary concern here.

Conflicts emerge when four conditions are minimally satisfied (Kriesberg, 1998c). First, one or more parties in a conflict have a sense of collective identity, distinct from another group with a different collective identity. Communal identities are widespread and often formed in distinction or even opposition to other communal groups. This conception of identity draws much from the social constructivism approach (Anderson, 1991).

Second, members or representatives of one or more social groups feel that they have a grievance, that they are enduring conditions that are wrong. Past conflicts may result in one communal group feeling wronged or humiliated by another group, a grievance likely to lead to further destructive conflicts. This condition is stressed in the human needs approach, and also in those emphasizing relative deprivation (Gurr, 1970).

Third, members of a social group believe that the source of their grievance lies in the conduct or existence of another social group. Prevailing ways of thinking tend to attribute group members' unsatisfactory conditions to different sources: the members' own behavior, the will of God, or to the actions of another communal group. For a conflict to emerge, the group members must formulate a goal that requires another group to change its conduct. Leaders who formulate and propagate ideologies fixing responsibility for their people's grievances on particular others, therefore, are often essential in the emergence and escalation of conflicts.

Finally, the members of an aggrieved group must believe that they can induce the group causing the grievance to change in ways that reduce their grievance. Without such confidence, they may believe they are better off living with the unsatisfactory conditions than struggling to change them and being worse off for their attempt, as realists stress. The method the group members choose to bring about the desired change is critical in whether or not the conflict is waged destructively or constructively. The availability of legitimate

institutionalized ways of conducting conflicts lessens the likelihood of resorting to destructive methods.

Once conflicts emerge they follow many different courses, escalating in
diverse ways and in varying degrees of intensity. They may become protracted
and mutually destructive, with episodic intense escalations. Some may end by
unilateral imposition. But at some point many conflicts begin to deescalate,
are transformed, and then a tacit or a negotiated accommodation may be
reached. Changes in identities, grievances, goals, and beliefs about attaining
them are crucial in the trajectory of conflicts. Here, I examine the role of
reconciliation actions in affecting those core elements of conflicts and hence
their constructive transformations.

Domestic and International Contexts for Reconciliation

The focus of this chapter is on the way contentious relations are affected by
reconciliation actions, in domestic compared to international settings. Before
discussing that subject, I want to call attention to three other conditions that
affect the nature of reconciliation and the accommodations reached between
antagonists: the asymmetry between the adversaries, particularly differences
in their relative power; the severity and symmetry of past conflicts and oppression; and the stage of the conflict in which the reconciliation actions are
being taken.

Asymmetries, Historical Experiences, and Conflict Stage

Antagonistic groups often have very unequal control of resources; they differ
in population size, military capability, wealth, and many other bases of power.
The stronger group is likely to be able to greatly shape the nature of the relationship with the weaker. Members of the stronger group generally are better
able to coerce and also to persuade the other side to yield.

The relative power of any two groups or societies, however, depends on
the boundaries of the system within which they function. One of the striking
features of many social conflicts is that each side sees itself as endangered and
threatened by the other side. Thus, on the island of Sri Lanka, the Hindu Tamils
see themselves as an ill-treated, vulnerable minority, whereas the Buddhist
Sinhalese feel threatened by the large Tamil community in southern India. The
Palestinians feel themselves victims of the powerful Jewish state of Israel,
whereas the Jews of Israel feel threatened by the large Arab and even larger
Muslim worlds. Northern Ireland and Cyprus offer further examples. Conse-

quently, changes in international borders, where they are drawn, or how significantly they constrain conduct, often greatly alter the relative power of ethnic or other communal groups. For example, the dissolution of the Soviet Union changed the relative standing of Russians in many of the Republics that had been part of the Soviet Union and are now independent states.

Relations between peoples also vary in the degree and nature of their historical experience with each other. Some peoples have suffered severe repression or injuries, even at a genocidal level. The suffering may be highly asymmetrical, one side having inflicted great harms on another people with little resistance or retaliation. In some cases, each side has experienced widespread horrors at the hands of the other. Obviously, the parties usually do not agree about the degree and direction of the asymmetry. Moreover, some persons on each side of a terrible conflict may gain benefits as well as suffer injuries from the other side.

Historical experiences, moreover, can go back a long way and certain ones are chosen and held dear (Volkan, 1988). Which experience is selected for attention tends to shift, as contemporary conditions change. Thus, indigenous peoples in the Americas suffered devastating losses as Europeans conquered them and settled their land. In some places new peoples with hybrid cultures emerged; in others indigenous people died or were killed; and in still other places the indigenous people were moved into small, restricted reservations. The sense of grievance among various indigenous peoples has varied over time, partly as a result of changing government policies toward them, changing social norms, and changes in resources available to the indigenous people to try to redress their grievances.

The degree of asymmetry between possible antagonists does not consistently differ within societies as compared to between societies. Nevertheless, the differences between the societal and international systems are relevant for the asymmetry in power and in historical experiences of particular antagonists. Within a country, ethnic, religious, linguistic, or other communal identities often are related to intense conflicts. If one such communal group is dominant, controls the state, and holds an ideology that regards the state as a defender of its ethnicity, religion, or language, then the socioeconomic and power asymmetry relative to other such groups is great and those other groups are likely to feel sorely aggrieved (Rouhana, 1997). In addition, the dominant group is likely to regard communal groups seeking political and economic equality or the right to practice their religion or to use their language to be challenging the legitimacy of the state. However, within countries with relatively neutral governments upholding civic nationalism rather than ethnonationalism, the government may foster equal rights for all ethnic and religious groups within the country (Smith, 1991; Hechter, 2000). To some degree all members of the country are the constituents of the political leaders.

In the international system, at least by international law, each state has equal sovereignty and legitimacy, providing some protections against domination by the stronger of the weaker countries. In actuality, however, countries differ greatly in economic, military, and other capabilities, as illustrated by instances of neocolonial relations. Furthermore, in the international system there is relatively little international authority that would protect the rights of weak states against the powerful ones. The leaders of each country understandably believe their primary obligation is to the people of their own country.

In addition, reconciliation actions may be taken in various stages of a conflict. They may be part of a transforming deescalation, part of negotiating a conflict settlement, or part of a peacebuilding effort after an accommodation has been negotiated or imposed. Different kinds of actions are feasible and effective at different conflict stages.

Comparing Contexts

In discussing the differences between domestic and international contexts, I sometimes refer to the two contexts as though they were distinct.[6] In reality, however, they are different ends of a continuum. Many cases lie somewhere between these two poles. This is true for colonies of distant colonial powers ruling indirectly, or for indigenous peoples with recognized national authority within a settler country, as in the case of Native Americans in the United States. It is also true for countries that are dominated politically and militarily by other states, as were the countries of the Soviet bloc by the USSR, or as economically dependent countries are by one or more dominant economic powers. The territory of the West Bank and the Gaza Strip is another illustration. Finally, in global settings transnational nonstate actors, such as churches, also may engage in reconciliation actions.

In many cases, moreover, the contending parties are in dispute about where they fit along this continuum. When one people is seeking independence or secession, it is claiming that the relationship should be regarded as international, whereas the government and its supporters treat the fight as domestic. Outside parties may decide whether to treat the conflict as domestic or not depending on geopolitical considerations or communal ties with the contending parties.

Whether an analyst or a partisan regards a particular case as domestic or international also depends on the time in question, as the change from Yugoslavia to the former Yugoslavia makes evident. The placement of many cases, then, should be recognized as dynamic and not static. This is evident in the relations between Israeli Jews and Arab Palestinians in the territory that was under the British Mandate for many years (Kriesberg, 2000).

Domestic and international settings tend to differ along four dimensions that influence the consequences of reconciliation actions: (1) the degree of integration, (2) the extent of shared identity and culture, (3) the boundedness of entities, and (4) the multiplicity of parties and identities.

LEVEL OF INTEGRATION. The degree to which peoples are integrated with each other is a particularly important variation between domestic and international contexts. The level of social interaction and economic interdependence of people within countries tends to be much greater than between people in different countries. This is a matter of degree, however, with peoples in some neighboring countries economically and otherwise highly integrated with each other while some peoples within a country are highly segregated.

Integration tends to be associated with lower levels of destructive conflicts and unreconciled differences. Generally, the need to achieve a high level of reconciliation is greater in domestic than in international contexts. Consequently, the failure to achieve a high degree of reconciliation tends to be more disruptive of social relations and conducive to recurrent intense conflicts within than between even neighboring countries.

SHARED IDENTITY AND CULTURE. Generally, people within a society, compared to peoples in different societies, have a greater sense of common identity. A shared identity eases the difficulties in achieving reconciliation. Moreover, people within a society, compared to peoples in different societies, tend to have a common culture, which also helps overcome the difficulties in deescalating a conflict and moving toward reconciliation. The American civil rights struggle of the 1950s and 1960s is illustrative, since members of the movement for equality appealed to shared American values.

Peoples who believe they share the same culture tend to have a decent regard for each other and resist dehumanizing each other. This also helps inhibit the destructive escalation of a conflict. Peoples in different countries may also have some degree of a shared culture and insofar as they do, conflict escalation is limited. This is one of the explanations for the finding that democratic societies do not wage wars against each other.[7]

Generally, the standards about justice, legitimate means of struggle, and other conflict-relevant matters are more similar at the country than at the global level. Thus, equality among members of a society is more likely to be valued by society members than by the peoples of the world regarding all other peoples. Thus, too, members of a society, more than people in the world as a whole, are likely to view recourse to violence as an illegitimate means to conduct a conflict.

CLEAR BOUNDARIES AND DECISION-MAKING STRUCTURES. In the international system of sovereign states, on one hand, the state borders are clearly demarked and constrain many aspects of social interaction within and across the borders. On the other hand, within a country, the borders around various ethnic, religious, and other communal, class, and ideological groups are often unclear and porous. Furthermore, the political institutions of countries establish hierarchies and have procedures for collective decision-making and reaching binding agreements. Most extremely totalitarian governments can make extraordinary accommodations with each other, as the Nazi and Soviet governments did in signing a nonaggression pact in 1939. Within a country, however, the amorphous character of classes and ethnicities often makes reaching formal decisions or binding agreements problematic.

These differences between the domestic and the international systems have distinctive implications for reconciliation. Within societies, it is relatively easy to find partners for reconciliation. Particular persons, groups, and organizations can reach out toward each other across divisions that had been the source of severe conflicts. However, it is more difficult within a society than between countries to make official agreements that commit communal groups as a whole to reconciliation and stable accommodations. In either context, the process of reconciliation goes on and on.

MULTIPLE PARTIES, INTERESTS, AND IDENTITIES. Despite the differences in scale, the relevant number of parties, interests, and identities involved in a conflict often is larger in domestic than in international relations. The international state system is powerful enough to subordinate many secondary concerns, organizations, and identities, thus reducing their relevance. Within a society, however, family, class, occupational, regional, religious, and many other identities and interests provide the basis for organizations and groupings that press concerns related to those identities. Crosscutting ties then serve to mitigate any single division as the basis for a severe conflict (Dahrendorf, 1959). Of course, if many of these identities coincide, the basis is laid for a protracted, destructive conflict. The international state system tends to channel identities and organizations so that they do coincide. The increasing globalization of the world, however, is fostering more and more crosscutting identities, interests, and organizations across state borders.

The prevalence of multiple identities, concerns, and organizations, insofar as they do not crosscut each other but simply coincide and reinforce each other, increases the likelihood that acts of reconciliation will be attempted and will be effective. Holding some shared identifications with people who are opponents on the basis of other identities facilitates discerning the common interests with those opponents and their shared humanity. Those identities may be based on religion, corporations, occupations, sports, or music, for example.

CHANGING CONTEXTS. Often, the contexts of relationships between antagonistic peoples are ambiguous and in flux. Sometimes they are matters of contention, as one ethnic community seeks to bring about a change in its relationship to its social-political context, for example, by seeking to secede from a country.

The Consequences of Reconciliation Actions

This chapter examines how reconciliation actions, within and between societies, contribute to reaching a mutually satisfactory and equitable accommodation between peoples. Not every action taken with the ostensible purpose of moving the reconciliation process forward actually does so. Thus, acknowledging the truth of committing past wrongs can fail to make amends and actually escalate a conflict. Admitting having committed past atrocities can certainly undermine the legitimacy of continuing to benefit from those wrongs, encouraging further claims for justice by the previously injured party. For example, in the late 1980s, many activists and elite members from Lithuania, Estonia, and Latvia struggled to have the Soviet leadership acknowledge the secret protocol of the 1939 Molotov-Ribbentrop pact and its role in the forced annexation of their countries (Lapidus, 1992). In August 1989, the Supreme Soviet acknowledged signing the protocol but still denied its implications. The demands for independence were not appeased and indeed escalated; independence was soon achieved, as the Soviet Union dissolved.

Developments relating to the ethnic Germans who were expelled from the Sudetenland area of Czechoslovakia at the end of World War II are also illustrative (Ryback, 1996–97). Soon after Vaclav Havel was elected president of Czechoslovakia, he denounced the expulsions as deeply immoral. Czechoslovak leaders made other reconciliatory gestures. But this reconciliation process broke down in an escalating exchange of charges and demands between the Sudeten Germans living in Germany and the Czechoslovaks. Public exchanges of recriminations endangered what had otherwise become a rapprochement between Germany and the Czech Republic. In secrecy, senior Czech and German officials tried to fashion a declaration that could be acceptable to both countries. On January 21, 1997, Czech Premier Vaclav Klaus and German Chancellor Helmut Kohl signed a joint declaration, which was approved by both countries' parliaments. Ultimately, the government policies helped attain a higher level of mutual accommodation and reconciliation than existed earlier.

Acts of reconciliation, whether substantial or symbolic, do not ensure appreciation or equivalent reciprocation in response. Sometimes, sensing political weakness on the other side and increased moral strength, those to whom the conciliatory actions were directed raise their expectations and their claims about what they should receive. However, persons who made the conciliatory moves may feel that they are now being disadvantaged and seek to regain what they have lost; the result is a backlash. Or they may feel they have been generous and then are resentful when the response is less grateful than they think it should be.

Nevertheless, there is systematic evidence that reconciliation actions contribute to stable accommodations. In a recent study of civil wars of the twentieth century, 12 cases were found in which genuine reconciliation events had occurred.[8] In eight of the 12 cases, 67 percent, war did not recur; but in only 9 percent of the cases without such reconciliation attempts did war not recur during the period of the reconciled cases, 1957–1999. Furthermore, all the reconciled cases that did not experience a subsequent war included a truth commission.

Given the very many kinds of actions that might contribute to reconciliation, it is not clear which actions have what consequences, under various conditions, and why. To clarify these matters, I note several kinds of actions relevant for each dimension of reconciliation and discuss how they are likely to affect the major conditions of conflict within a domestic and an international context. A variety of actions and their impacts in different contexts are set forth in tables 1–4. Since all of them cannot be examined at length in this chapter, I will discuss a few to illustrate the kind of analysis that may be done, utilizing the framework presented.

It should be recognized that every reconciliation action usually has consequences for the party carrying out the action, as well as for the recipient. Thus, those performing an action tend to become committed to the action by having taken it. Cognitive dissonance theory and a variety of evidence indicate that people tend to change their attitudes so that the attitudes are consistent with their behavior (Festinger, 1957; Deutscher, 1973).

Actions Promoting Truth

Many official and unofficial actions can reveal truths that were not known to important segments of the populations in a conflict, as indicated in table 4.1. Thus, official commissions of inquiry can be an instrument to reveal conditions relating to violence and oppression. For instance, in the United States, the Kerner Commission (1968) provided a comprehensive report about the causes of the urban riots in the late 1960s and made recommendations for the future.

Truth commissions are increasingly established within societies recovering from destructive conflicts or repressive relationships to report on human rights abuses in a particular country or relating to a particular conflict.[9] They are often part of a negotiated settlement and consider atrocities committed by members of both sides in a struggle, and some even offer protection to the alleged perpetrators of gross human rights violations. They are sometimes instituted to help increase mutual understanding, not to punish wrongdoers.

In international relations, official truth commissions have not occurred. In recent years, officials and perpetrators of gross human rights violations have been prosecuted by special international tribunals, as in the case of the Nuremberg trials after World War II and the International Criminal Tribunal for

TABLE 4.1 Truth Actions' Impacts by Context

Context and Truth Actions	Impacts of Truth Actions on Conflict Conditions			
	Identity	Grievance	Goal	Method
Relatively Domestic				
Truth commission	Revise history and self-concept	Lower for some	More shared	Less coercive
Cultural media			Less ethnocentric	Negotiated agreements
Curricular material		Raise expectations for others		
Scholarship				Cooperation
Trials				Persuasion
Admit doing harm				
Relatively International				
Trials	Revise history and self-concept	Lower for some	More complementary	Less purely coercive
Cultural media				
Curricular material		Raise expectations for others		
Scholarship				
Admit doing harm				

the former Yugoslavia. Trials have often also been held within countries against persons accused of crimes relating to terrorism or oppression.

Trials can provide some of the same benefits that truth commissions do by revealing previously unacknowledged truths. They also, however, can appear to be one-sided and vindictive. Furthermore, they are often tools of an oppressive regime to maintain domestic domination. They then arouse resentment and enhance the sense of grievance among the persons prosecuted and their associates.

In addition, private citizens often undertake kinds of actions that can help promote truths contributing to reconciliation. Scholars and other intellectuals have played important roles in documenting ongoing and past atrocities and oppression. This may occur in the face of official denials, as revealed in analyses of the Armenian genocide in Turkey (Dadrian, 1995). Furthermore, such research and journalistic accounts contribute to additional kinds of action: films and other popular-culture depictions, as well as curricular material for primary and secondary schools.

The greater integration within countries, compared to between countries, raises the likelihood that actions taken domestically will have more extensive effects than actions taken internationally. International actions generally must be dramatic and cumulative to have great impact (Mitchell, 2000). These various truth-promoting actions can enhance the equity and durability of accommodations. Knowledge of past and ongoing oppression by people within the oppressor community or country can alter their self-identity. They may come to see themselves as being complicit in wrongly harming others; having accepted that responsibility they will be more likely to apologize and offer some degree of compensation for past injuries. This has been the case notably for Germans, domestically and internationally.

Revelations can reduce grievances among members of the communal groups that had suffered injuries, for which the perpetrators had denied responsibility. The perpetrators' acknowledgment of having done harm can be gratifying to victims, and their goals are then less likely to incorporate seeking vengeance.

In addition, truth-promoting actions encourage the harmed persons, in their struggle for improved conditions, to use methods that include persuasion and legitimate institutional means rather than violence. For all parties, recourse to violence that would be regarded as an abuse of human rights is more likely to be viewed as illegitimate.

Actions Promoting Justice

Partisans may take many kinds of actions that can enhance justice as part of reconciliation (see table 4.2). Here I consider three such categories: (1) they may undertake actions, such as criminal trials, to punish those who have done wrong or benefited from the wrongs; (2) they may seek monetary payments, or other forms of restitution or compensation, for the injuries they or their people have suffered; or (3) they may promote policies and institutional arrangements that will end and prevent future injustices, for example, by instituting anti-discrimination laws.

In international relations, treaties ending a war may include reparations for harm inflicted by the losing side. Other punishments may be imposed as well, such as loss of territory or prosecution of alleged war criminals. However, some members of the defeated side may well regard such actions as one-sided and as creating new injustices.

Every particular justice-promoting action has diverse consequences. It may change identities, reduce grievances, or affect the choice of conflict methods. Thus, in the United States, many past acts of repression against African Americans are only recently being investigated and adjudicated. In past decades, particular crimes have been tried in federal courts when local courts failed to convict alleged perpetrators even when strong evidence pointed to their guilt. Recently, local legislative as well as judicial investigations have reached well back in time to particularly egregious violence against blacks. For example, in February 2000 a commission created by the Oklahoma legislature recom-

TABLE 4.2 Justice Actions' Impacts by Context

Context and Justice Actions	Impacts of Justice Actions on Conflict Conditions			
	Identity	Grievance	Goal	Method
Relatively Domestic				
Trials and punishment	More inclusive	Lower for some	More delimited	Judicial,
Restitution		Raise for others	alternatives	political
Future equity				
Relatively International				
Trials and punishment	More inclusive	Lower for some	More delimited	Political
Reparations		Raise for others	claims	aternatives
New structures				
External aid				

mended that reparations be paid to the black survivors of the United States' bloodiest race riot, in which as many as 300 people were killed in Tulsa in 1921.[10]

Also in the United States, responding to the civil rights struggle of the 1950s and 1960s, many actions fostered a new accommodation between Americans of European and of African descent. The federal government took several steps that contributed to building reconciliation. For example, during President Lyndon B. Johnson's administration, the Civil Rights Act of 1964 and the Voting Rights Act of 1965 were ratified. The latter authorized federal examiners to register qualified voters and eliminate devices aimed at preventing African Americans from voting.

Such actions have manifold impacts on the conditions that inhibit destructive conflict and foster equitable and enduring accommodations. In the case of the changing accommodation of African Americans and European Americans in the 1950s and early 1960s, the nonviolent way the civil rights struggle was waged and the way the country as a whole responded affected conflict components relating to collective identity and grievance as well as goals and methods of reducing them. Thus, the nature of the collective identities of African and European Americans changed. This included augmenting the civic character of American identity rather than its ethnic character. Furthermore, the content of American identity significantly changed, becoming less a melting pot within which "foreign" elements assimilated and more an enduring multicultural society.

On the one hand, presumably actions that increase justice tend to reduce a sense of grievance. However, gains that are achieved may raise expectations for more progress and provide resources to demand it. On the other hand, some people may believe that the justice-promoting actions, such as affirmative action programs, create new injustices. The expanding economy of the 1950s and 1960s mitigated such counterproductive effects in the United States, but the 1970s period of economic stagnation contributed to the backlash against affirmative action policies by white men.

Justice-promoting actions also affect the goals a party constructs. Thus, if one side is forthcoming about providing compensatory benefits for past injustices or providing assurances that past injustices will end, the other side tends to pursue limited and non-vindictive goals. There is a risk, however, that the compensations and assurances are seen as signs of weakness and the goals are raised higher. Attribution theory suggests another possibility (Kelley, 1973). It holds that people tend to believe that members of their own ingroup are good by nature, whereas members of an outgroup act well only because of their circumstances. It follows that if those others have done some good deed, it is only because they were forced to do so and more coercion will yield even greater benefits.

Insofar as justice-promoting actions do not seem to result purely from coercive pressure, those seeking greater justice are less prone to resort to coercion to advance their claims. Persuasive efforts will appear relatively promising and attractive. Furthermore, institutionalized channels for reducing injustice will appear feasible and effective. Domestically, official and nonofficial organizations promoting programs of affirmative action or the protection of human rights are illustrative. Internationally, effective actions by the United Nations and other regional governmental organizations that enhance social, economic, and political justice encourage reliance on such avenues in further pursuit of greater justice.

Actions Promoting Regard

A fundamental aspect of reconciliation is the recognition by members of each adversary of the humanity of the people in the other camp (see table 4.3). Three major kinds of actions demonstrate such regard. First, regard may take the form of respectful recognition of the other. This includes people on each side using the name for the other people that is preferred by them, as well as respectful tolerance of differences in ways of life. Second, regard may be demonstrated in friendly social interaction, whether in dialogue groups, informal interactions, or intimate relations. Finally, one party apologizing for its past conduct to the injured party demonstrates regard to members of that party. It is also shown when members of one side express forgiveness to members of the side that had inflicted harm.

In domestic affairs, regard can be demonstrated by many kinds of official and nonofficial actions such as ending discriminatory practices, celebrating diversity, giving a hearing to those who suffered past indignities, and expressing regrets and remorse for past behavior that denied the human equality of others. This was the case when the U.S. Supreme Court ruled in May 1954, in *Brown v. Board of Education*, that separate education could not be equal education (Kluger, 1976). That decision constituted a minimal amount of at least one aspect of reconciliation. It declared that legally maintained segregation in schools imposed an injury on those discriminated against and was wrong. The Supreme Court ordered that segregation end, in all deliberate speed. Neither the Supreme Court nor any other government agency expressed apologies or offered restitution for past wrongs. But by saying that past practices must stop, the Supreme Court acknowledged that improper impositions had been made.

TABLE 4.3 Regard Actions' Impacts by Context

Context and Regard Actions	Impacts of Regard Actions on Conflict Conditions			
	Identity	Grievance	Goal	Method
Relatively Domestic				
Recognition	Pluralistic	Justify claims	More shared	Consider others' humanity
Official apology	Includes sense of responsibility	Mitigate past grievance	More inward	
Group dialogue				
Interpersonal forgiveness	Civic nationalism			Symbolism
Media portrayals				
Relatively International				
Official apology	Includes sense of responsibility	Mitigate past grievance	More shared	Consider others' humanity
Group dialogue			Inward	
International forgiveness				Alternative channels
Recognition				

Domestically, various workshops and dialogue groups are increasingly used to reduce prejudice and intolerance between religious, ethnic, and other kinds of communities. They may be sponsored by and supported by local governments, schools, employers, or private associations. They are more and more often used by humanitarian assistance organizations helping to build peace in countries that are recovering from destructive conflicts.

Internationally, the significance of official recognition is embedded in international protocol and law. In addition, ad hoc reconciliatory actions demonstrating regard may be taken by state officials and by ordinary citizens. This includes apologies for past grievous actions; for example, in March 1999, President Bill Clinton, at a forum of Guatemalan leaders, admitted the wrongful U.S. support for military forces and intelligence units that engaged in violence and widespread repression (Broder, 1999).

Regard is also demonstrated by people in countries with a history of conflicts developing history texts that incorporate each other's accounts and perspectives. In the immediate aftermath of the Second World War, UNESCO began to promote the revision of textbooks so as to eliminate biases and nationalistic prejudices.[11] In recent years it has helped support projects contributing to peacebuilding in war-torn countries such as Somalia, Rwanda, and

Burundi; these projects include training journalists and producing radio programs.

Reconciliatory actions promoting regard for others have impacts on the identity of those undertaking the actions as well as of their recipients. Taking such actions reduces the likelihood of holding identities that incorporate sentiments and beliefs that people sharing one's collective identity are superior to other peoples and that others are inferior and less wholly human. Certainly, such reconciliatory actions reduce the grievance of those who previously had suffered the indignities of low regard. Obviously, people in subordinated and denigrated communities are distressed and feel aggrieved at being treated as unworthy human beings.

Viewing enemies as subhuman fosters inhumane methods of struggle. As clashes escalate and become destructive, the members of the other side are more and more likely to be referred to as vermin, pigs, or other animal names (Thompson, 1990). Recognizing the enemy's humanity provides some check to using destructive methods.

Actions Promoting Security

Actions that foster security also tend to differ in international and in domestic contexts (see table 4.4). In international relations, realists tend to regard security as based on mutual threat and deterrence, but adherents of other theoretical approaches argue that security comes from each side demonstrating that it is not threatening the other. Confidence-building measures are one way of enhancing security in relations that have significant levels of mistrust and mutual fear. More enduring and stable security is based on high levels of interaction and integration (Deutsch et al., 1957; Kacowicz et al., 2000). Actions taken to increase such aspects of relations between countries can be viewed as promoting security. These include cultural exchanges and economic activities such as trade and investment.

In domestic relations, overarching political institutions typically are supposed to provide security for residents of a country, exercising a monopoly on legitimate violence. In addition, particular laws and constitutional arrangements can protect specific minorities and other vulnerable categories of people. These arrangements may include systems of power sharing and provisions for autonomy in regard to culture, language, and religion. Measures assuring citizens of basic civil rights are embedded in the laws, if not the practices, of most countries. Reconciliation actions in this realm would include the inclu-

TABLE 4.4 Security Actions' Impacts by Context

Context and Security Actions	Impacts of Security Actions on Conflict Conditions			
	Identity	Grievance	Goal	Method
Relatively Domestic				
Laws protecting rights	Less vulnerable	Reduce harassment	More mutual	Authoritative structures
Autonomy				
Integrated security agencies	Overarching			Legitimate channels
	Pluralistic			
Affirmative action				
Relatively International				
Integration	More overarching	Reduce fear	More mutual	Authoritative structures
Confidence-building measures		Promise gain		Legitimate channels
International organizations				Alternative channels
Economic aid				

sion of formerly deprived groups in the police and judicial bodies and in all other areas of employment.

In contexts that are more in-between international and domestic settings, such as occupations and uprisings, rules limiting the means of repression may be stipulated by high authorities. In implementing them, however, soldiers and police may act with "restrained savagery," believing they are carrying out unstated policies (Ron, 2000).

Reconciliation actions promoting security can affect identity, grievance, goals, and methods of struggle in ways that increase the likelihood of equitable and enduring relations, domestically and internationally. Collective identities may incorporate a lessened sense of vulnerability, so that people sharing the identity are less likely to regard others as threatening them. This will reduce their sense of grievance as well.

With an increased sense of security, antagonistic groups can explore the possibility of advancing mutual benefits by cooperative or complementary conduct. This tends to reshape goals so that they are less likely to be regarded as mutually exclusive, internationally as well as domestically.

Finally, the methods of pursuing contentious goals are likely to be less confrontational with an increased sense of security. Domestically, this may include greater joint participation by persons from antagonistic sides in government agencies and nongovernmental organizations. In international relations, it may involve greater reliance on nonprovocative means of defense.

Combinations and Sequences of Actions

Each reconciliation action has diverse effects on identity, grievance, goals, and methods of struggle. Furthermore, these actions and their diverse consequences are not independent of each other. Their implementation occurs in many combinations and sequences, and each action and its consequences are shaped by the context other actions provide. Thus, the profound effects of the Truth and Reconciliation Commission in South Africa are attributable to its own manifold activities and to the many other changes under way in South African society.

Established in 1996, it consists of three committees, implemented sequentially. The members and staff of the first committee heard the accounts of gross human rights violations, many of which were publicly presented and some of them shown on television. Victims and survivors and alleged and acknowledged perpetrators gave accounts that captured intense, widespread attention. The second committee gathered information from victims, witnesses, and records and heard testimony from alleged perpetrators. The committee then recommended amnesty for individuals who had been cooperative and forthcoming; alleged perpetrators who were not granted amnesty were subject to criminal prosecution. The third committee is charged with developing a system of compensation for those who suffered injuries as a result of apartheid and the struggle to end it, a matter that is not yet fully resolved.

The TRC with its televised hearings prompted great interest among South Africans and stimulated public discussions and personal reflections for more than two years (Theissen, n.d.). It reduced some of the grievance among many of those who had suffered under apartheid. Nevertheless, public opinion data indicate that it did not fundamentally change the views of many who had supported apartheid.

In the case of protracted destructive conflicts, small, begrudging reconciliatory gestures do not have a transforming impact. This is evident in the difficulties associated with transforming the Israeli-Palestinian conflict. Even before the breakdown of negotiations and the eruption of the al-Akasa Intifada in September 2000, many people on each side did not believe that the conflict had been fundamentally transformed. For example, grievances remained large and whatever mitigation may have occurred was the result of reluctant concessions (Hadi, 2000).

Conclusions

Actions to promote reconciliation have many possible effects that contribute to fostering enduring, mutually acceptable accommodations between peoples who in varying degrees have committed injuries against the other and also suffered them. These reconciliation actions and their effects are to some degree independent of other factors shaping the relationship. Without significant and consistent reconciliation actions, transforming a protracted conflict to attain a mutually acceptable accommodation is extremely difficult. This seems to be illustrated by the breakdown in Israeli-Palestinian negotiations and the eruption of violence (Kriesberg, forthcoming). This is not to deny the relevance of many other factors in transforming and resolving conflicts.

These conclusions are not consistent with the realist approach, which would treat reconciliation actions as essentially epiphenomenal. The self-interest approach also appears to have only limited value in explaining the complex ways reconciliation actions affect conflict transformation and the emergence of mutually acceptable and enduring relations. People do calculate, but the very notion of "self" is problematic because people form and change the collective identities they hold. Similarly, the values they wish to maximize are diverse and their nature and relative importance tend to shift, in part as a result of interactions with peoples in other camps.

The human needs approach contributes considerations that are relevant to creating a durable, mutually acceptable relationship between peoples. Needs, however, are not immutable nor are their meanings universally shared. There may be consensus about some needs, at an abstract level, but how they are to be satisfied is variable and often contested.

The constructivist approach in some ways is a useful corrective to the other approaches. Interpreted too strongly, however, its application can underestimate the role of power, economic calculations, and social relations in shaping the construction of norms, values, and other ideas.

Finally, the institutional approach has much more relevance for reconciliation actions in the domestic context than in the international. Alternative political and social structures are more important for countries than for the international system, which lacks powerful political and social structures.

In this chapter, I have drawn from all these approaches and incorporated them into a broad social conflict approach. This approach, as used here, stresses the interaction between contending parties and various intermediaries. This, I believe, indicates how people attempt to reconcile with each other and helps account for the difficulties as well as effectiveness of various kinds of reconciliation actions.

Reconciliation actions and their sequencing differ significantly between domestic and international settings. Generally, less profound and widespread reconciliation is needed in international relations than in domestic relations. After all, peoples in different countries can have much less integrated relationships, and often do, than peoples living in the same country. That is why partition or secession, under some circumstances, may be a relatively stable resolution to a domestic conflict between communal groups (Hechter, 2000; Sambanis, 2000).

The relative priority and the sequence of the four dimensions of reconciliation tend to differ in domestic and in international settings. Matters of higher priority often precede matters of lower priority. In domestic settings, regard frequently has the highest priority, with truth also relatively high, whereas justice has somewhat lower priority, and security, perhaps because it is more generally realized, has the least primacy. In international settings, however, security is often given the highest priority and its assurance usually precedes the implementation of other aspects of reconciliation. Regard also has relative high priority, followed by justice, with shared truths having the least priority.

In international affairs, this is illustrated by the effectiveness of the West German Ostpolitik in the early 1970s. German acceptance of the results of World War II, embodied in the borders and regimes in Eastern Europe, offered security to those regimes and relative regard. That also contributed to the development of East-West détente in the early 1970s, and détente contributed to the exchanges that fostered the transformation of the Soviet Union (Kriesberg, 1992). Justice and truth were advanced in subsequent years, with the collapse of the Soviet Union.

These observations have implications for Jewish-Arab relations within Israel and between Israel and a future Palestine. The issues between Israel and Palestine, once they both are established by mutual agreement, may be more stable and less likely to result in destructive conflict than are the issues between Jews and Arabs within Israel. As I have noted, the level of reconciliation required between countries is less than what is needed for peoples sharing a country. Reaching a mutually acceptable accommodation about the establishment of a Palestinian state, of course, is presently extremely difficult and requires a fundamental transformation of the conflict based on profound changes within the Jewish Israeli and Arab Palestinian societies. Once Palestine is thus established, however, requisite changes in the components of the conflict may be more attainable than between Jews and Arabs within Israel.

The subordinate position of the large Palestinian minority within a country guided by an ethnonationalist ideology poses a severe challenge.

The analysis in this chapter indicates that comparing the variations in reconciliation actions and their consequences in international and domestic contexts helps us understand the impact of reconciliation efforts in each. The analysis also suggests additional actions that may be taken to effectively construct stable and equitable accommodations. Finally, it suggests how to avoid or limit counterproductive effects of some reconciliation actions, for example, by mutual deliberations about the exchange of actions and reactions.

Reconciliation actions are important components of domestic and international peacemaking. Even if a comprehensive and complete reconciliation is never achieved, taking appropriate steps toward it helps transform destructive conflicts and relationships into constructive ones.

NOTES

1. Many writers stress this dimension and the element of forgiveness as the primary factor in reconciliation. However, that may reflect the centrality of forgiveness within Christianity, whereas it may be less significant in non-Christian cultures. Furthermore, it tends to be part of a high degree of reconciliation, and other kinds of regard for the former adversary should be recognized. (See Cohen, this volume.)

2. Steinberg observes, "Indeed, the Jewish sages noted that when the demands of pure justice are met, there is no peace and when peace is the exclusive consideration, there is no justice" (2001, 7).

3. I use the term *approach*, rather than *theory*, to indicate that I do not assume that the perspectives discussed are precise theoretical explanations. These approaches are not held and used only by academic analysts, but rather are ways of thinking that many people use without much reflection.

4. Three additional approaches are not discussed here. One is based on genetics, asserting high genetic closeness within each communal group and a primordial sense of identity. This may be coupled with beliefs about human genetic proclivity for violence. These ideas cannot explain the great variations in human conduct over time and space in the matters of interest here. The second approach is evolutionary psychology (Long and Brecke, 2000). According to the evolutionary view, the human mind has developed an array of reasoning abilities and also includes emotional processes; this could be hypothesized to include a forgiveness and reconciliation process. Granting such a universal human capacity, however, in itself does not help explain the great variations in reconciliation among humans. Finally, the third approach argues that every relationship is unique, with its own history and course of development. My purpose here, however, is to search for some patterns of regularity, taking into account particular histories.

5. Religious faith might be the basis for another approach to explaining conflict transformation and the role of reconciliation in such transformation. In this chapter,

however, I am discussing only empirically based social science approaches. Religious convictions are obviously an important factor in influencing people to take reconciliation actions (Henderson, 1996). I seek to explain, here, the consequences of such actions for the transformation of intercommunal conflicts.

6. At those times, I will be treating them as ideal types, in Max Weber's sense.

7. See, e.g., Gleditsch and Hegre (1997); Russett and Oneal (2001).

8. Reconciliation events include the following elements: "(1) direct physical contact or proximity between opponents, usually senior representatives of the respective factions; (2) a public ceremony accompanied by substantial publicity or media attention. . . . ; and (3) ritualistic or symbolic behavior that indicates the parties consider the dispute resolved and that more amiable relations are expected to follow" (Long and Brecke, 2000, 2).

9. The United States Institute of Peace has an extensive library of material, with relevant documents, on truth commissions. See http://www.usip.org/library/truth .html.

10. Also, in 1994, the Florida legislature provided up to $2 million to compensate survivors of a white mob's destruction of Rosewood, Florida (an African American community) and the killing of at least six black residents in 1923 (Yardley, 2000).

11. Reports about many studies of history textbooks can be found in the *Newsletter of the UNESCO International Textbook Research Network*, available at http://www.gei .de/newsletter/nlprojm.htm. For reports of other UNESCO programs, see http://www .unesco.org.

5

Reconciliation as Identity Change: A Social-Psychological Perspective

Herbert C. Kelman

This chapter focuses on reconciliation in the context of and in relation to an emerging or recently completed process of conflict resolution. The cases that particularly inform my analysis are the Israeli-Palestinian conflict and other protracted conflicts between identity groups—such as those in Bosnia or Northern Ireland—that are characterized by the existence of incomplete, fragile peace agreements (cf. Rothstein, 1999a). I hope, however, that the analysis also has some relevance to reconciliation in postconflict situations—both those of recent origin, such as South Africa or Guatemala, and those of long standing, such as the German-Jewish or the Franco-German relationship in the wake of World War II. Clearly, there are differences in the nature of reconciliation processes as a function of the stage of the conflict and the time that has elapsed since the end of active hostilities, but such differences need to be accounted for in a comprehensive theory of reconciliation.

Reconciliation and Conflict Resolution

The concept of reconciliation has had a place in my writings over the years about the goals of conflict resolution, both in general (for example, Kelman, 1999a) and in the Israeli-Palestinian case in particular (for example, Kelman, 1998a). But I have not treated reconciliation systematically as a distinct analytic category. The central distinction for my colleagues and myself, following John Burton, has been between *settlement* and *resolution* of conflict (see, for example, Burton, 1969, chs. 11, 12). In contrast to the negotiation of a political settlement, a process of conflict resolution goes beyond a realist view of national interests. It explores the causes of the conflict, particularly causes in the form of unmet or threatened needs for identity, security, recognition, autonomy, and justice. It seeks solutions responsive to the needs of both sides through active engagement in joint problem solving. Hence, agreements achieved through a process of genuine conflict resolution—unlike compromises achieved through a bargaining process brokered or imposed by third parties—are likely to engender the two parties' long-term commitment to the outcome and to transform their relationship. We have argued that an agreement emerging from such a process of conflict resolution and the new relationship it promotes are conducive to stable peace, mutually enhancing cooperation, and ultimate reconciliation.

Thus, reconciliation, in this view, is a consequence of successful conflict resolution. It comes at the end of the process, with time: the test of a good agreement, and of the process that generates it, is its conduciveness to *ultimate* reconciliation. This does not mean (and has never meant, in my view) that reconciliation comes into play only after an agreement has been reached. Reconciliation is, after all, a *process* as well as an outcome; as such, it should ideally be set into motion from the beginning of a peace process and as an integral part of it. In this spirit, I have described the exchange of the letters of mutual recognition between the PLO and the state of Israel—which I have always regarded as the most important feature of the Oslo accord (see Kelman, 1997a)—as "a product of a rudimentary process of reconciliation" (Kelman, 1998a: 37). In the same spirit, the problem-solving workshops between politically influential Israelis and Palestinians that my colleagues and I have organized for some years (see Kelman, 1992; Rouhana and Kelman, 1994) represent tentative steps toward reconciliation, insofar as participants are encouraged to listen to and to try to appreciate each other's narrative and to engage in a process of "negotiating identity" (Kelman, 2001).

During the Netanyahu period I went further, arguing that the pragmatic, step-by-step approach of the Oslo process was no longer feasible, because of the breakdown of trust and partnership between the two sides, and that a new process was needed in which reconciliation would move to the fore. I would make that point even more strongly today, in the second year of the second Intifada. I am not proposing that reconciliation is a precondition for negotiation or that it must precede a peace agreement. But significant steps toward reconciliation—in the form of mutual acceptance of the other's nationhood and humanity—are necessary in order to resume negotiations and move them forward. "The process and outcome of negotiations must be consistent with the requirements for ultimate reconciliation" (Kelman, 1998a: 37). In my view, this requires negotiations committed to the search for a principled peace, anchored in a historic compromise.

Although reconciliation has been central to my thinking in these different ways, I tended to conceive of it not so much as a separate process but as a component and logical outcome of conflict resolution as my colleagues and I have conceptualized and practiced it. However, along with many analysts and practitioners of conflict resolution, my thinking has been influenced by a variety of recent events that have brought the issue of reconciliation into focus: the truth and reconciliation commissions in South Africa and in Latin America; the signing of incomplete peace agreements, which have failed to lead to a new relationship and a stable peace between the antagonists; the efforts of external powers to intervene in internal conflicts, which may have succeeded in reducing the immediate violence but lacked a strategy to enable the warring communities to live together; and the new wave of attention to the unfinished business of World War II, both in the form of restitution for Holocaust victims and in the form of psychological efforts to promote healing, best exemplified by the work of Bar-On (1995b, 2000) and others to bring together children of Nazi victims and Nazi perpetrators. The cumulative effect of these experiences has been to encourage me, along with my colleagues, to view reconciliation as a distinct process, qualitatively different from conflict resolution—even conflict resolution within a needs-oriented, interactive problem-solving framework. Reconciliation is obviously continuous with and linked to conflict resolution and it certainly is not an alternative to it. But whereas conflict resolution refers to the process of achieving a mutually satisfactory and hence durable agreement between the two societies, reconciliation refers to the process whereby the societies learn to live together in the postconflict environment.

Combining the customary differentiation between conflict settlement and resolution, and the more recent differentiation between conflict resolution and reconciliation, suggests a conceptual model based on three qualitatively distinct processes of peacemaking: conflict settlement, conflict resolution, and reconciliation. In adopting such a model, I am following in the footsteps of my colleague, Nadim Rouhana (in press), although my formulation of the process of reconciliation, in particular, differs from his in some important respects. As an analytic approach I find the three-way distinction very appealing, for reasons that will become clearer in the next section.

Three Processes of Peacemaking

Although settlement, resolution, and reconciliation represent three approaches to peacemaking, they should not be viewed as three different ways of achieving the same goal. Instead, they are three ways of achieving different—though often overlapping—goals, all broadly linked to changing the relationship between groups, communities, societies, or states from one of hostility to one of peaceful coexistence. The specific goals and emphases of the three processes may be congruent and mutually supportive, but they may also be contradictory to one another.

I have already suggested that reconciliation is continuous with and linked to conflict resolution. In a sense, it can be argued that reconciliation, at least in its full form, presupposes conflict resolution: a long-term, cooperative relationship, based on mutual acceptance and respect, is not likely to take hold without a peace agreement that addresses the fundamental needs and sense of justice of both sides. Similarly, it can be argued that conflict resolution presupposes conflict settlement, at least in the sense that a political agreement negotiated by the legitimate leaderships of the conflicting parties and endorsed by relevant outside powers and international organizations must be in place if the two societies are to consider their conflict to have ended in a fair and mutually satisfactory way. The three processes may thus be related in a sequential way, with settlement as the first step, which may or may not be followed by resolution, which in turn may or may not be followed by reconciliation. However, there is no reason to assume that the three processes necessarily follow such a sequence. Steps in the direction or in the spirit of settlement, resolution, or reconciliation may occur quite independently, in any order and in any combination.

In short, possible relationships between the three processes need to be explored, conceptually and empirically, rather than assumed—or dismissed. The main purpose of the present exercise is to see whether we can gain some analytical leverage by thinking of settlement, resolution, and reconciliation as qualitatively different (though not necessarily always empirically separate) processes and identifying the distinct antecedents and consequences of each.

My special perspective on the distinction among conflict settlement, conflict resolution, and reconciliation derives from the proposition that they broadly correspond to the three processes of social influence—compliance, identification, and internalization—that I distinguished in my earlier work (Kelman, 1958, 1961; Kelman and Hamilton, 1989). Very briefly, *compliance* refers to acceptance of influence from another in order to achieve a favorable reaction from the other, to gain a reward or approval from the other, or to avoid punishment or disapproval. *Identification* refers to acceptance of influence from another in order to maintain a desired relationship to the other and the self-definition anchored in that relationship; identification may involve taking on the role of the other or a role reciprocal to that of the other. *Internalization* refers to acceptance of influence from another in order to maintain the congruence of one's own value system; internalization may involve adopting new behavior because it is consistent with one's beliefs or consonant with one's identity.

I arrived at this three-way distinction early in my work on attitude and behavior change in individuals, out of an abiding interest in the quality of the changes induced by social influence: the depth of change, the durability of change, the independence of change from the external source from which it was originally derived, and the integration of the new elements into preexisting structures such as the person's belief system, value system, or personal identity. Each of the three processes is characterized by a distinct set of antecedent conditions. For example, the source of the power of the influencing agent to induce change varies for the three processes. In the case of compliance, it is the agent's means of control, that is, control over rewards and punishments, which constitute material or psychological resources that are consequential to the person. In the case of identification, it is the agent's attractiveness, that is, desirability as a partner in a continuing relationship. In the case of internalization, it is the agent's credibility, that is, expertise and trustworthiness as a conveyor of value-relevant information (Kelman, 1958).

At the output end, each of the three processes is characterized by a distinct set of consequent conditions. Most important here are the conditions under which the new opinion or behavior is likely to manifest itself. The manifestation of compliance-induced behavior depends on surveillance by the influencing agent. Identification-based behavior is not contingent on surveillance, but it does depend on the continuing salience of the person's relationship to the influencing agent. That is, it is likely to manifest itself only when the person acts within the role defined by that relationship. Finally, internalized behavior becomes independent of the original source and is likely to manifest itself whenever it is relevant to the issue at hand, regardless of the surveillance or salience of the influencing agent.

I have extended this model to analysis of the relationship of individuals to the state or other social systems (Kelman, 1969), and to the nation or other collective entities (Kelman, 1998b). In this connection, we have distinguished between three types of political orientation—rule-, role-, and value-orientation (Kelman and Hamilton, 1989)—that are coordinated with the three processes of influence. The rule, role, and value distinction has also been useful in analyzing people's relationship to legitimate authority and their emotional reactions to their own deviations from social norms. I have also distinguished between rule-oriented, role-oriented, and value-oriented movements of social protest. In an entirely different context, in my writing on the ethics of social research, I drew on my three-processes model to distinguish among three types of ethical concerns that our research may arouse: concerns about the impact of the research on the interests of the individuals and communities who are the subjects of our investigations, on the quality of the relationship between investigators and research participants, and on broader societal values.

I mention these various extensions of the original model because they suggest the possibility, or at least the hope, that it might also have some relevance to the analysis of conflict settlement, conflict resolution, and reconciliation as three distinct processes of peacemaking. My original model of social influence emerged out of research on persuasive communication, but it has broadened to capture the interaction of individuals or groups with each other and with larger social systems in a variety of social contexts, and their integration within these social systems. In essence, my trichotomy distinguishes three foci for these interactions. The first centers on individual and group *interests*, whose coordination is governed by a system of enforceable *rules*, with which individuals are expected to *comply*. The second centers on the *relationships* between individuals or groups, which are managed through a system of shared *roles*, with which individuals *identify*. The third centers on personal and group *identities*, expressing a *value* system that individuals *internalize*.

As indicated, my original three-process model grew out of an interest in the quality of changes induced by social influence—their depth, durability, independence, and integration. My approach to conflict resolution has involved a very similar problematique: I have always been interested in the conditions under which negotiations to end a conflict will produce a high-quality agreement—an agreement that will be deeper, more durable, more sustainable, and more fully integrated into the political cultures or societal belief systems (cf. Bar-Tal and Bennink, this volume) of the conflicting societies than the settlements that are so often hammered together under the pressure of external powers. I have always assumed, therefore, that it should be possible to forge a link between my work on conflict resolution and the three processes of influence. Now, I feel, I have found that link. This is, of course, esthetically pleasing, but the important question is whether it is analytically useful. Does that link give us handles for distinguishing between qualitatively different ways of making peace, with distinct antecedent and consequent conditions? Specifically, for present purposes, does the proposed correspondence of reconciliation to internalization suggest a useful way of defining and conceptualizing reconciliation?

Let me make clear that I am not proposing an exact correspondence because we are dealing with different levels of analysis. In my original model of social influence, the unit of analysis is the individual—albeit the individual embedded in a social system. In a model of peacemaking, the unit of analysis is a pair of actors—the relationship between two parties, whether two individuals or two collectivities. My purpose here is to explore whether conceptualizing peacemaking processes in terms of the broader trichotomy suggested by the three processes of compliance, identification, and internalization is useful in suggesting relevant hypotheses about the determinants and outcomes of different approaches to peacemaking.

In this spirit, I propose that it may be useful to conceive of conflict settlement as operating primarily at the level of *interests*, conflict resolution at the level of *relationships*, and reconciliation at the level of *identity*. It is interesting that this distinction may have been anticipated by the late James Laue, when he suggested that Roger Fisher's approach focused on interests, Burton's on needs, and mine on values. At the time, I had some question about this formulation because my approach to conflict resolution has always been—and indeed continues to be—needs-based, in the Burton tradition. But Laue may well have detected in my work an incipient interest in moving beyond conflict resolution to reconciliation, where societal values have to be addressed.

Conflict Settlement and Resolution

Let me turn first to conflict settlement and resolution in terms of the distinction I have proposed. Conflict settlement can be described as a process yielding an agreement that meets the interests of both parties to the extent that their respective power positions enable them to prevail. In other words, the terms of their agreement are heavily determined by the power they can bring to bear in the negotiations. Third parties—outside powers or international organizations—often play a role in brokering or even imposing an agreement, using their own power by way of threats or inducements. The agreement may be supported by the publics on the two sides because they are tired of war and have found the status quo of continuing hostility and uncertainty increasingly intolerable. Such support for the agreement does not rest in any particular change in public attitudes toward the adversary. The settlement process is not designed to change the quality of the relationship between the societies. As is the case with compliance as a form of social influence, the stability of a political settlement ultimately depends on surveillance—by the parties themselves, in keeping with their deterrent capacities, by outside powers, and by international organizations.

Conflict settlement is not a negligible achievement in a violent and destructive relationship with escalatory potential. In fact, conflict resolution can often build on political settlements, insofar as these involve a negotiating process in which each side pursues its interests and in which they are able to reach agreement on many outstanding issues through distributive bargaining in which power as well as international norms play a role. But conflict resolution, particularly if we think of it within an interactive problem-solving framework, goes beyond conflict settlement in many of the ways to which I already alluded at the beginning of this paper:

- It refers to an agreement that is arrived at interactively, rather than imposed or sponsored by outside powers, and to which the parties therefore have a higher level of commitment.
- It addresses the parties' basic needs and fears and therefore has a greater capacity to sustain itself over time.
- It builds a degree of working trust between the parties—a pragmatic trust in the other's interest in achieving and maintaining peace—and therefore is not entirely dependent on surveillance as the guarantor of the agreement.
- It establishes a new relationship between the parties, best described as a partnership, in which the parties are responsive to each other's needs and constraints and are committed to reciprocity.
- It generates public support for the agreement and encourages the development of new images of the other.

In all of these ways, conflict resolution moves beyond the interest-based settlement of the conflict and its dependence on the balance of power. It represents a strategic change in the relationship between the parties, expressed in terms of a pragmatic partnership, in which each side is persuaded that stable peace and cooperation are both in its own best interest and in the interest of the other. This is the kind of partnership that began to emerge, especially at the leadership level, in the early post-Oslo environment (cf. Lustick, 1997).

But there are limits to this change in the relationship, which make it vulnerable to changes in interests, circumstances, and leadership. Conflict resolution as a process of peacemaking—like identification as a process of social influence—involves the development of a new relationship, with an associated set of new attitudes *alongside* or perhaps on top of the old attitudes. The new attitudes are not necessarily integrated with one's preexisting value structure and belief system—with one's worldview. This means that the old attitudes—including attitudes of fundamental distrust and negation of the other—remain intact even as new attitudes, associated with the new relationship, take shape. The coexistence of new attitudes toward the other as a potential partner in peace with old attitudes toward the other as a mortal enemy creates instability in the new relationship, particularly in the context of an existential identity conflict. Changing circumstances may trigger the old attitudes in their full force.

Reconciliation

The third process, reconciliation, presupposes conflict resolution of the type that I have described: the development of working trust, the transformation of the relationship toward a partnership based on reciprocity and mutual responsiveness, and an agreement that addresses both parties' basic needs. But it goes beyond conflict resolution in representing a change in each party's identity.

The primary feature of the identity change constituting reconciliation is the removal of the negation of the other as a central component of one's own identity. My main empirical reference point here is the Israeli-Palestinian case, in which mutual denial of the other's identity has been a central feature of the conflict over the decades (cf. Kelman, 1978, 1999b). The mutual negation of the other's identity is perhaps not as central in other cases of conflict and reconciliation—such as those of Chile, Guatemala, or South Africa, or the German-Jewish, the Franco-German, or even the Egyptian-Israeli case—yet in each case the negation of the other is somehow embedded in the identity of each of the conflicting parties and must be addressed in the reconciliation process.

Changing one's collective identity by removing the negation of the other from it implies a degree of acceptance of the other's identity—at least in the sense of acknowledging the legitimacy of the other's narrative without necessarily fully agreeing with that narrative. The change in each party's identity may go further by moving toward the development of a common, transcendent identity—not in lieu of, but alongside of each group's particularistic identity. Development of a transcendent identity becomes possible with reconciliation and, in turn, reinforces reconciliation, but is not a necessary condition or consequence of reconciliation. What is essential to reconciliation, in my view, is that each party revise its own identity just enough to accommodate the identity of the other. As the parties overcome the negative interdependence of their identities, they can build on the positive interdependence of their identities that often characterizes parties living in close proximity to each other (Kelman, 1999b).

Reconciliation goes beyond conflict resolution in that it moves past the level of pragmatic partnership—which is the hallmark of identification and is essential to peacemaking—and enables the parties to internalize the new relationship, integrating it into their own identities. New attitudes toward the other can thus develop, not just alongside of the old attitudes but in place of them. In contrast to the attitude-change process that characterizes identification, internalized attitudes are not just taken over in full measure but are reworked. As the new attitudes become integrated into the group's own identity, they gradually replace the old attitudes. Working trust can gradually turn into personal trust. This does not foreclose the possibility that old fears and suspicions will reemerge, but the relationship is less vulnerable to situational changes.

Viewing reconciliation as identity change linked to the process of internalization has important implications for the nature of the identity change that it involves. Internalization represents a readiness to change an attitude because the new attitude—though induced by influence from an external source—is more consistent with the person's own, preexisting value system. Thus, the change in a particular attitude actually strengthens the preexisting structure in which it is embedded by responding to a potential challenge to that structure: one might say that we change in order to remain the same. By the same token, the change in each party's identity—the revision in its narrative—that I am defining as reconciliation implies a strengthening, rather than a weakening, of each party's core identity. I would argue that a revision in the group's identity and the associated narrative is possible only if the core of the identity remains intact. In fact, changes in more peripheral elements of identity are often seen as necessary in order to preserve the core of the identity—just as changes in specific attitudes may be seen as necessary in order to maintain the consistency and integrity of a person's value framework. This was the basis, for example, on which a majority of Israelis and Palestinians were (and I believe continue to be) prepared to revise the territorial dimension of their national identity in order to maintain the essence of that identity (Kelman, 2001).

This analysis points to a major dilemma of reconciliation. Reconciliation requires parties to change an element of their identity—the negation of the other—which is far from trivial for parties engaged in an existential identity conflict, while at the same time preserving, even strengthening, the core of their identity. This is more easily achieved in situations in which one of the parties has already rejected part of its identity—as was the case for many Germans in post-Nazi Germany and many whites in post-apartheid South Africa—although even in these situations resistances are bound to arise. It is particularly difficult, however, in conflicts in which each side insists on the justice of its cause and sees itself as having been wronged by the other. The dilemma is that the amount and kind of identity change that A requires from B in order to be ready for reconciliation may be perceived by B as undermining the core of *its* identity. A good example here would be the demand to acknowledge collective guilt to which even post-Nazi Germany was reluctant to accede (Auerbach, this volume).

It is important to emphasize here that, in conflicts such as that between Palestinians and Israelis, negation of the other is a *central* element of each party's own identity, which it cannot give up easily. Given the nature of the conflict, each party finds it necessary to deny the other's authenticity as a people, the other's links to the land, and the other's national rights, especially its right to national self-determination through the establishment of an independent state in the land both claim, because the other's claims to peoplehood and to rights in the land are seen as competitive with each party's own claims and rights. Moreover, negation of the other is also important to each party in a violent conflict as a protection against negative elements in its own identity (cf. Kelman, 1999b). Insofar as the other can be demonized and dehumanized, it becomes easier for each party to minimize guilt feelings for acts of violence and oppression against the other and to avoid seeing itself in the role of victimizer, rather than only the role of victim.

Thus, in protracted identity conflicts, negation of the other is not a peripheral, marginal element of each party's identity that can be easily discarded. My argument is merely that, from an "objective" point of view, negating the other's identity is not a *necessary* condition for preserving, and indeed enhancing the core of one's own identity. However, for conflicting parties to arrive at a point where they can be free to relegate negation of the other to the periphery of their own identities and eventually discard it requires the hard work of reconciliation. What is central to that work is the growing assurance that the other is not a threat to one's own identity. In that process of assurance, the conditions for reconciliation play a vital role.

Parties in a conflict in which both sides perceive themselves as victims are helped to deal with the dilemma of abandoning some elements of identity without threatening the core of their identity by the reciprocal nature of reconciliation. Changes on the part of one group make changes on the other's part more attainable. But this view suggests that the process of reconciliation requires a certain amount of "negotiation" of identity, including negotiation of the conditions for reconciliation, which turn on such issues as truth, justice, and responsibility. I contend that reconciliation—especially in cases in which neither party is prepared to adopt the role of perpetrator—cannot be achieved on the basis of purely objective criteria of truth, justice, or responsibility, anchored in historical scholarship or international law, but requires some degree of mutual accommodation in the course of negotiating the conditions for reconciliation. I briefly discuss these conditions in the concluding section.

Conditions for Reconciliation

I want to identify five conditions that can help groups in conflict arrive at the difficult point of revising their identity so as to accommodate to the identity of the other. One might also think of these as indicators of reconciliation, or steps in a process of reconciliation. They are both indicators of movement toward reconciliation and conditions for further movement in that direction.

Mutual Acknowledgment of the Other's Nationhood and Humanity

Such acknowledgment is, of course, implicit in my very definition of reconciliation. Insofar as reconciliation means removing the negation and exclusion of the other from one's own identity, it requires the accumulation of steps that indicate acceptance of the other as an authentic nation and inclusion of the other in one's own moral community. Such steps include political recognition and acknowledgment of the other's legitimacy, the authenticity of their links to the land, and their national rights, including the right to national self-determination. Equally important are steps toward the humanization of the other, including respect for their dignity, concern for their welfare, and attachment of value to the other's lives and security.

Development of a Common Moral Basis for Peace

To create the conditions for reconciliation, it is necessary to move beyond a peace anchored entirely in pragmatic considerations—essential as these are—to a peace based on moral considerations. This condition is relatively easy to meet when the moral basis is widely accepted and shared from the beginning of the peacemaking effort, as in the rejection of Nazism or the rejection of apartheid. It is much more difficult to achieve in a conflict in which the common moral basis is not a given, such as the Israeli-Palestinian conflict or the conflicts in Sri Lanka or Northern Ireland. In the Israeli-Palestinian case, I have emphasized, in this connection, the need for commitment to a principled peace, which finds its moral basis in a historic compromise—a compromise that is presented to the publics as not just the best that can be achieved under the circumstances, but as the foundation for a peace that is right because it is consistent with the principles of fairness and justice for both sides (Kelman, 1998a). The definition of justice, in this and other such cases, will to some extent have to be negotiated between the parties, recognizing that there is some inevitable tension between justice and reconciliation. Such negotiations must experiment with different kinds of justice that an agreement might try to achieve, such as

- Substantive justice, achieved through an agreement that meets the fundamental needs of both sides
- Future justice, achieved through the establishment of just institutions, arrangements, and relationships
- Procedural justice, achieved through a fair and reciprocal process of negotiating the agreement
- Emotional justice, achieved through the sense that the negotiations have seriously sought and to a significant degree shaped a just outcome

Confrontation with History

Confronting history and coming to terms with the truth is an essential component of any reconciliation effort. The reexamination of historical narratives and the reevaluation of national myths—on both sides of a conflict—are valuable contributions to such an effort. Here again, however, I maintain that it is unrealistic to aim for the establishment of a single, objective truth and that one has to accept the need to negotiate the historical truth to a certain degree. I want to avoid the simple relativistic stance that each side has its own truth and that their conflicting narratives are therefore equally valid. But we have to recognize that the different narratives of different groups reflect different historical *experiences*—occasioned by the same set of facts and figures—and that, therefore, their experienced truths can in fact not be identical. Reconciliation, in my view, does not require writing a joint consensual history, but it does require admitting the other's truth into one's own narrative.

Acknowledgment of Responsibility

Reconciliation also requires acceptance, by each side, of responsibility for the wrong it has done to the other and for the course of the conflict. Responsibility must be expressed symbolically in acknowledgment of one's actions and their effect on the other and appropriate apologies and concretely in appropriate steps of compensation, reparation, and restitution. The German distinction between *Aussöhnung* and *Versöhnung* (as pointed out in Feldman, 1999) is very helpful in reminding us that the practical/material dimension and the philosophical/emotional dimension (or instrumental and moral dimensions) are both key elements of reconciliation. It is not surprising that I again take the view that the acknowledgment of responsibility cannot be based entirely on an objective set of legal or moral norms, but requires a process of negotiation in which different types of responsibility are identified and agreed upon.

Establishment of Patterns and Institutional Mechanisms of Cooperation

Cooperation on functional issues cannot in itself lead to reconciliation in the absence of a mutually satisfactory political agreement. It can, however, help increase openness to the search for political solutions and it can play an important role in peacebuilding in the wake of a political solution. To contribute to reconciliation, the patterns and mechanisms of cooperation must themselves meet certain critical conditions: they must be genuinely useful to both parties in meeting societal needs and achieving societal goals, they must be based on the principles of equality and reciprocity, and they must undercut rather than reinforce old patterns of dependency of one party on the other. An important variety of cooperative institutional mechanisms consists of institutions and arrangements focusing on conflict resolution through joint problem solving in order to deal constructively, on a continuing basis, with the conflicts that will inevitably arise in the relations between the two societies.

In sum, all of these conditions are designed to facilitate changes in the collective identities of the conflicting parties, with particular emphasis on removing the negation of the other as a key element of each group's own identity.

6

Leadership and Reconciliation

David Bargal
Emmanuel Sivan

The process of building peaceful relations following the attainment
of a formal peace agreement requires a basic transformation in former adversaries' attitudes toward each other. Intractable conflicts
that have persisted for decades generate hostile relations between
the groups in conflict, leaving them divided on such essential dimensions as security, identity, territory, and narratives. These hostilities are ingrained in the nation's collective memory and highlight
the adversary's role in the conflict. According to Rouhana and Bar-
Tal (1998), intractable conflict embraces many facets of each group's
political and cultural existence. It is total, persists for several generations, and is fostered by each party's national consciousness. Each
party feels it has the sole claim to justice and legitimacy, and views
itself as the main victim of the conflict. To reinforce the adversary's
alleged negative attributes, each side adopts a set of cognitive, emotional, and behavioral mechanisms that emphasize and perpetuate
erroneous perceptions of the other. This is done by using cognitive
beliefs that support and justify each party's image of itself and of the
other side.

Especially when peace is a consequence of formal treaties
signed by representatives of the two parties, the cognitive distortions, the anger and fear, and the one-sided narratives that have ac-
cumulated over the years of conflict cannot simply be eliminated.
Thus, to build long-term peace, the parties need to experience constructive reconciliatory events. Such events may enable them to per-

ceive each other more realistically and develop positive relationships between the respective communities and states.

Most of the literature on reconciliation and leadership is based on the bottom-up approach, which emphasizes encounters between individuals. A well-known encounter of this kind between German and French young people took place in Switzerland at Mountain House in 1946 (Henderson, 1996). In South Africa, truth commissions played an important role in bringing about interpersonal (and intergroup) reconciliation (Krog, 1998; Tutu, 1999).

This chapter will, however, discuss the top-down approach, which focuses on the role of national political leadership in reconciliation processes. This approach acknowledges that other types of leaders, usually secondary and tertiary elites in civil society, also play a role in these processes. Regarding the societies considered in this chapter, there is evidence that German and French religious leaders contributed to the rapprochement between their countries during the early 1950s. In addition, socialist activists and leaders of the Sign of Atonement movement helped mend Germany's rift with Israel. In Spain, reconciliation between Republicans and Loyalist war veterans, who constituted a secondary elite, began in the later phase of the Franco regime. During other phases of the reconciliation processes in those countries, however, top-ranking political leaders were the ones who made the difference.

The chapter begins by introducing three historical case studies, involving the role of political leaders in reconciliation processes in the societies in question. The case studies are then analyzed on the basis of conceptual and theoretical principles derived from the social and psychological literature. The first principle has to do with the new leadership paradigm and the qualities of transformational leadership, which include several qualities relevant to explaining reconciliation activities. Another set of principles that explains how leadership contributes to reconciliation derives from theories dealing with the bases of social power. Two of these power bases, informational power and legitimate power, are outlined here, with emphasis on their relevance to explaining leaders' channels of influence (French and Raven, 1959; Raven, 1993). The chapter then discusses the change process involved in reconciliation, illustrating it in the context of the three cases. A final section offers concluding remarks.

Table 6.1 presents a mapping sentence that shows the facets (that is, content areas and conceptual domains) that define the variables relevant to the chapter and the relationships between them (Guttman, 1968).

The mapping sentence identifies nine different facets that form the process in which political leadership contributes to reconciliation. Facet A is based

TABLE 6.1. A Mapping Sentence to Describe the Impact of Political Leadership on the Reconciliation Process

A. *Leadership (Transformational)*		B. *Bases of Social Power*		C. *Nature of the Conflict*
a_1 Idealized influence	that also relies on	b_1 Informational	in the context of the following components	c_1 Intractability
a_2 Inspirational motivation		b_2 Legitimate		c_2 Perpetrator-victim relations
a_3 Intellectual stimulation				c_3 Ripeness for resolution efforts
a_4 Individualized consideration				c_4 Costs to parties

	D. *Activity Measures*		E. *Target Audiences*		F. *Extent of Legitimacy*
will activate	d_1 Psychological	toward	e_1 Internal: one's own constituencies	that will	f_1 Legitimize leader's activities
	d_2 Political		e_2 International		f_2 Delegitimize leader's activities
	d_3 Economic		e_3 The adversarial party		

	G. *Phases of Change/ Stagnation*		H. *Outcome*		I. *Reconciliation*
toward	g_1 Unfreezing	with the	h_1 Internalization	which will indicate	i_1 High extent of reconciliation
	g_2 Moving		h_2 Identification		i_2 Low extent of reconciliation
	g_3 Refreezing		h_3 Compliance		
	g_4 Stagnation		h_4 Denial		
			h_5 Revolt		

on knowledge derived from leadership theory. This knowledge is used to characterize the transformational components of leadership, which may serve as a resource for politicians seeking to promote the reconciliation process. Facet B concerns the two bases of social power: the informational base, which pertains to control of information at the disposal of a political leader, and the base of legitimate power deriving from the leader's formal position. Facet C deals with the nature of the conflict that generated adversarial relations between the two parties. Specific characteristics addressed in this facet are the intractability of the conflict, perpetrator-victim relations, the ripeness of efforts for a solution, and the costs of these efforts for each of the parties. Facet D involves activity measures adopted by the leaders in attempting to normalize relations between the former adversaries. These measures may be psychological in nature (for example, initiating a dialogue or encounter between representatives of the two parties), or they may be political and economic. Facet E pertains to the target audiences in which the political leaders seek to implement change.

Facet F concerns the extent of legitimacy granted by the leader's constituency to pursue reconciliatory relations with adversary groups. Facet G deals with three phases of the change process: generating motivation for change (unfreezing), moving toward change (movement), and stabilizing the change (refreezing). Facet H addresses the outcomes of the reconciliatory efforts. These may be superficial and cool, or they may represent a real transformation in the adversaries' attitudes and behavior toward each other. At the other extreme, reconciliatory efforts may result in resistance to relations or even lead to revolt. Facet I reflects the extent to which reconciliation is achieved.

The facets of the mapping sentence will serve as the theoretical anchors for this chapter's arguments. We now turn to three case studies that illustrate the applicability of these principles.

Germany-France

Reconciliation efforts were initiated in the late 1940s by German Protestant pastors and laymen, with special emphasis on youth encounters. These efforts were pursued at the institutional level by French statesmen and the technocrat Jean Monet, who founded the Coal and Steel Community in 1952. Charles de Gaulle, then leader of the Rally of the French People party, opposed this process at the time. Having previously proposed placing the Rhineland and the Ruhr under long-term Allied control, de Gaulle expressed serious reservations about reunifying the three western sectors of Germany into the Federal Republic in 1948. Upon his return to power in 1958, however, he changed his mind about the West German state, and even came to see it (with France) as one of the two pillars of Europe. Thus, much to the surprise of his own ultranationalist party, his first foreign policy initiative was to work openly toward rapprochement with Adenauer's Germany. Five years later this initiative culminated in a formal treaty (Maillard, 1990; Herf, 1997; Gardner-Feldman, 1999).

Germany-Israel

Adenauer's 1951 reparations initiative, which followed proposals by Jewish and Zionist groups, was motivated by a desire to improve Germany's position in the international community, as well as being a first step toward atoning for the Holocaust. The Israeli prime minister, David Ben-Gurion, took part in formulating the idea but did not believe reconciliation could actually be achieved. He entered the negotiations with the aim of securing long-term financial support for immigrant absorption, but was not interested in establishing diplomatic relations right away. Only in 1960, six years after the Reparations Agreement took effect, did Ben-Gurion change his perception of the new Germany and come to regard establishing close relations with the country as a major asset for Israel. From 1951 to 1953 this policy had met with considerable domestic opposition in both countries, especially Israel. By contrast, it should be noted that the German-French reconciliation was opposed only in France by the Gaullists and the Communists (Shinar, 1967; Herf, 1997).

Spain

This is a domestic policy case involving reconciliation between Republicans and Francoists in post-Civil War Spain. Here, key roles were played by King Juan Carlos and his two main political allies, parliamentary speaker Miranda and Prime Minister Suarez, in the period from 1975 (the year Franco died) to 1981 (the year a new constitution was ratified). Some degree of rapprochement between the opposing political camps had already been achieved during the 1960s and early 1970s, when there was a certain trend toward political liberalization, an orientation toward economic prosperity, as well as a stronger European influence. Nevertheless, numerous obstacles remained: the Francoists remained highly suspicious of the Communists, who were a major opposition force, and refused to grant amnesty to political prisoners. Moreover, the democratic opposition insisted on returning to a republican regime and had deep reservations about the monarchy, which had been Franco's ally (Carr and Fusi, 1979; Powell, 1996).

Reconciliation

Gardner-Feldman (1999) highlights two components of the term reconciliation, the philosophical-emotional and the practical-material. Based on the German reconciliation efforts, Gardner-Feldman argues that these components are interwoven, since they involve "cooperation and confrontation between government and societies: long-range vision and short-term strategy; political support and opposition. In reconciliation, the mix of pragmatism and morality differs depending on history, institutions, leadership and international or political dynamics of the process" (334). This mix of components will be illustrated later in the context of the three historical cases.

Based on a sociological perspective, Kriesberg (1998a) characterizes reconciliation as accommodative ways members of the adversarial entities have come to regard each other after having engaged in intense and often destructive struggle. They have somehow become able to put aside feelings of hate, fear, and loathing, to discard views of the other as dangerous and subhuman, and to abandon the desire for revenge and retribution. To set aside does not mean to have no such feelings, perceptions, and goals, but not to make them paramount nor to act on them against the former adversary (184). This definition suggests that reconciliation requires former adversaries to undergo a significant cognitive, emotional, and behavioral transformation involving movement toward each other. Political leaders are the major actors in initiating the reconciliation process in their societies. They do this via personality resources (charisma) and their high position (legitimate power) in the system, which enable them to mobilize legitimacy among followers within their society.

Leadership

There are numerous definitions of leadership, many of which emphasize the process of influencing others as the core behavior of leaders. A recent review lists over seven thousands books, articles, and presentations dealing with the subject (Bass, 1990). Hogan, Curphy, and Hogan (1994) maintain, for example, that "leadership involves persuading other people to set aside for a period of time their individual concerns and pursue a common goal that is important for the responsibilities and welfare of a group" (493). This definition represents the traditional, social psychological research perspective on leadership and leadership processes.

Burns (1978) offers another definition, which represents a different school of thought based on holistic, humanistic, and interactive perspectives: "Leaders influence followers to act for certain goals that represent the values and motivations—the wants and needs, the aspirations and expectations of *both leaders and followers* and the genius of leadership lies in the manner in which leaders see and act on their own and their followers' values and motivations" (19). This definition portrays leaders as possessing values and needs in common with their followers. Certain qualities of leadership, that is, fellowship and interaction, play an important role in leaders' involvement in reconciliatory processes.

One unique type of leadership, namely, transformational leadership, is characterized by the special qualities that make reconciliation activities possible.

Transformational Leadership

Burns (1978) coined the term "transforming leadership." According to Burns's definition, "such leadership occurs when one or more persons *engage* with others in such a way that leaders and followers raise one another to higher levels of motivation and morality. . . . Power bases are linked not as counterweights but as mutual support for a common purpose" (20). Bass (1985) uses this definition to formulate a typology of *transformational leadership*. The notion of transformational (and transactional) leadership is anchored in empirical research conducted among business executives, agency administrators, and U.S. army colonels, who responded to a list of statements related to leadership behavior (Bass, 1985, 1997; Bass and Avolio, 1993).

These studies revealed four interrelated components of transformational leadership behavior: idealized influence, inspirational motivation, intellectual stimulation, and individualized consideration (Bass, 1997).

- *Idealized influence* refers to leaders' ability to display conviction, emphasize trust, present their most important values, and highlight the importance of purpose, commitment, and ethical consequences of decisions. In this context, leaders are admired as role models. As such they generate pride, loyalty, and confidence, in addition to mobilizing support for a common cause.
- *Inspirational motivation* concerns leaders' ability to articulate an appealing vision of the future, challenge followers with high standards, express enthusiasm, and provide encouragement.
- *Intellectual stimulation* relates to the following leadership capabilities: to question existing assumptions, traditions, and beliefs; to stimulate others to adopt new perspectives and behavior patterns; and to encourage expression of new ideas and reasoning.
- *Individualized consideration* involves leaders' ability to deal with others as individuals.

These traits of transformational leadership can enhance and promote reconciliation processes via the leaders' activities.

Leadership and the Bases of Social Power

French and Raven (1959) and Raven (1990, 1993) analyze the bases of the social power that agents can exert on a target subject. Six bases of social power are proposed as a conceptual framework for describing the different influencing abilities that leaders can use among various target populations. In the case of reconciliation, the leader may use these abilities among different internal and external audiences. In the present context, the two relevant bases are informational power and legitimate power.

- *Informational power* refers to persuasion, and is based on the information or logical argument that the influencing agent may bring to the attention of the target audience so as to achieve change (Raven, 1990).
- *Legitimate power* refers to the influencing agent's structural position vis-à-vis the target, that is, the power to use authority that derives from the political leader's position as head of the system.

Political leaders, then, have two bases of social power that may affect their ability to change the negative image of the adversarial party among their constituencies, or at least to help modify beliefs about the former enemy. The leader's position as gatekeeper of information can be instrumental in reframing, for example, the dominant narrative about the enemy, which is usually distorted and biased through the eyes of the in-group (Rouhana and Bar-Tal, 1998). From the position of legitimate power, the leader may initiate political, economic, and cultural steps that will generate interpersonal and intergroup contact and cooperation. These are the most important tools for changing prejudice and other negative emotions toward the other side (Worchel, 1986; Pettigrew, 1998).

In addition to the legitimate power at their disposal, leaders need to gain legitimacy from their followers or constituencies for moves toward reconciliation. Lipset (1960) defines legitimacy as "the capacity of the system to engender and maintain the belief that the existing political institutions are the most appropriate ones for the society" (64). Katz and Kahn (1978) propose a different definition of legitimacy as "a social-psychological concept in that it refers to social situations in which widespread compliance occurs and to the psychological processes within individuals that account for their compliance" (300). In other words, leaders gain legitimacy when their followers trust their judgments and decisions. In this situation, followers consent to act according to their leader's vision. During periods of reconciliation, leaders need strong support (legitimacy) from their followers in order to initiate behaviors that were previously proscribed.

Phases of the Change Process

The reconciliation process requires the parties in conflict to change their cognitive, emotional, and behavioral reactions to each other. As a rule, new attitudes and behaviors are not easily adopted by social groups or collective communities. The process of establishing new relationships between former adversaries involves, however, several phases of change. Lewin (1947) proposes three phases: unfreezing, movement, and refreezing.

Unfreezing

The first phase in the change process is that of unfreezing, which involves opening up to new information. In Lewin's terms, unfreezing refers to melting the current "quasi-stationary equilibrium state," or status quo. According to this conceptual approach, current attitudes toward the other party in the conflict derive from two kinds of forces—driving and restraining forces—that act simultaneously on a target audience. The driving forces are the ones that promote change. In the case of reconciliation, political leaders use beliefs, attitudes, and knowledge that advocate peace-building and normalization between the conflicting groups. The restraining forces, in contrast, draw the target audience away from that goal. The two forces differ, however, in the extent to which they promote or obstruct attainment of the goal.

For the change process to begin, the driving forces must be stronger than the restraining forces. Two further factors will help stimulate motivation for change at this stage. First, there is a need to generate tension so as to "melt" or "unfreeze" the status quo. In the personal, interpersonal, and collective realms, this means that the target audience experiences feelings of tension that include stress, discomfort, and anxiety. These unpleasant feelings may drive the target audience to open itself to the goal of change. Second, as Lewin recommends, the change agent can begin neutralizing the restraining forces before strengthening the driving forces. In the case of reconciliation, for example, among the restraining forces that act against normalizing relations between groups in conflict are hatred or hostility that develops during the period of war, or fear of being destroyed by the enemy. In any attempt to advocate normalizing relations between former adversaries, the target audience for change should be assured that their hatred and fear are being taken into account.

A by-product of the unfreezing phase, which generates motivation and energy for change, is the growing *ambiguity about the unknown* felt by the actors in the process. With respect to reconciliation, this means the parties may express concern and anxiety about the unknown consequences of a peace agreement. The need for the parties to abandon beliefs about the former enemy, legitimize the new image of the enemy, and develop relatively unbiased relations entails a major "mental earthquake" for many members of groups that were once adversaries.

An additional by-product of the unfreezing phase, according to recent research, is the emergence of *ambivalent feelings toward the process*. Piderit (2000) quotes Pratt and Barnett's assertion that "ambivalence is needed to stimulate unlearning the discarding of obsolete and misleading knowledge, which is a necessary precursor to change" (790). Piderit acknowledges that ambivalence is beneficial at this phase because it contributes to "reframing our understanding of the status quo" (790). As far as reconciliation processes are concerned, this means unsettling previous attitudes toward the enemy, pointing to characteristics of the enemy that were not recognized previously, and acknowledging one's own biased perception of the enemy.

At this stage, the role of political leaders is to contain the feelings of ambiguity about the unknown expressed by parts of society, and to deal with the ambivalence toward the proposed process of change. The concept of containment, which derives from the field of clinical psychology, refers to the ability of change agents to absorb and tolerate feelings of anxiety, anger, and uncertainty among the target audience. Literature in clinical psychology points to the need for change agents at this stage to focus on providing assurance to the target audience so as to contain negative feelings and instill a sense of hope (Yalom, 1985).

Movement

The transition from the phase of unfreezing and preparation for change to the phase of change itself is not clear-cut. During the initial process of unfreezing, members of adversarial groups begin to reframe their cognitive beliefs and perceptions as they move toward a new level of behavior. Rouhana and Bar-Tal (1998) suggest that during the phase of reconciliation, the parties in conflict need to "change their beliefs of conflictive ethos that help perpetuate the conflict" (768). They also point out that at this stage, there is a need to construct a new ethos of peace that consists of "societal beliefs about the utility of cooperative relationship mechanisms that maintain peaceful relations, a vision of peace and the necessity of providing the conditions for trustful and empathic relations with yesterday's enemy" (768).

The movement phase also includes changing stereotypes about the former enemy and humanizing his image. In regard to change, it should be emphasized that the driving forces are not the only relevant factors at this point. According to Watson (1969) and Klein (1976), the restraining forces continue to exert their influence during the movement phase in the form of "resistance to change." Such resistance is expressed by mobilizing energy to prevent disruption of the status quo.

Several types of forces may hinder the reconciliation process at this phase. Some groups may resist attempts by leaders to reframe attitudes toward the former enemy from the very outset. These groups deny the new reality of peace and continue to relate and behave toward the former enemy as if war is still in progress. Another resistance strategy is even more extreme and may take the form of major denigrations of the leadership, including claims that the leadership's legitimization of the former enemy is an act of treason. These claims are supported by catastrophic scenarios of the future fate of the peace treaty and its reconciliatory concomitants. These arguments may also portray the former enemy as unreliable and having a history of broken promises. Opposition groups may perceive the peace treaty and efforts to achieve reconciliation as signs of weakness to be avoided at all costs.

According to theorists of change (Zander, in Marcus, 2000; Deutsch, 1973), restraining forces manifest major resistance to the change effort, and to succeed the movement phase must cope with them successfully. Zander suggests two main approaches to weakening these forces: enhancing understanding of the need for change among the group or society, and encouraging active participation in preparing for change. Political leaders are able to use the most effective channels of communication such as television, radio, and newspapers to convey the ideas and values of change. Continuous efforts by the political leadership to legitimize the steps of peacebuilding may help mobilize their followers toward actively taking part in the process. This, in turn, may weaken manifestations of resistance.

Several other approaches may contribute to weakening the restraining forces: starting with a smaller change, letting the parties involved in the conflict mourn the loss that the change may bring about, and providing abundant resources during the change process (Marcus, 2000). The first condition, that is, change in small doses, means that from the outset of the reconciliation process the political leaders ensure that the parties will not be required to make extreme changes in behavior toward former enemies. At the same time, the leadership works to initiate relations between the groups or states in the cultural, economic, psychological, and religious spheres. Such efforts call for re-examining former images and narratives about the other party in all of those domains.

Refreezing

Refreezing refers to institutionalization of the change products, whether they are new attitudes and emotions or concrete programs in the economic and political domains. In reconciliation terms, this means enabling the former adversarial parties to coexist on the basis of mutual respect and tolerance. This change in attitudes, emotions, and behavior brought about by reconciliatory coexistence is not an isolated event; it should be regard as a long-term and continuous process in which "ongoing adaptation and adjustment occur" (Weick and Quinn, 1999). The two former adversaries gain deeper and more significant knowledge about each other. Thus, strangeness, intolerance, demonization, and delegitimization are replaced by manifestations of mutual respect and cooperation.

It should be mentioned, however, that by no means are the three phases of change necessarily adopted at all levels of former adversarial societies. Certain groups may maintain their former views of the "enemy," which they support ideologically and historically with arguments and factual examples.

Outcomes of the Change Efforts

Facet H in the mapping sentence in table 6.1 indicates the various degrees to which the society's target audiences are persuaded to adopt the reconciliatory attitudes and behavior advocated by the political leadership. These outcomes range from deep and thorough internalization of the reconciliation at one extreme to total rejection and revolt against it at the other. It is necessary to distinguish varying levels of intensity in these outcomes because leadership activity is aimed at multiple audiences both within and outside the state.

Three types of outcomes may be specified on the basis of three processes defined by Kelman (1958, 1961): compliance, identification, and internalization. "Compliance can be said to occur when an individual accepts the influence from another person or from a group because he hopes to achieve a favorable reaction from the other" (1961: 62). In the context of political leadership and reconciliation, this means citizens or constituencies may transform their attitudes toward the former enemy only as lip service so as to gain approval from the leaders or authorities. Identification, according to Kelman, means that "an individual adopts behavior derived from another person or group because this behavior is associated with a satisfying self-defining relationship to this person or group" (1961: 63). As far as the influence of political leadership is concerned, this means target audiences may adopt attitudes and behavior that are considerate and forgiving toward the former enemy because they esteem their leader, that is, as a result of "referent power" in Raven's (1990) typology.

Internalization means that "an individual accepts influence because the induced behavior is congruent with his value system. It is the content of the induced behavior that is intrinsically rewarding here" (Kelman, 1961: 65). In our context, this means the target audience transforms its attitudes and behavior toward the enemy in an optimal way. Thus, the influence of internalization in generating attitude change does not depend on an external source. Because members of the target audience profoundly believe that the attitude or behavior acquired is true, useful, and consistent with their basic values, they will maintain the attitude and behavior even apart from the awareness of the leader.

Nevertheless, as noted, not all groups in a society are willing to transform their attitudes and behavior toward the former enemy at whatever degree of intensity. Opposition to the reconciliatory endeavors may be passive or active. Passive opposition involves denial of the new reality created by the reconciliation, and may be manifested by neglecting to reframe one's views and test old stereotypes in light of the changing relations with the former enemy. Active opposition is often adopted by groups that have opposed any dialogue with the former enemy from the outset. These groups may make concerted efforts to preserve the enemy's negative image and prove the futility of reconciliation, based on the nature of the enemy, the circumstances of reconciliation, or both.

Case Illustrations and Discussion

The following cases illustrate the conceptual framework in light of historical facts. Clearly, all three of the historical cases discussed here fall into the category of intractable conflict. As such, they could not be resolved through transactional leadership, instead requiring intervention on the level of transformational leadership. The three conflicts were all total, affecting every aspect of life for the societies involved. All were protracted (eighty years in the German-French case, forty years in the Spanish case). Although the German-Jewish conflict was much shorter, the compromise that was reached had to address acts of mass slaughter. The savage violence and heavy human and material losses engendered by the Holocaust had a profound and lasting affective impact on the Jewish people, breeding fear and hostility toward the other party.

Such emotions—which are crucial for mobilizing forces to sustain the conflict—are bolstered at the cognitive level by the belief in the exclusive legitimacy
of one's own claims, with one's own side viewed as the victim and the other
as the perennial perpetrator. In short, the change in attitudes and beliefs required for reconciliation can be protracted and difficult because of the strength
of subjective and objective restraining forces.

Subjective forces refer to the cognitive and affective legacy of years of
conflict; objective forces to the formal or de facto manner in which armed
hostilities are terminated. In the German-French case, the war culminated in
a total defeat of Germany followed by a change in the German regime. Thus,
it was easier for the French people to change their attitudes toward the former
adversary than it was for the Jewish people after World War II, during which
one-third of the Jewish population was exterminated. After the German-French
conflict, the French people satisfied some of their desire for vengeance and
many of their fears were alleviated. The Jewish people, however, were clearly
not in the same position. In Spain, the results of the Republican-Francoist
struggle were mixed. At first, the Republicans were crushed and ruthlessly
repressed. However, Francoism subsequently lost much of its ideological zeal
with the decline of the Franco regime, growing prosperity, and the opening
toward Europe. Nevertheless, the Francoists continued to hold the tools of
repression and the fear of (and desire for) retribution ran high in both camps.

In none of the three cases did the parties reach the refreezing stage. What
is important, however, is that the movement toward reconciliation steadily pro-
ceeded, albeit at a snail's pace. No real setbacks or changes of direction can be
singled out. Even the crisis between Israel and Germany over arms shipments
to the Arabs was rather brief and ultimately led to the establishment of diplomatic relations. (As with the attempted coup d'état in Spain in 1981, this moment of tension essentially served to further the reconciliation process.)

In both the Spanish and German-French cases, the process reached an
advanced point in the movement phase, whereas the German-Israeli reconciliation process involved unfreezing and an early stage of movement.

How was some measure of change achieved in each of the three cases?

In the German-Israeli case, which was the least ripe for reconciliation, the
restraining forces were so powerful that Ben-Gurion had to operate in an wily
fashion. In public he declared that full reconciliation with the Germans was
out of the question, and that he was merely negotiating an agreement to obtain
reparations for immigrants (most of whom were Holocaust survivors at that
time). But as the opposition was quick to point out, Ben-Gurion must have
been aware that some form of reconciliation would inevitably result from the
negotiations. Along with the belief in the impossibility of full reconciliation,

the other restraining force was the notion that the Germans were unreliable. Ben-Gurion, however, firmly rejected the argument that Germany would not honor a commitment to pay reparations. He stressed that the Federal Republic had assumed this responsibility so as to be accepted into the world community, and therefore had every reason to keep its word. On the German side, Adenauer also had to confront opposition to the agreement within his own party, where some believed that the amount of the reparations was too high a price to pay for admittance into the society of nations. Adenauer countered this argument by warning of the alleged menace of reprisal against Germany by the Jewish lobby in Washington.

In Spain, one of the restraining forces was the Francoist military's uncertain attitude toward the transition to democracy. It was King Juan Carlos who allayed the reservations by appealing to the people's sense of loyalty to the legitimate power, that is, the regime, as well as by reinforcing their fear of another civil war. When military rebels tried to stage a coup d'état in 1981, the king's insistence on maintaining the legitimate power and preventing anarchy prevailed. The Left's excessive demands for restoring the Republic constituted another restraining force. Ultimately, this force played into the hands of the Right, as the king presented the Left with the choice between a constitutional monarchy or chaos and the end of prosperity.

In France, most of the restraining forces emanated from the nationalist Right and were neutralized in effect by de Gaulle, who was a paragon of rightist virtues. Specifically, he characterized the Communists as inveterate adversaries who had to be marginalized because they were working on the Soviet Union's behalf, thereby allaying the fears of the Right. On the other side of the spectrum from the Right, the Socialists, much like their counterparts in Germany, advocated reconciliation in the name of the universal fraternity of peoples. The centrist parties and the industrialists' associations, for their part, favored a united Europe.

This is not to underestimate the important role of the driving forces that, in the Spanish case, stimulated the people's desire to achieve freedom, stability, and prosperity and banish the specters of the past. But just as de Gaulle had to allay French fears of a return of German militarism before he could promote the vision of a united Europe resting on the twin pillars of France and Germany, the fears of the Spanish people had to be assuaged. Ben-Gurion, for his part, had to dispel fears that the memory of the Holocaust would be erased, as well as the suspicions that the Germans would not honor their financial commitments, before he could express the hope that the reparations would promote immigrant absorption and economic progress. In all these cases, the restraining forces were more powerful than the driving ones.

To cope with the challenges, the respective leaders had to rely on all or some of the four characteristics outlined by Bass.

De Gaulle

De Gaulle wielded the *idealized influence* of a lone and daring hero who had waved the flag of rebellion against the Vichy regime and resistance to Nazism. When he argued that the time had come to heal the rift with Germany, this could hardly be seen as unpatriotic. Since he was a role model for the Right, the Right could not disavow him.

Inspirational motivation was provided, among other things, by de Gaulle's mastery of the French language and the art of rhetoric. His words projected a vision of a peaceful and prosperous Europe extending from the Atlantic to the Urals.

De Gaulle offered *intellectual stimulation* by questioning the assumptions about the age-old animosity between Germany and France, the alleged strong influence of Nazism in Germany, and the indefinite continuation of the Cold War. Believing that nations are "cold monsters" that have only interests, he maintained that rapprochement with an increasingly democratic Federal Republic was in France's interest, and would bolster those democratic tendencies while emphasizing the failure of the Versailles Treaty. In addition, renewing relations would put an end to a conflict that had lasted from 1870 to 1945, and had stemmed from Prussian ambitions to take over Europe that had been dealt a mortal blow by Hitler's defeat. Last but not least, rapprochement would enable France and Germany to lay the foundations for a post-Cold War Europe— even though the Cold War was bound to end in any case with the eventual dissolution of the Soviet Union.

De Gaulle lavished *individualized consideration* on Adenauer, whom he courted as his senior in statesmanship. De Gaulle showed his appreciation for Adenauer's Francophile inclinations and expressed his own deep respect for the German genius, thereby also humanizing the former enemy.

Ben-Gurion

Ben-Gurion, for his part, exhibited similar qualities, although he faced tougher restraining forces. As a savvy elder statesman and founder of the state of Israel, Ben-Gurion had exercised *idealized influence* over the Israeli population during the crisis of the 1948 War of Independence, his arguments about Israel's supreme interests at that moment playing a decisive role. Ben-Gurion's much-glorified historical vision as the so-called unique leader of his generation lent credibility to his perception of the current phase of Jewish history and how it was interwoven with earlier periods in that history. The phrase "from Holocaust to Redemption" represents Ben-Gurion's *inspirational motivation*: the extermination of European Jewry had helped bring about or hastened, in a dialectical way, the birth of the state of Israel. The Jewish state also constituted a sort of revenge against the enemies of the Jewish people, while offering an ultimate guarantee of a safe haven if Jews' physical survival were ever to be threatened again. According to this perspective, anything that strengthened Israel, no matter what its source, was desirable.

The *intellectual stimulation* that Ben-Gurion provided had to do with the special nature of realpolitik, the calculation of interests in light of the state's needs for survival. Thus as of 1948, when the Jewish state emerged as a culmination of the Zionist movement, a change in modus operandi was required. It was now necessary to focus on the major task of absorbing new immigrants and to subordinate the emotions of grief generated by the Holocaust to rational considerations of state-building.

Ben-Gurion showed *individualized consideration* toward Adenauer, especially when he refrained from openly challenging Adenauer's claim that it was Germans, "in the name of the German people"—and not the German people as such—who had perpetrated the Holocaust. When the two leaders met in 1960, Adenauer thanked Ben-Gurion for this.

Juan Carlos

Juan Carlos exerted the *idealized influence* of a young and dynamic role model, symbolizing what most Spaniards hoped to see in their "restored" nation, that is, the integration of future-directed change with a reassuring (but not oppressive) dose of tradition in the form of the Bourbon dynastic monarchy. The dream, or *inspirational motivation*, that Juan Carlos embodied was that of economic and technological progress, along with greater integration into the prosperous (and democratic) West European community while overcoming the rifts of the past.

Intellectual stimulation was provided by a traditional force, namely, the monarchy, which questioned the Francoist assumption that Spain needed authoritarianism to ensure stability and economic progress. Wherever the young ruling couple traveled in Spain they generated a sense of personalized attention among the masses, and this, in turn, fostered a sense of the republican monarchy that freed the Left of its obsessive perception of the Republic as a cure-all. This personal touch was also helpful during the 1981 coup d'état crisis, enabling Juan Carlos to channel the heightened tensions toward further reconciliation.

Adenauer

Adenauer enjoyed the *idealized influence* of a wise old man, and indeed was affectionately nicknamed *Der Alte,* much as Ben-Gurion was called *ha-Zaken.* Adenauer had proved his political and moral mettle as mayor of Cologne under the Nazis, and thus was able to serve as a bridge between the old and new. His position as ruler of non-Nazi West Germany provided a sort of guarantee, for at least some of the Israeli population, that he represented "another Germany."

The *inspirational motivation* he provided was to atone for the Nazi atrocities, albeit in a limited and restrained manner, as a horrendous crime committed, as we saw, by people operating "in the name of the German people" though not by the German nation itself. This approach was tailor-made to reassure the German population, if not necessarily the Israeli one. Adenauer offered *intellectual stimulation* by showing that payment of reparations, alliance with France, and conveying remorse were conditions for integration into the world community. As for *individualized consideration,* Adenauer developed a certain personal relationship with de Gaulle and later with Ben-Gurion.

Leaders' Tools and Approaches

In terms of the bases of power in leadership suggested by Raven, there were two instances in which leaders within this group used legitimate power to combat challenges to their policy. In 1981, Juan Carlos used his legitimate power to quell the coup d'etat; earlier, in 1952, Ben-Gurion used his legitimate power in deploying the police against Menachem Begin's supporters when they tried to storm the Knesset while a debate was being held on reparations. Informational power was almost never used in these cases. In one rare instance, Adenauer warned ultraconservatives that he had received information from "reliable sources" that the Jewish lobby in Washington would vent its anger against Germany if the Bundestag did not pass the Reparations Law.

These actions may be viewed from another analytical perspective, which specifies the range of tools available to leaders:

1. *Affective* tools, which address fears and hopes.
2. *Cognitive* tools, which involve explaining the need for change—such as achieving democracy and ending isolation and backwardness (in

the case of Spain); the vision of a united Europe (in the cases of Germany and France); or overcoming stereotypes of a former enemy that nurture fears. Initiatives taken in that context include Juan Carlos's fostering the image of a fraternal Spain; de Gaulle's homage to the great German cultural heritage, his statement that the FRG was France's equal in Europe, and his belittlement of the three wars between France and Germany as a "duel"; Adenauer's praise for the Jewish contribution to German culture; and Ben-Gurion's reference to "another Germany."

3. *Behavioral* tools, which can be either symbolic (German-French summits, the 1960 meeting between Ben-Gurion and Adenauer, the encounters of the king and queen of Spain with ordinary citizens throughout the country) or substantive and institutional (reparations, amnesty, and constitutional changes in Spain; German-French economic cooperation, and cultural encounters between youth). Such activities generally constitute confidence-building measures and efforts to promote common interests.

Although moral and intellectual leaders may operate just as effectively as political leaders on the affective and cognitive levels, political leaders have an overwhelming advantage on the behavioral level. At the first two levels, the political leadership deploys its legitimacy, prominence, and "resonance power" to set the agenda and influence hearts and minds. At the behavioral level, leaders use material and coercive resources to create faits accomplis that will hopefully endure. Taken together, these tools encompass all the major levels of social action (psychological, political, and economic). This, essentially, is the "abundance of resources" referred to by Zander (1950, cited in Marcus, 2000).

Zander seems to have been correct in suggesting that the reconciliation process should begin cautiously, taking care to reassure the parties and allay their fears of the unknown. Thus, Ben-Gurion denied that the Holocaust could ever be forgotten, but recognized that reconciliation with Germany was inevitable. Juan Carlos gave his word that no retribution would be exacted for acts committed under the Francoist regime, but conferred legal status on the Communists. This need for a cautious, measured approach—especially with respect to the older generations—reflects the fact that restraining forces recede slowly and should be taken into account even long after the reconciliation has been established.

To a large extent this involves the endurance of remnants from the past, and leaders' attitudes toward the past are indeed important. In the examples cited here, the leaders opted for partial amnesia. Adenauer feared that because of the nondemocratic tendencies among the Germans, addressing the past openly would hamper the task of reconstruction. Hence he put a stop to the denazification efforts and asked the world community to pardon Germany—a term used in this context only in Catholic parlance—for crimes committed "in the name of the German people." Likewise de Gaulle, in the interest of promoting reconciliation among the French people and, yet again, rebuilding the country, downplayed the impact of Vichy and helped create a myth of a widely popular resistance. Juan Carlos, for his part, joined the effort to set aside the past, which was initiated as early as the 1960s by associations for war veterans and the handicapped. As for Ben-Gurion, he was less preoccupied by the Holocaust than other Israeli leaders and parties in the 1950s. Although groups close to his own centrist party were strongly concerned about the Holocaust, he worked to ensure that the Holocaust would not constitute part of the Israeli founding mythology.

That is not to say reconciliation cannot be furthered by leaders who cope directly and openly with the past (for example, Willy Brandt's contribution in the late 1960s). But in the early phases of the reconciliation process, when restraining forces are still powerful, some willful ignorance may be advantageous.

It should be mentioned that we have not distinguished here among different target audiences. These include internal audiences (for example, domestic public opinion, which is particularly crucial in democracies), external audiences (the former enemy), and the international arena (which was important in the case of German reparations). Indeed, in a world of open communications, messages to different audiences may collide. For example, Adenauer's ambiguous request for pardon, which catered to his home audience, was quickly picked up by Menachem Begin in the Knesset debate on reparations, and used as proof of Germany's duplicity and Ben-Gurion's hypocrisy. Moreover, internal audiences may be multiple, and however deftly they are managed by the leader, resistance to change may persist in some sectors. This could take the form of sullen acquiescence (as expressed toward Germany by parts of the Gaullist Right), behind-the-scenes manipulation, incendiary propaganda (used by some of the Francoist party and security forces), street-protest politics (used by Begin's supporters against Ben-Gurion), and even armed revolt (such as the putsch attempt in the Spanish parliament). It should also be noted that even those who do not resist are not always persuaded.

The opposition is often induced to accept reconciliation out of identification with the leader. For example, the French Right was induced to accept de Gaulle's policies out of respect for him, and the Israeli public accepted the German reparations plan out of respect for Ben-Gurion. In more difficult cases, however, movement toward reconciliation does not progress beyond the level of mere compliance. That, for example, was the response of the Spanish armed forces and some members of the Francoist Right to Juan Carlos. Even within Ben-Gurion's ruling Labor Party, a considerable number of members supported the Reparations Agreement only so as to appease him.

Finally, the three cases of Germany-France, Germany-Israel, and Spain seem to show that internalization occurs gradually and follows patterns set by the political leader. It takes time and generational change for reconciliation to reach the refreezing stage. In Spain, Germany, and France, the younger age groups were indeed the ones that internalized the future-oriented messages of Juan Carlos, Adenauer, and de Gaulle most rapidly and agreed to close the door on the past. Older cohorts, in contrast, were more likely to identify with the charismatic leader and his policy without necessarily cleaning the slate.

Concluding Remarks

It could be argued that the cases presented here all belong to a sort of Age of Giants, in which leaders like Churchill, Roosevelt, and Stalin shaped the destinies of their nations and the world at large. This argument implies that such giants no longer exist in the contemporary era of ungovernability. But is that the case? What of Nelson Mandela, who dressed himself up in a Springboks shirt, or King Hussein, who knelt before the bereaved parents of an Israeli girl killed by a mentally deranged Jordanian soldier and asked them for forgiveness? Without such leadership, how can one account for the abolition of apartheid in South Africa or the reconciliation process between Israel and Jordan?

The importance of leaders may also be viewed negatively, such as when their acts hamper reconciliation by altering the public agenda. Take, for example, Netanyahu's longstanding refusal to meet with Arafat or shake his hand (the obverse of the famous handshake between Rabin and Arafat on the White House lawn). Then there was Barak, who showed arrogant disregard for the Palestinian leader. And there was Egyptian President Mubarak who, contrary to Hussein, performed no ritual of contrition after a deranged Egyptian soldier murdered Israelis vacationing on the Sinai coast. Moreover, the Egyptian president has adamantly refused to visit Israel, except on the occasion of Rabin's funeral.

In such contexts, leaders have a greater impact on liberal democracies, which are characterized by free-for-all power competition, than on illiberal democracies characterized by "soft authoritarianism." That explains why Sadat had less influence on his domestic audience than on the Israeli public. The

Egyptian masses followed him because of his pseudo-Pharaonic, legal, and charismatic power, out of acquiescence rather than internalization. However, this by no means diminishes Sadat's major role in convincing the Egyptian military elites to accept the military and economic rationale of peace with Israel. For their part, the Egyptian military forces were prepared for internalization of the concept "no more war" following preliminary talks with their Israeli counterparts in 1975, when they became familiar with Israel's security concerns. Even today this internalization has retained some significance in Egypt, despite the outbreak of the second intifada. Indeed, a wide-ranging opinion poll in December 2000 revealed divergent views among Egyptian elite groups on issues related to Israel. For instance, although two-thirds of the Egyptian journalists surveyed voiced adamant opposition to economic relations with Israel, over half of the businessmen welcomed such relations. The lower classes, however, were indifferent to this issue, their primary concerns focusing on unemployment and housing (*Al-Ahram* Weekly, May 3–9, 2001).

A major (and unexpected) conclusion of this study is that research on reconciliation should devote more attention to secondary elites in both liberal and illiberal democracies. Whether or not the era of gigantic leaders is over, secondary elite groups still have an impact and enjoy growing sway in the global village. Such groups include, for instance, the Protestant pastors of postwar Germany, the Confédération du Patronat (the employers' organization) during the decolonization of France, and associations of war veterans and disabled veterans in Francoist Spain. All these groups remind us that even the giants did not operate on their own, and that civil society and the public sphere count in politics. Civil societies, for that matter, do not have their own dynamics; rather, secondary elites help shape civil society and set the agenda for debate on the reconciliation process.

The role and motivations of those who follow these elites (as well as top political, intellectual, and religious leaders) may be assessed to some extent through contemporary opinion polls. In the French case, for instance, the polls indicate that pubic disenchantment with the Algerian War—especially among the middle classes though less so among the peasants and workers—was already prevalent by late 1957, that is, well before the rise of de Gaulle and following the alleged victory of General Massu in the Battle of Algiers; hence, secondary elites such as the Communisty Party and the trade unions had gained support. Likewise, in Germany of the early 1950s, polls conducted by the occupation authorities show how well Adenauer perceived his public: most West German adults believed that on the whole, the Nazi regime had made positive achievements during 1933–1939.

This last example points to a second conclusion emerging from the present study, namely, the need to pay more attention to the "usable" past. The term usable past was coined in the course of intellectual debates in the United States in the early twentieth century. In 1918, the culture critic Van Wyck Brooks posed the question: "What, out of all multifarious achievements and impulses and desires of the American literary mind, ought we to elect to remember?" The question of "what we elect to remember" has gained intensity and political relevance in recent times. Most notably, Germany has been concerned with the question of whether and how the people can be proud of their national identity. There has also been a heated debate in France on torture during the Algerian War.

For our purposes, the most pertinent question concerns the role of primary, secondary, and tertiary elites in shaping public debate on which aspects of the nation's history to emphasize, commemorate, and teach. What are the ethical dimensions of this debate, and how does it relate to the formation of civic identities, patriotism, or cosmopolitanism? The cosmopolitan option is, of course, closely related to the debate on globalization. The role of the elites is also important in shaping the image of the enemy. The language in which the image is couched is no less important than its content, or than the stories that people tell about the conflict. Here, again, elite groups and individuals (such as writers and poets) are likely to play an active role.

7

The Role of Forgiveness in Reconciliation

Yehudith Auerbach

One witnesses these days a worldwide phenomenon of peoples and leaders asking forgiveness or offering apologies to one another for past wrongdoing. These apologies are occasionally made by one nation-state to another. An example of this kind is provided by the Czech-German "Declaration of Mutual Relations and Their Future Relations" issued in January 1997 whereby the two countries apologized to each other for past grievances caused by each of them to the other's population or part of it (Handl, 1997). More often a nation-state apologizes for its misconduct to the group that was the object of this transgression. An example of this kind is President de Klerk's apology in August 1996 to the black majority in Africa for the brutal violation of their rights under the Apartheid rule (Kriesberg, 1998a: 186).

Another attempt to redress past injustice and bring about peace within torn societies is truth commissions. This technique is usually based on an informal understanding between a majority group that has previously been subjected to the oppressive rule of a minority group, on the one hand, and the minority, now afraid of reprisals, on the other. According to this agreement the past perpetrators confess their crimes and in return receive immunity from prosecution. The best known example of such a truth commission is the Truth and Reconciliation Commission (TRC) in South Africa initiated by Nelson Mandela with the blessing of Desmond Tutu (Tutu, 1999).

Similar commissions have been established in Argentina, Chile, El Salvador, Honduras, Rwanda, and Uruguay.

What are the reasons for this recent phenomenon of collective forgiveness? One explanation is changes in the international system. With the end of the Cold War and military hostilities across recognized frontiers becoming increasingly rare, at least in the Western world, communal conflicts, some of them extremely brutal, have come to the fore. Ethnic and religious minorities that have been the objects of deprivation, discrimination, and even mass killings are asking for redress of the injustice done to them.

In the West this trend has been fueled by the growing wealth in which the younger generation of once-deprived people has been taking an increasing share. The self-confidence of these groups has been strengthened and correspondingly they become more and more aware of their rights and of their power to claim them. Electronic media, which were developing at a rapid pace toward the end of the twentieth century, serve as efficient channels for diffusing the often heart-breaking stories of injustices done to these groups' ancestors. A case of this kind is the recent growing demand for redress of injustice done to the blacks in the United States. As a result, leaders, stimulated either by moral instincts or by more political motives, issue authentic or quasi-authentic declarations of forgiveness or apologies (for example, Israeli Prime Minister Barak apologizing in September 1997 to Israel's non-European "eastern" immigrant communities for their sufferings caused by misdeeds of the Labor Party when in power). In other cases apology is accompanied by the offer of compensation for past injustice (for example, the apology and compensation offered by the Reagan Administration to Japanese-Americans who had been interned during World War II).

The increasing number of efforts made toward redressing past wrongdoing within multinational countries (for example, the willingness of Australia, New Zealand, and Canada to compensate their respective indigenous minorities) may corroborate the thesis that we are entering an era of neo-Enlightenment. Proponents of this thesis argue that "as the so-called realism of the cold war vanished, the UN, NATO, and individual countries struggled to define their places in a world that is paying increased attention to moral values" (Barkan, 2000: xvi). Against the apparent proof of neo-idealism one can assemble evidence of the continuation of old-Realism into the twenty-first century. The unsuccessful enforcement of international sanctions against Iraq is only one example out of many. Still, it is hard to overlook the growing tendency toward the morality, or at least morality as conceived by Western values, that has been permeating the international community in the last years.

Another reason for the growing wave of goodwill toward underprivileged communities maybe the fears and hopes that have accompanied the end of the millenium. Along with the continuation and even acceleration of the mundane race for money and consumerism, one may also notice a trend toward spirituality and nonmaterial self-fulfillment. More and more young people find their way to India and other Far-East countries in search of spirituality and a meaningful life. This search may have found its way to the political arena, where it was translated into various manifestations of goodwill toward past victims.

Concurrently with these developments, scholars of conflict and conflict-ending strategies have gradually shifted their focus from conflict resolution to such concepts as reconciliation and forgiveness that reflect more correctly the spirit and practice of the "New Age" (for example, Gardner-Feldman, 1999; Kriesberg, 1998a; Montville, 1993; Rothstein, 1999a).

However, there is still need for further research on both the theoretical and empirical levels regarding the feasibility of forgiveness between groups and nations and the relationship of forgiveness to reconciliation. Is forgiveness a necessary condition for reconciliation between former enemies? Is it sufficient for bringing about real and stable peace between them?

This chapter will examine the role of "forgiveness" in the process of group reconciliation, including among states and nations. It will concentrate on forgiveness and try to see whether it is a necessary condition for furthering peace among nations. It will explore the different conditions needed for the success of forgiveness in the process of reconciliation. The case of Israel-West Germany will be examined in light of the above.

Conflict Resolution and Reconciliation

Conflict resolution as a means of ending rivalries between nation-states was mainly examined within the framework of the realist paradigm, which has long dominated the study of international relations. According to this paradigm, conflicts erupt usually over resources such as territory, oil, and spheres of influence. When pushed, by realistic power calculations, to terminate their conflict, the rivals usually do not aspire to more than the cessation of hostilities and the settlement of their dispute.

Scholars who wished both to understand the process and to contribute to its realization developed the conflict resolution concept as a vehicle for this double successful outcome (for example, Boulding, 1962; Coser, 1961; Fisher,

1964; Holsti, 1966; and Luard, 1970). The concept was defined and elaborated within the limited contours of the relevant era. According to Kriesberg, the conflict resolution approach "presumes that conflicts are never wholly zero-sum . . . consequently there is the possibility of . . . an integrative outcome whereby all parties gain much of what they need or want" (Kriesberg, 1992: 9). Studied from a cognitive perspective, conflict resolution is defined as a "political process through which the parties in conflict eliminate the perceived incompatibility between their goals and interests and establish a new situation of perceived compatibility" (Bar-Tal, 2000b: 354).

Reconciliation

Conflict resolution is an important but not a sufficient condition for stable and harmonious peace between former enemies. *Reconciliation*, often used inter-changeably with *stable peace*, is considered "the long-term goal of any process of conflict resolution" (Rothstein, 1999a: 237).

The concept of reconciliation has a much broader meaning than conflict resolution. It involves psychological processes, both cognitive and emotional, and thus adds an important element to the analysis of conflict termination. True, social-psychological contributions have been introduced into the study of conflict and conflict resolution for over the last thirty years (for example, Burton, 1969, 1988; Kelman, 1979, 1997b). Usually, however, these ap-proaches conceptualize conflict resolution as a *process*, through which former enemies settle or rather try to mitigate their disputes. A typical example is provided by Kelman who notes: "Conflict resolution does not imply that past grievances and historical traumas have been forgotten and a consistently har-monious relationship has been put in place. It simply implies that a *process* has been set into motion that addresses central needs and fears of the societies and establishes continuing *mechanisms* to confront them" (Kelman, 1997b: 197; emphases added). Although the debate between those who see reconcili-ation as an outcome and others who view it as a process is still going on (for a discussion of this debate see Bar-Tal and Bennink, this volume), this chapter will follow those who emphasize the *outcome* aspect of reconciliation. One of these is Kriesberg, who views reconciliation as a "relatively amicable relation-ship typically established after a rupture in relations involving one sided or mutual infliction of extreme injury" (Kriesberg, 1998c: 351).

Kriesberg describes the four steps that former rivals take on the way to reconciliation: "They acknowledge the reality of the terrible acts that were per-petrated." This point incorporates an important aspect of reconciliation, emphasized by social psychologists (for example, Kelman, 1997b: 206), as well as by historians (e.g. Barkan, 2000: xxii), namely, the mutual acceptance of the adversaries' narratives as legitimate. Kriesberg goes beyond this point and argues that in a genuine process of reconciliation the former enemies "accept with compassion those who committed injurious conduct, as well as acknowledging each other's sufferings; believe that their injustices are being redressed; anticipate mutual security and well-being" (Kriesberg, 1998c: 352).

The last phase marks, in fact, the culmination of the reconciliation process and embodies the hopes for trust, respect, and harmony that motivated both the study of reconciliation and its practice by former enemies.

Kriesberg notes that full and complete reconciliation is almost never accomplished between former enemies. Nonetheless, he encourages rivals to mobilize their efforts toward this goal, since "the failure to carry out any measure of reconciliation endangers the stability in relations between former enemies" (Kriesberg, 1998c: 354).

Whereas reconciliation emphasizes the psychological aspect of conflict termination, forgiveness adds the spiritual-moral flavor to the discussion.

Forgiveness

Forgiveness is a religious concept prevalent in the Judeo-Christian culture but much more accentuated in Christianity (Shriver, 1998: 134).

In the Old Testament forgiveness is represented as one of the basic qualities of God. It emanates from his love for his people and is given to the sinners as a gift, independently of their actions (Smitt, 1943: 230, 376). Forgiveness is the expression of love and mercy and goes beyond Justice. The incompatibility between justice and forgiveness had troubled the Jewish sages. They suggested that God sometimes quarrels with himself about this issue and prays. "What is His prayer? May it be my will that My love of compassion [that is, forgiveness: Y. A.] overwhelm my demand for strict justice" (Berakot 7a, quoted in Murphy and Hampton, 1998: 4).

Forgiveness between man and God is possible because man is aware of his own weakness vis-à-vis God and is, therefore, not afraid of being humiliated through his plea for forgiveness. No power calculations are involved in this story. Giving pardon does not diminish God's power, and man does not feel patronized by receiving it, as is often the case when one human being grants forgiveness to another, thus placing himself morally above the transgressor. The person that atones for his sins knows that God loves him and wants him to repent.

Forgiveness is typically defined as "the forswearing of resentment, the resolute overcoming of anger and hatred that are naturally directed toward a person who has done an unjustified and non-excused moral injury" (Murphy and Hampton, 1998: 15).

The transaction of asking for and giving forgiveness presupposes the following: "[Recognition of] . . . the commission of an *evil* act by one agent against another and the effort of the victim to repair the relationship fractured by the evil. . . . the willingness of offenders to acknowledge their offenses . . . this is the *repentance* side of the transaction . . . [which is the condition] for moving on toward a reconciliation . . . Moral forgiveness begins with the memory of immorality, with *moral judgement.* To forgive . . . is to value the hope of relation repair. . . . forgiveness always involves a certain *forbearance,* a step back from revenge. It . . . involves some degree of *empathy* with the one who has committed the wrong" (Shriver, 1998: 133; emphasis in original).

The six components outlined above are not of equal importance or difficulty. The *sine qua non* for forgiveness seems to be the recognition on both sides to the conflict that one side has committed a crime against the other. Forgiveness is only possible when the sides involved in the conflict acknowledge that injustice has been done and agree upon the identity of the victim and the perpetrator.

In the literature there is some vagueness concerning the similarities and differences between *forgiveness* and *apology. Forgiveness* seems to be wider than apology, incorporating both the request for forgiveness made by the perpetrator and the victim's response. It has thus the connotation of a transaction. *Apology* on the other hand seems to denote only the action of asking for forgiveness. But for the present discussion I'll refer to these two concepts interchangeably, relying on authors such as Tavuchis, who actually suggests that the one incorporates the other: "One who *apologizes* seeks *forgiveness* and redemption for what is unreasonable, unjustified, undeserving and inequitable" (Tavuchis, 1991: 17; emphasis added). Stating it differently, one can say that apology is the operational definition of forgiveness, that is, "apology is essentially a speech act that seeks forgiveness" (Tavuchis, 1991: 27).

Tavuchis differentiates between four modes of apology:

From one to one (individual to individual)
From one to many (individual to collectivity)
From many to one (collectivity to individual)
From many to many (collectivity to collectivity)

The mode that is most relevant to the discussion of the role of forgiveness (or apology) in the process of reconciliation between societies across or within borders is the fourth, namely, from many to many. True, in most cases it is the one, usually the leader, who makes the apology speech, but in fact he is apologizing on behalf—though not always with the full approval—of his people, and he addresses his plea to the many, namely to the other people.

The collective apology differs from the individual apology in its tone and style. It is not as spontaneous and emotional as the bid for forgiveness addressed by one person to another. Being "a diplomatic accomplishment" (Tavuchis, 1991: 100), it tends to be "couched in abstract, remote, measured and emotionally neutral terms" (Tavuchis, 1991: 102).

This qualitative difference notwithstanding, the collective apology, like the individual apology, is an act of expressing remorse and asking for forgiveness, and as such it is regarded as "a prelude to reconciliation" between offenders and victims. The process culminates in "the forgiveness of the offender which symbolizes reconciliation and allows for the resumption of normal social relations" (Tavuchis, 1991:121)

There is disagreement regarding the merits of forgiveness. A contending psychotherapeutic approach argues that resentment is a legitimate and healthy way of expressing self-respect (Hampton, 1988) that makes people "feel alive and wards off the threat of emptiness" (Montville, 1993: 120).

The literature dealing with forgiveness from a philosophical perspective (see particularly Arendt, 1958; Tavuchis, 1991; Wiesenthal, 1997) raises a host of intriguing questions concerning the virtue and feasibility of forgiveness in cases of genocide and other heinous crimes: Are all crimes forgivable? Is there no danger that cheap and easy forgiveness will lead rather to the perpetuation of the evil instead of eradicating it? Do survivors have the right to forgive in the names of the dead victims? And alternately, should and can the descendants of perpetrators ask for forgiveness in the names of their late fathers?

One of the most problematic aspects of forgiveness is its relation to memory and past. Archbishop Tutu argues that forgiveness is the only way to liberate oneself from the prison of past animosities and rancor (Tutu, 1999: 272). But is the past, including the difficult and horrendous part of it, not the fabric of nations' consciousness and common identity? Forgiving means giving up an important part of the history of the victimized collectivity. Paraphrasing the title Tutu gave to his moving book, namely, "no future without forgiveness," one can claim with equal strength: "no past with forgiveness."

Among activists who have been working with the victims of the Apartheid regime in South Africa, there is some skepticism concerning the compatibility of the noble phenomenon of forgiveness with the harsh realities of intrasocietal conflicts. One of these skeptics warns: "This notion of healing and reconciliation which is so closely associated with 'forgiveness' . . . poses great dangers to any realistic or meaningful prospects of building reconciliation" (Simpson, 2000: 5). Asking for forgiveness in the context of intractable and sometimes bloody conflicts may seem "extreme and perhaps paralyzing" argues a scholar of conflict resolution (Gardner-Feldman, 1999: 335).

Nevertheless, leaders and scholars alike seem to be attracted by the potential of forgiveness for furthering reconciliation and stable peace between former enemies. Tutu, who was deeply involved in the work of the TRC in South Africa, rejects all the allegations against forgiveness: "In forgiving people are not being asked to forget. On the contrary it is important to remember, so that we should not let such atrocities happen again. Forgiveness does not mean condoning what has been done. . . . Forgiveness is not being sentimental . . ." (Tutu, 1999: 271–272). Another proponent of forgiveness emphasizes its *healing* effect: "The value of forgiveness for the 'victim' is that it cleans the wound and allows it to heal." The intuitive rejection of forgiveness as a humiliating process is met by this author with a counter-argument: "[Forgiveness] erases the humiliation that was suffered, replacing it with pride and positive self-esteem. It encourages the expression of love, even love for the 'perpetrator'. . . . It supports the victim morally and emotionally, with less cost to both sides, and the society as well" (Cloke, 2001: 13).

Proponents of forgiveness marshal numerous examples of successful cases of apologies and forgiveness pleas to substantiate their arguments. Among them, a Franco German commission of historians whose task was to revise German and French texts that presumably laid the psychological foundation for the establishment of the European Community (Montville, 1993: 121); a similar work done in Soviet State Archives leading to a formal Soviet apology to the Polish people for the murder of 15,000 Polish reserve officers in Katyn; Poland's President Lech Walesa asking for Israeli forgiveness in the Israeli Parliament in May 1991; and Austrian President Frantz Vranitsky apologizing to the Jewish people for the Austrian part in the Holocaust in July 1991 (Montville, 1993: 122–123). Montville admits, though, that the common denominator of most of the cases reviewed above is individuals motivated by personal dignity and sense of duty, who could not earnestly claim that they reflect or are in position to influence public opinion in their respective countries.

The literature dealing with forgiveness in the context of international or intranational conflict examines the relation and links between the act of forgiveness and the process of reconciliation. Some would argue that reconciliation brings upon and facilitates forgiveness and healing (Lederach, 1998; Staub, 2000). Others hold that forgiveness is a step toward reconciliation. Among those who see forgiveness as a phase in the process of reaching genuine reconciliation there are still some differences regarding the nature of this phase. Is it a necessary or sufficient condition for reconciliation? There are scholars who claim that forgiveness is not a necessary condition for reconciliation, relying on cases such as the reconciliation between West Germany and Israel (Gardner-Feldman, 1999). I will use the same example, namely Israeli—German relations, in order to substantiate the argument that forgiveness is important, and in some cases—most notably when a crime of the scale of the Holocaust has been committed—necessary for a *full and genuine* reconciliation between former enemies. If no real effort at achieving forgiveness is made, reconciliation is doomed to be partial and vulnerable. In some cases, most paradoxically when forgiveness is most needed, the way to forgiveness may be hampered (for reasons that will be detailed below). However, forgiveness does not inevitably lead to reconciliation. People may forgive each other without necessarily becoming friends (Cloke, 2001: 17).

Forgiveness is, therefore, a *necessary—though not always possible—*and not sufficient condition for *full* and *perfect* reconciliation between former adversaries. Forgiveness is only possible if and when the two sides that engage in the process of reconciliation agree about the crime committed by one of them and about the identity of the perpetrator. In many of the ongoing bitter conflicts that attract world attention (for example, the Israeli-Palestinian conflict) the contradicting arguments about who is or was the criminal and who is or was the victim is one of the most serious stumbling blocks on the way to reconciliation. Every side has its version of the dispute and cultivates its own historical narrative. The conflicting narratives serve as the cornerstones of the respective collective identities and are, therefore, almost immune to change. If the sides have come to agree on the issues of crime, perpetrator, and victim, most of the work toward conflict resolution has already been done. Then and only then can and should the reconciling sides enter into a process of forgiveness in order to achieve full and perfect reconciliation.

However, there are cases where the assertions about the nature of the crime and identity of perpetrator are beyond dispute. The fact the Nazis tried to disguise their deeds and cheat the whole world about the real function of the concentration camps proves that they were completely aware of the criminal nature of their behavior. In most cases of genocide, or even of less brutal wrongdoing toward indigenous inhabitants, there is no doubt about the share of guilt. These are the cases where forgiveness is both needed and possible though not easy to undertake.

Reaching true reconciliation through genuine forgiveness is difficult and consequently rare. It depends on a variety of factors, which can further or hamper the process. What are the conditions for the success of forgiveness in the process of reconciliation? This will be the subject of the next section.

Conditions for the Success of Reconciliation through Forgiveness

Several factors have to be considered when trying to assess the success of reconciliation via forgiveness.

The Religious-Cultural Context

Since forgiveness is basically a spiritual-moral phenomenon, the religious-cultural context in which it is carried out is crucial. The extent of compatibility between the parties that wish to reconcile is one of the main predictors of the success of forgiveness. Incompatibility in the convictions regarding forgiveness will make it hard for the sides to get into a genuine process of forgiveness.

A quick glance at references to forgiveness in the most prevalent religions will reveal the potential for misunderstanding between antagonists that consider forgiveness as a way to reconciliation.

Christianity teaches its believers to cherish love and mercy and to express these noble feelings through forgiveness of their enemies. The devout Christian is required to follow the example of Jesus, who forgave his enemies on the Cross without even waiting for them to ask for forgiveness (Tutu, 1999).

The literature that studies the place of forgiveness in Christianity emphasizes its importance and centrality for true believers. Forgiveness is one of the cornerstones of Christian theology. It should be given unconditionally to friends and enemies alike independently of the size of the crime or the behavior of the perpetrator. (For an excellent review of this literature as well as the literature regarding Islam's approach to forgiveness see the appendix to Bar-On, 2001.)

Judaism, however, has stricter rules regarding forgiveness. Forgiveness can be asked only from the victim himself, and only the victim can forgive. Maimonides says: "Sins between one man and his fellow, such as striking, cursing, or stealing are never forgiven until one pays up his debt and appeases his fellow. Even if he returns the money he owes he must still ask for forgiveness" (Rambam, *Mishneh Torah, Hilchoth Teshuvah* 2:9–10). According to Rambam (Maimonides), there are three essential stages in the process of *Teshuvah*, that is, repentance. First, sinners have to confess their sin; thereafter they are requested to repent their wrongdoing; and finally they must undertake not to repeat their sins (Rambam, *Mishneh Torah, Hilchoth Teshuvah* 1:1).

Teshuvah—repentance—is the *sine qua non* for forgiveness. Without *Te-*

shuvah there is no forgiveness. Judaism puts greater emphasis on *Teshuva* than on forgiveness. The prominent Jewish thinkers, Rabbi Abraham Yitzhak Hacohen Kook and Rabbi Yosef Dov Halevi Soloveitchk, imbue *Teshuva* with the halo of truth, love, and light and elevate it to the highest degree of religious accomplishment (Kook, 1994; Peli, 1974).

It is noteworthy that the Old Testament does not speak about forgiveness between human beings. Only God—not even the Great Priest on the Day of Atonement—has the authority to forgive.

In Islam, forgiveness has been given major attention. *Tawba* (repentance), like its Jewish equivalent *Teshuvah*, is a demanding process consisting of three phases identical to those requested by the Jewish law (EI,² 1991, 10: 385) and considered a necessary condition for *ghufran*—forgiveness granted by God to the repenting sinner (EI,² 1991, 2:1078). The rituals of *sulha* (settlement) and *musalaha* (reconciliation), usually performed within a communal framework, are meant to end conflicts among believers and establish peace through acknowledgment of and forgiveness to the injuries between individuals and groups (Irani, 1999).

With its strong emphasis on compassion, tolerance, and nonviolence, Buddhism places forgiveness on top of the hierarchy of values. "For a Buddhist, forgiveness is always possible and one should always forgive" (Matthiew Richard, a Buddhist monk, in Wiesenthal, 1998: 235).

The different approaches to forgiveness may hamper understanding and, in fact, the reconciliation process between parties of different religious convictions. An example of such incongruity is provided by Simon Wiesenthal. Wiesenthal shares with his readers his past dilemma when he was unable to forgive a Catholic Nazi-SS soldier, who, on his deathbed, begged and felt entitled to forgiveness for his terrible crimes against Jews (Wiesenthal, 1998). Fifty-three people, among them philosophers, theologians, authors, and religious authorities, have tried to cope with Wiesenthal's disturbing question: "What would I have done [if I were in Wiesenthal's place]"? All the Jewish respondents answered that Wiesenthal was right in not granting forgiveness to the Nazi soldier. All those who said they would have forgiven were non-Jewish (one Buddhist and the others Catholics). It is of course quite understandable that the Jews would identify with their Jewish brother and through him with the Jewish victims of the Nazis. Still, the answers of the participants reveal to what extent they have been influenced by their respective religions. For example, one of the respondents, a Catholic priest, said: "My whole instinct is to forgive. Perhaps that is because I am a Catholic priest. In a sense I am in the forgiving business. I sit in a confessional for hours and forgive everyone who comes in, confesses, and is sorry" (Dr. Theodore M. Hesburgh, in Wiesenthal, 1998: 169).

The different approaches of the central religions to forgiveness can thus create a gap between the parties who wish to reconcile their dispute through forgiveness. This factor is, however, relevant only if religion plays a significant role in the mindset of either one or both contenders.

Religion is part of a broader cultural context consisting of values, norms, myths, and manners inculcated in a society for generations. Japanese society, which makes such frequent and intensive use of "*Sumanai*," meaning "I'm sorry," is considered "the apologetic society par excellence" (Tavuchis quoting Doi in Tavuchis, 1991: 37). However, Tavuchis quotes Foucault as saying that it is the "Western man [who] has become a confessing animal" (Tavuchis, 1991: 41). Tavuchis suggests that the real distinction is between collectivities and individuals. Whereas "[Western] collectivities are sociopathic: they are incapable ... of acknowledging regret and expressing remorse," Japanese corporations find it natural to apologize for misdeeds (Tavuchis, 1991: 43).

National Interests Promoted through Reconciliation and Forgiveness

A crucial factor is the importance of the interests perceived to be promoted through forgiveness versus other interests that can be harmed by it. On the one hand, the greater the perceived importance of the interests to be achieved through forgiveness, the greater the chances for forgiveness. On the other hand, when expediency seems to be the only or main motivation for asking for forgiveness, the request is likely to sound hollow and therefore difficult to realize (Tavuchis, 1991: 62).

The need for forgiveness is particularly conspicuous in cases of intrasocietal conflict, and even more so if the divided society is in its nation-building stage. Disputes of this kind, namely, among two or more ethnic, racial, or ideological groups, are usually extremely brutal and sanguinary (for example, the civil wars in Cambodia, Rwanda, and Yugoslavia). When the sides decide to settle their dispute and direct their efforts to the structuring of a united national framework, they will generally look for a mechanism that will prevent revenge and further bloodshed. Truth and reconciliation committees are frequently geared toward this aim. Forgiveness may then serve as a psychological healer, and contribute to a healthy process of nation building.

But when forgiveness is perceived as touching the nerves of the dispute and hurting fundamental and crucial beliefs that relate to the identity or legitimacy of one of the parties involved in the conflict, the path to *reconciliation via forgiveness* may be more difficult. Israeli psychiatrist Rafi Moses tells the story of a Israeli-Palestinian workshop where the Israelis refused the Palestinian request to acknowledge the suffering of the Palestinian people in 1948. "The Israelis were frightened of the consequences of what it might imply to make such an acknowledgement" (Montville, 1993: 119). The Prime Minister of Israel was advised not to apologize to the Palestinians for their suffering during the 1948 war, lest this plea for forgiveness serve as leverage for further Palestinians demands and for the delegitimization of the State of Israel (Blumental, 2001).

Power Asymmetry

Forgiveness takes place in an inherently asymmetrical power context. The perpetrator, who asks for forgiveness, is usually the stronger side in this equation, or at least was stronger when he committed the crime. For him to apologize to the once weak victim is obviously humiliating, particularly if he has reasons to believe that his plea would be denied. Furthermore, the victim may feel patronized by the request and refuse to play the game. But granting forgiveness too quickly may convey the offensive message: "You are not meaningful enough to have hurt me." In the international domain, it is more common that a very powerful "perpetrator" will avoid asking for forgiveness if he feels that he is not obliged to do so. An illustrative example is Turkey's refusal to acknowledge, let alone accept responsibility for, the Armenian genocide.

In view of the centrality of power considerations in the international system it seems that forgiveness between national groups is hardly possible. The rarity of cases of genuine forgiveness between nations can be used by proponents of the realistic paradigm to substantiate their gloomy predictions regarding the role of morality in international relations. Still, even under the realistic assumptions there is room for forgiveness in balance of power cases, when the two enemies exploring ways to resolve their conflict are more or less even, and consequently don't feel humiliated by either asking for or granting forgiveness to each other.

Status of the Leaders

The act of asking forgiveness is usually made by the leader of the wrongdoers. A possible hindrance to the success of this plea may be the feeling either of the victimized group or of his own group that this leader is not an authentic representative of the group that was involved in the injustice. In the case of Israeli Prime Minister Barak's apology, it was claimed by many members of the Labor Party in whose name Barak spoke, as well as by the non-Western community to whom he apologized, that Barak had no right to speak in the name of the present and past Labor party (Artzi, 1997; Yehoshua, 1998: 179).

Authenticity of the Request

A related point may be the extent to which the quest for forgiveness is perceived as genuine. If it seems that the leader is motivated solely by political expediency and does not really regret the wrongdoing, the victim will reject what he considers an empty gesture. Obviously it is hard to tell if a plea for forgiveness is a sincere act of remorse or just a ruse for gaining political benefits. Sometimes circumstances can serve as a litmus test. When, for example, the apology takes place close to election day and the transgressor needs the votes of the people to whom he offers his apology, they have good reasons to doubt his sincerity.

Time

Time plays an ambivalent role in the forgiveness transaction. If forgiveness is sought immediately after the crime has been committed, "it may easily or reasonably be construed as self-serving, a hollow courtesy, or merely a sign of patronizing indifference" (Tavuchis, 1991: 88).

Time is also known to be the great healer. With the passage of time it may become easier for the children of the victimizers and victimized generations to ask for forgiveness and to forgive. However, time does not necessarily heal old wounds. Sometimes the opposite occurs. The first generation may be unable or unwilling to dwell on its past agonies, and it remains for the young generation to find out and consequently condemn even more harshly the full scale of atrocities committed against their parents. If and when they become ready to show generosity toward the wrongdoer and grant forgiveness in the names of their ancestors, they may be troubled with the moral question: Do we have the right to forgive?

International Environment

An international environment can support the forgiveness process either through offering rewards to or imposing sanctions on the "perpetrator." The greater the dependency on the international community of the country asked to repent for its wrongdoing, and the more unanimous the international community is in its demand for reconciliation and forgiveness, the greater the chances for the countries involved to get into a process of reconciliation. The pervasive international sanctions on South Africa were undoubtedly one of the catalysts for the reconciliation process there. However, the international environment, though potentially conducive to reconciliation, is less significant in shaping the process and leading to forgiveness than the other conditions mentioned above.

The list of conditions suggested in this chapter is by no means exhaustive. It represents a tentative frame of reference for analyzing concrete cases of *reconciliation via forgiveness*. In the next section I will examine the German-Israeli case in light of this analytical framework.

The Israel–West Germany Case

The Israel-Germany case represents a special and rare case of state A apologizing to state B for crimes committed by state's A former regime toward the people represented by state B, which had not existed at the time of the crimes.[1] Its uniqueness puts a challenge before anyone who tries to explain it within a wider framework. Moreover, the Holocaust, the root of the deep hostility between the German and the Jewish people, was of such satanic dimensions that one can reasonably argue that the case deserves a special discussion and that the lessons drawn from it are of limited applicability.

If one accepts the legitimacy of theorizing about German-Israeli relations after and following the Shoah (in fact this has been done before, for example: Auerbach 1980; Gardner-Feldman, 1984; 1999), one may still argue that the conflict-reconciliation framework is not suitable for dealing with the case. After all, what kind of conflict is there between Israel and Germany today or even during the last 53 years?

I suggest that although the conflict between these countries is not a typical case of an *intractable conflict needing reconciliation* as commonly defined by researchers (Bar-Tal, 1998; 2000b), it has some of the characteristics of such a conflict and thus is suitable for discussion within the conflict-reconciliation frame of reference.

First and most important, the Shoah represents an intrasocietal conflict, in which one side, the ruling majority, declared total war against an ethnic minority. When considering the degree of violence used for the goal of anni-hilating the Jews this case can be seen as a zero-sum and intractable conflict pushed to its utmost. True, unlike the typical case of intrasocietal conflict, where hostility and violence are reciprocal, in this case the hostility emanated from one side, Germany, while the otherside, the Jews, was the innocent victim that did not wish to and was totally incapable of striking back. However, the war declared by Germany against the Jews was not limited to Germany, but in fact took place all over the world, including the United States and Palestine where the Jews could and tried (to a very limited effect) to retaliate. Further-more, the conflict did not end with the termination of the war and the estab-lishment of two quasi-new entities: the State of Israel, on the one hand, and democratic West Germany, on the other. The State of Israel was conceived by the Jewish people, as well as by the international community, as the realization of the Jewish right to, and indeed need of, sovereign existence, so tragically proved by the Shoah. Israel has been built on the foundations of history, and the past, certainly the recent past, is part and parcel of its identity and ethos. For many Israelis the Shoah is not merely a remote memory, but a live expe-rience that underlies their attitudes toward many aspects of their daily life, such as planning a tour to Europe, purchasing valuables made in Germany, or listening to Wagner's music. By the same token, the evaluation of Germany's policy toward Israel and the Middle East has been greatly affected by the mem-ory of the Shoah. Germany is constantly under examination: Did it really re-pent? Does it try to please the Palestinians at Israel's expense in order to ease its conscience burdened with the Palestinian plight allegedly created by the Holocaust?

I assume that both Israel and Germany would like to free their relations from the heavy chains of the past. Both would like to reach genuine normali-zation and eventually harmony in their reciprocal contacts.

Thus, though not a typical case of an intractable conflict, the German-Israeli relationship represents an interesting case study of two communities who are wishing to heal past wounds, or, in other words, who are seeking reconciliation.

More substantially, the German-Israeli conflict has the characteristics of a case suitable for discussion within the framework of *forgiveness*. There is a distinct and agreed-upon victim: the Jewish people, and an indisputable per-petrator: the German people (or, according to a more extenuating approach, the German Nazi regime). The decisions that Germany and Israel took regarding their relations involved the mixture of morality and pragmatism, emotions and mind, shame and pride that so often accompanies the forgiveness process between antagonists. I therefore believe that along with awareness of its uniqueness the Germany-Israel case can be studied within a general framework of *reconciliation via forgiveness* and be used to test the propositions mentioned in the first section of the paper regarding this process.

I begin with a brief description of the Reparation Agreement between Israel and West Germany in 1952, which paved the way to slowly expanding relations between the two countries and which would not have materialized without a symbolic act of apology on the part of Germany toward Israel. I will not enter into a detailed description of the unfolding relations between the two countries. My aim is to shed some light on the role of forgiveness and apology in this relationship. I will then discuss the implications of this case for the possibility and necessity of forgiveness and apology in the process of reconciliation between enemies.

The Reparations Agreement: A Necessary Step toward Normalization

Israel and Germany were enemies according to a law approved by the Israeli parliament, the Knesset, in 1949. Israel boycotted Germany and avoided any contact with its representatives (Auerbach, 1980).[2]

By 1950 the economic situation in Israel deteriorated gravely. All measures taken to improve the situation seemed doomed to failure. Finance Ministry Director-General David Horowitz suggested an approach to Germany with a bid for reparations for the damage in life and property to the Jewish people. Prime Minister David Ben Gurion endorsed the idea for two reasons. First, the grant would be a significant contribution to the ailing economy of Israel. No less important, Ben Gurion perceived the contact with Germany as an opportunity for the young State of Israel, threatened by millions of hostile Arabs, to break out of its political isolation. Ben Gurion believed that Germany's need of the Jewish people's "seal of approval" in order to be admitted into the family of nations would dissipate within a short while, in direct correlation with its expected economic and political recovery. When this happened, so Ben Gurion estimated, Germany would be in no hurry to offer Israel the kind of economic and other rewards that it was willing to grant Israel in 1950.

In view of the deep hostility toward Germany, the Israeli government tried to approach Germany indirectly, through the occupying powers, but the three

Western countries—the USSR didn't even respond—refused to acquiesce in Israel's request. So Israel was left with a tough choice either to give up reparations altogether or to approach Germany directly, in contradiction to its moral and legal commitment to shun Germany.

The Israeli government, led by Ben Gurion, opted for the second alternative but realized that there would be need of a dramatic gesture on behalf of Germany in order to alleviate the anger of many in Israel and among the Jewish people all over the world.

In a secret meeting that took place in Paris, April 1951, between Israeli representatives and the German Chancellor, Konrad Adenauer, it was made clear to Adenauer that before any negotiation began, the German government would have to issue a public declaration including the following points:

> Admission of responsibility and expression of shock and regret concerning the crimes committed by the German people against the Jewish people during the period of Nazi rule
> Willingness to pay individual restitution as well as collective reparations for the damage in life and property,
> Agreement to the sum Israel specified, namely $1.5 billion (Auerbach, 1991: 279–280)

On September 27, 1951, Adenauer delivered his historic declaration before a fully packed Bundestag. The chancellor acknowledged that "in the name of the German people terrible crimes were committed which require the provision of moral and material recompense for the damages suffered by individual Jews and for Jewish property for which no claimants remain." He tempered his admission: "The decisive majority of the German people related with disgust to the crimes committed against the Jews and did not take part in them." Adenauer then ensured himself against exaggerated claims: "Thought should be given to the limits placed on Germany's ability to pay, because [Germany must face] the distressing necessity of taking care of the innumerable victims of war and providing for the refugees and the expelled persons" (Auerbach, 1991: 281).

Adenauer eschewed all expressions of genuine remorse and admission of responsibility demanded by Ben Gurion as *a sine qua non* for getting into contact with Germany. But the strategic course of starting a dialogue with Germany had already taken off, and the decision makers in Jerusalem did not wish to halt it. Jerusalem cited Adenauer's declaration as indicating that "the Federal German Government admits *without reservation* that crimes indescribable by man were committed in the name of the German people and this implies an obligation to provide moral and material reparations *to both, the individual and the aggregate"* (emphasis added by the author to indicate the significant difference between Adenauer's original statement and the Israeli version of it).

With this statement the government of Israel agreed to enter direct negotiations with Germany on reparations. Germany thus received the rehabilitation it so much needed without genuinely taking responsibility for the crimes against the Jewish people or asking forgiveness.

The Reparations Agreement was signed on September 10, 1952. Despite gloomy predictions in Israel, the accord was fully carried out with implementation completed in 1965.

In the years that followed the Reparations Agreement, Israel and West Germany built a wide and intricate network of relations of all kinds: economic, political, and military. These contacts culminated in the establishment of diplomatic relations between the two states in March 1965.

Normalization without Reconciliation

Today, relations between Germany and Israel can be termed normal. Some analysts go as far as calling them "special," implying that the two countries have given each other more than what each of them gives any other country (Gardner-Feldman, 1984). Others see the relations as a zig-zag path whose course between friendliness and mutual criticism has been to a large extent influenced by the personalities of the leaders of the two countries (Wolffsohn, 1993).

Still others, studying the role of the media in the relationship between Germany and Israel, argue that normalcy in relations has always been accompanied by mutual demonization in images and perceptions (Witztum, 1993). According to this thesis, the image of Germany in Israel is stereotypic, reflecting a deep-seated mistrust toward the former Nazi country. The study cites a poll by Dahaf in February 1991 that showed that 68 percent of the Israelis believed that the Germans have not changed since World War II. Young people (age 18–29) are even more suspicious toward Germany (Witztum, 1993; 122).

The image of Israel in Germany also suffers from stereotypic perceptions. Many Germans relieve their conscience vis-à-vis the Jews by blaming Israel for the "holocaust" of the Palestinians (Zimmerman, 1993).

There are different ways to tell the story of Israel-Germany relations. I would like to suggest that even though the relations are normal, maybe even "special," there is still no *full* reconciliation between Israel and Germany.

Some of the elements of reconciliation mentioned in the analytical section of this paper have been accomplished, among them:

(partial) acknowledgement by Germany of the acts that were perpetrated
Anticipation of mutual security and well-being
A belief in Germany as well as in Israel that injustice had been at least
    partly redressed

However, it would be going too far to suggest that the parties "accept [ed] with compassion those who committed injurious conduct, as well as acknowledging each other's sufferings" (Kriesberg, 1998c: 352). On the contrary, the polls cited above show that there are still a lot of bad feelings between Israel and Germany. The zig-zag pattern of mutual appreciation and mistrust that has been characterizing Israeli-German relations is still far from the ideal of reconciliation demanding that "members of the two groups come to see the humanity of one another . . . accept each other and . . . develop mutual trust" (Staub, 2000: 376). This has still not happened. The relations between the two sides still bear the stamp of the past and the reconciliation between the two peoples is partial and crippled.

One of the main reasons for this incomplete process is that Germany never expressed genuine remorse for the crimes of the Nazi era. The Jewish people, whether in Israel or in the Diaspora, had not been given a serious chance to contemplate the possibility of forgiving Germany for the crimes of the past. In what follows I will try to substantiate this thesis and examine, in light of the frame of reference suggested in the analytical part of the paper, the factors that influenced the process of forgiveness between Israel and Germany.

Factors Related to the Process of Forgiveness between Israel and Germany

Before examining the factors that influenced the forgiveness process between the two countries one has to see whether, in fact, there has been a genuine process of forgiveness. Of the six elements of forgiveness cited in the analytical discussion, one stood out as the *sine qua non* for forgiveness, that is, the recognition on both sides that a crime has been committed by one side against the other. In the German-Israeli case there is no doubt that a terrible crime was committed. The number of people who deny the occurrence of the Holocaust—as opposed to those who doubt the number of victims—is negligible. By the same token, there is no confusion regarding the identity of victim and victimizer. However, the German leaders tried throughout the postwar period to distance West Germany from the Third Reich. Adenauer set the tone in his declaration of September 1951 and was consistently followed by the successor decision makers. Apart from some notable political figures, mostly from the Social-Democratic Party, almost every German leader who was related to the Holocaust acknowledged the evil done but avoided taking full responsibility for it. (For a more detailed description and examples from German leaders' speeches see Shriver, 1998; Wolffsohn, 1993.)

Furthermore, it may be suggested that Israel helped Germany evade full repentance by showing premature magnanimity toward the country, which had not even started coping with its past. Ben Gurion, whose policy toward Germany was dictated almost solely by pragmatic considerations, wanted to justify it in moral terms. Toward this end he introduced the thesis of a "different Germany," implying that the Germany of 1950 was not the Germany that had massacred the Jewish people. In light of the prophets' rule that a man shall die for his own sins and not for the sins of his forefathers, Ben Gurion concluded that "The sins of the Nazis should not be visited on the German people." Along this line of advocacy, normalization with Germany was presented as the realization of the vision of the prophets, and boycotting Germany became racist (Auerbach, 1991: 288).

The "other Germany" thesis advocated by Ben Gurion may have blocked the process of soul-searching in Germany. People in Germany, and in that respect in Israel too, may have wondered: If today Germany is "other," namely a separate entity not connected to the Germany that had killed six million Jews, why should it atone for the crimes done by another entity?

To sum up, it is suggested that there was no genuine forgiveness between Germany and Israel, and that consequently the process of reconciliation between the two has been hindered. I will now examine the factors that affected the process of forgiveness between Israel and Germany in light of the factors suggested in the analytical section.

National Interests Promoted through Reconciliation and Forgiveness

Political expediency was perhaps not the only but undoubtedly was the most important input to Adenauer's decision to make the declaration that paved the way to reparations and to the subsequent unfolding of relations between Israel and West Germany. Adenauer was first and foremost a realist leader, completely aware of Germany's pariah status, who understood that Germany could pave its way back into the international community only through apologizing to the State of Israel and to world Jewry. The same spirit of real politik was what guided Ben Gurion when he initiated the process and showed a willingness to accept Adenuer's partial admission of responsibility as a genuine expression of remorse and atonement. Both were farsighted statesmen who disdained the politicians from left and right for trying to stop them in the name of what they considered false national pride (in Germany as well as in Israel) or economic calculations (particularly in Germany). Moral considerations played a significant role but were not strong enough to push Adenauer to issue a sincere apology. Ben Gurion, for his part, let political realism blind him to the deficiency of that quasi-apology.

Power Asymmetry

As noted in the analytical section of this chapter, the process of forgiveness between groups and within societies usually takes place in an asymmetrical power context. This factor usually hampers the process. The stronger side usually does not want to humble itself before the weaker side, particularly if it has reasons to believe that its request would be refused. This pattern appeared also in the case of Israel and Germany. Moreover, this was not the typical case, where the strong side apologizes to the weak side, thus exposing itself to humiliation. Here was conquered and humiliated Germany apologizing to the state of the survivors, which was weak materially but enjoyed internationally wide acceptance and sympathy. Furthermore, Germany had to apologize not only to the State of Israel but also to world Jewry, considered as very strong and influential. In view of the tremendous antagonism manifested toward Germany by Israel and by Jews all over the world, Adenuer could have feared that his apology would be met with a loud "no." In fact, Adenauer's readiness first to exchange drafts of his declaration with the government of Israel and his subsequent unwillingness to fully acknowledge Germany's responsibility for the Holocaust stemmed, apparently, from his concern that his own as well as his country's pride would be hurt. (For details and evidence regarding the exchange of drafts of the 1951 declaration between Israel and Germany see Auerbach, 1991: 281.)

Status of Leaders

The two leaders under discussion, Adenauer and Ben Gurion, were perceived both by their respective communities and by the other side as genuine leaders in full capacity to represent their nations. West Germany and Israel were young states, too much preoccupied with problems of survival to challenge the charismatic leaders who contributed so much to their revival. There were objections on both sides to the 1952 agreement, particularly in Israel, where the government's decision to get into direct contact with Germany for the sake of reparations was met with furious objection. In the late 1950s political crises erupted in Israel in the wake of revelations of military cooperation with West Germany. But it may well be that if other than these two leaders were in power in those early days after WWII, the way toward reparations and widening relations between Germany and Israel would have been much harder.

Authenticity of Request for Forgiveness

As shown above, Adenauer's declaration in 1951 was far from an unqualified apology. This is not to say that Adenauer did not harbor any genuine feelings of guilt or repentance. In his memoirs he acknowledged Germany's moral commitment toward the Jews. At the same time he would belittle Germany's guilt by emphasizing that "not all the Germans are responsible for the atrocity, many heard about it later. . . ." (Adenauer, 1966: 132). Reparations were presented not only as a moral but also as a political endeavor which aims at repairing the huge damage caused to Germany's reputation by the crime of the former regime (Adenauer, 1966: 137, 140, 142).

Adenauer's 1951 declaration reflects accurately this double concern for the conscience as well as the interests of a humiliated state trying to pave its way back to the international community with the Jewish people's approval as an entry license. This was not an authentic plea for atonement.

It can be surmised that if the international media would have been more developed in the early 1950s, enabling the people of Israel to watch Adenauer's 1951 speech on TV, the anger toward Germany would have increased to the point of forcing Israel's government to withdraw its request for reparations.

True, it was mainly due to Adenauer's steadfastness that Germany signed and subsequently carried out the reparation agreement to the letter, despite pressures to suspend the payments that came both from within Germany and from outside (for example, U.S. pressures following the Israeli-British-French Suez Operation in 1956). However, whenever there seemed to be a clash between Israel's wishes and needs, on the one hand, and German interests, on the other, Adenauer gave priority to his country's interests. For example, he did not hesitate to criticize Israel for abducting Eichmann from Argentina and putting him on trial in Jerusalem. He avoided exerting his influence to bring about the extension of the statute of limitation on National-Socialist crimes. He blatantly evaded unofficial Israeli requests for establishing diplomatic relations between the two states.

To sum up, Adenauer was first and foremost a proud German leader whose primary goal was to elevate his country's status in the postwar international system and free it from the burden of the past. Taking full responsibility for Nazi crimes did not fit into this frame of mind. Adenauer's strategy was adopted by his successors, with minor variations due to personal style and political circumstances. Without authentic apology there could not be real forgiveness.

Supportive International Environment

The international community played an ambivalent role in the process of reconciliation between Israel and West Germany. The West, particularly the United States, encouraged Adenauer to settle Germany's relations with the Jewish people. It was argued that the willingness of Adenauer to proceed with the reparations increased and diminished in direct correlation with the degree of pressure put on Germany by the Western powers (Gardner-Feldman, 1984: 60).

However, the West needed a strong Germany as a buttress against the USSR and therefore refrained from putting too much pressure on Germany. Another factor that blocked rapprochement between Germany and Israel was Germany's fear that the Arab countries would retaliate by recognizing East Germany. According to the Hallstein Doctrine, which served as West Germany's blueprint in the Middle East in the 1950s, such recognition would have necessitated the severance of relations with these oil- and population-rich countries.

As Germany recovered economically and politically and regained its self-confidence, it became less apprehensive of the world's—including the Arab world's—reactions. Correspondingly, Germany's need of Israel or world Jewry decreased and, with it, the incentive for plunging into a genuine and painful soul-searching regarding Germany's past behavior.

The Religious-Cultural Context

There was a cultural and religious gap between Germany and Israel but it did not seem to play a major role in the contacts leading to and directly following reparations. I would like to stress again that this evaluation is confined to the macrolevel. At the microlevel, namely, the relations between Jewish and German individuals, things are different, and the religious aspect has been playing a crucial and painful role in the process of forgiveness, as evidenced so remarkably by Wiesenthal (Wiesenthal, 1998). Coming back to the macrolevel, Germany is by and large a religious country and was led at the time of the reparations by Konrad Adenauer, a devout Catholic. On the one hand, from the Christian and even more so the Catholic perspective, forgiveness is a necessary and possible step toward redemption. On the other hand, Judaism is very skeptical about the right of a person who was not directly subjected to wrongdoing to grant forgiveness on behalf of the victim. It may be that religion played some role in Adenauer's declaration. But, as indicated before, Adenauer and Ben Gurion were motivated almost solely by pragmatic considerations, and the religious significance of the dialogue between the two nations was put aside.

Time

Time played a paradoxical role in the case under discussion. When forgiveness was dearly needed (1940s and 1950s) it was not possible; when forgiveness became possible (1970s and after) it was, apparently, not needed any more. At the time of the negotiations for reparations, the wounds of the Shoah were still raw and the emotions on both sides were too strong and conflicting to allow for a genuine process of forgiveness. The victims, or for that matter the survivors, could not be expected to "let go" of their hatred. The perpetrators were still overwhelmed by their deeds and by the perceived detrimental impact of taking full responsibility for these deeds on their political and economical situation. But the need on both sides to get into contact was great and, consequently, Adenauer delivered a quasi-apology. Once the State of Israel accepted this "apology" as genuine and sufficient, the way toward normalization was cleared. With the passage of time, when a new generation took the place of the generation of victims and perpetrators, there could have been room for a genuine process of forgiveness on both sides. But apparently there was no need for such a process, because on the surface the relationships between Germany and Israel were already normal.

In an attempt to shed some light on the paradoxical effect of time on Israeli-German relations, Wolffsohn speaks about "dis-synchronism" between Germans and Jews: "[whereas] Israeli Jews and others view the Germans from the perspective of the German past . . . the Germans view themselves from the perspective of the present and the future" (Wolffsohn, 1993: 66). While Israeli youth goes every year by its thousands to Poland to identify with the victims of the Holocaust, and rituals commemorating the Shoah have become more personal and meaningful throughout the years, the Germans are gradually detaching themselves from Nazi Germany. In a poll conducted in 2001 in Germany, 60 percent of the participants said they do not feel responsible for Nazi crimes; 61 percent concurred with the sentence: "It's time to stop dealing with past wounds," and 45 percent—a meaningful minority—was ready to go even further and said they are fed up with the Third Reich and do not want to hear about it any longer (Der Spiegel, 2001: pp. 58–61).

These conflicting perspectives regarding the history and identity of both Germans and Israelis present a serious stumbling block on the way of reconciliation between the two peoples.

Implications and Conclusions

The German-Israeli case was presented in this chapter as a rare but not irrelevant case of *reconciliation via forgiveness* in a conflict that started as an intragroup and continued as an intergroup conflict. The fact that a formal act of apology was requested as a prerequisite for starting normalization between Germany and Israel proves its relevancy.

What can one learn from this case about the possibility and necessity of *forgiveness* as a route to *reconciliation*?

Seven conditions, presented in the analytical section as necessary for the success of this process, were examined. Three were found to be conducive to forgiveness in our case: national interests promoted through forgiveness, an international supportive environment, and strong leaders. Four inhibited the process: short time between the crime committed and the request of forgiveness, lack of authenticity of the request for forgiveness (itself a result of other factors), power asymmetry, and religious gap. The two lists are not equivalent and it seems that the factors that operated against forgiveness were stronger than those in favor of it. The result was that the act of forgiveness was carried out halfheartedly.

How did this semi-forgiveness influence the relations between Germany and Israel? It is my view that it paved the way to normalization but hampered full reconciliation. There are commentators who blame Israeli politicians for the lack of full reconciliation between Germany and Israel, arguing that the Israelis have used the Holocaust as an effective instrument against Germany (Wolffsohn, 1993: 210).

In my view this line of advocacy underestimates Germany's responsibility for the incomplete process of reconciliation between the two states. On a more general and theoretical level Wolffsohn's stipulation underestimates the potential of forgiveness to heal past wounds and bring about full reconciliation between former enemies.

Some would say that reconciliation in the full sense of the word is not needed in relations between societies that do not share the same land, particularly if the chances of eruption of violence between the two countries are remote as is the case in Israel-Germany relations. This may be true. But if we wish to go beyond formal peace between former enemies toward healing and harmony, reconciliation should be a goal worthy of our intellectual as well as practical endeavors.

In this respect the Israeli-German case is a particularly disenchanting example for all those who are harboring hopes for *reconciliation via forgiveness* between other enemies such as the Israelis and Palestinians, who are in great need of but for the time being so far away from reaching that goal.

ACKNOWLEDGMENTS   I would like to thank Liat Green- Zemach for her valuable assistance in the preparation of the bibliography, which served as important groundwork in the writing of this paper. In addition, I would like to thank three readers, Prof. Michael Brecher, Prof. Herb Kelman, and Prof. Shmuel Sandler, for their helpful comments on earlier versions of this chapter.

NOTES

1. In this section I will refer only to West Germany. The case of East Germany's relations with Israel deserves separate discussion.

2. The historical documents that served as evidence for this section can be found in Auerbach (1980, 1991).

8

Apology and Reconciliation in International Relations

Raymond Cohen

Apology has been succinctly defined as "a speech act that seeks forgiveness" (Tavuchis, 1991 :27). Directed at assuaging grievance, it is a remedy for conflict and an instrument of reconciliation. Assuming a variety of shapes and forms around the world, its scope ranges from trivial personal quarrels all the way up to complex international conflicts. It is an appealing concept because of its association with reconciliation and healing, and because it seems such a humane and efficient device for curtailing violence and conflict. At the international level, apology is one arrow in the quiver of diplomacy. Unfortunately, it is invariably granted grudgingly, received ungraciously, and as often avoided as used. Its utility on the ground is inconclusive and results inconsistent. Apology clearly arouses ambivalent attitudes on the part of both giver and receiver.

This chapter addresses in a preliminary and necessarily incomplete way the phenomenon of apology in international affairs. My intention here is to suggest a useful framework for analysis and some initial distinctions. A comparative, cross-cultural perspective is adopted, grounded in the dispute-processing philosophy of the law and society movement. This approach, which declines to privilege either the language or the methods of the West, is felt to be appropriate for a feature of human behavior found in many societies reflecting different beliefs and customs. Such an approach should help avoid some of the more obvious linguistic and cultural preconceptions underpinning the concept, especially in the English-speaking world.

Apology raises intriguing philosophical, social, and political issues. Not the least of these is establishing just what constitutes an apology, when it is appropriate, and why it works. Is there a generally valid paradigm of apology or at least essential shared features of the notion available for international conciliation? Are apology and its supposed correlate, forgiveness, either a necessary or a sufficient condition for resolving conflict? Of inherent fascination, this remarkable concept stimulates reflection on the quality of relationships and the very nature of conflict. If symbolic action can alleviate or remove the sources of contention, what does this tell us about conflict?

All of us are aware, from personal experience, that apology has the potential to appease the aggrieved, amend damaged relationships, and help curtail destructive spirals of conflict. Yet the apparent simplicity and efficient elegance of the device are matched by paralyzing inhibitions in the path both of its articulation and acceptance. Again, most of us have endured or witnessed, at one time or another, the excruciating dilemmas of self-accounting involved in this deceptively straightforward expedient.

A case has also been made for abandoning the entire discourse of confession and contrition altogether. Andrew Rigby, of the Centre for the Study of Forgiveness and Reconciliation at Coventry University, wonders whether apology is not more trouble than it is worth. He is "not convinced of the appropriateness of opening up the past and talking about it as a means of dealing with the hurt." He thinks "that you can have too much memory" and advocates amnesia and forgiveness. Amnesty for human rights violators can contribute to political stability whereas a spirit of revenge would tear society apart, and forgiveness should be the free gift of the victim: "Perpetrators have no right to expect forgiveness from those they have abused in some way or another" (Rigby, 2000).

A Dispute-Processing Approach

Rigby makes important points, and formal prosecution for crimes against human rights may indeed be feared as a counterproductive exercise in the transition to democracy; hence the preference for truth and reconciliation commissions. Similarly, countries that collaborated with or were involved with the Nazis in World War II expediently chose to avoid social strife by suppressing memories of their role and by selectively interpreting history. However, in conflicts between societies painful memories and grievances cannot simply be dismissed or suppressed, nor the same appeal to expediency made. For one thing, grievance can be an insidious source of disruptive behavior in international relations. If grievance has real effects, ignoring it will not make the problem go away. For another, contested claims about the past and competing versions of justice are the very stuff of international conflict. Talking of grievance immediately draws attention to psychic and affective aspects of conflict that are every bit as relevant as material factors.

To understand conflict and conflict resolution more fully thus requires an approach that can accommodate and not skirt conciliatory mechanisms as well as remedies for grievance, such as apology, regrets, reparation, damages, and commemoration. Grievance must be viewed as an organic part of conflict and disputing as an integral, indeed natural feature of relationships. Seen in this light, apology (with its corollaries the demand for apology and the response to apology) is simply an important feature of disputing behavior and not to be ignored.

An enlightening perspective on disputing behavior that meets these requirements is found in the work of the "law and society" school of researchers. A number of shared assumptions, ideas, observations, and methods distinguish this school of thought (see Mather, 1990). Originally conceived with domestic conflict in mind, most of the following points are equally relevant to international conflict:

- The key concept is *dispute*. This is a choice of researchers and not a self-evident feature of the material world. A dispute is deemed to be the stage in a relationship at which a quarrel becomes public. Indeed, disputes can only be understood as integral features of ongoing relationships, not as self-standing, isolated events.
- Analytical attention is focused on the *disputing process* and *disputing behavior*, namely, the interaction of disputants and other interested parties over a possibly extended period of time during which the dispute emerges, is transformed and reinterpreted, and handled by remedial mechanisms. This requires a *longitudinal*, that is, historical approach to the study of disputes.
- Researchers insist that disputes must be viewed and understood within the social and political structures in which they are played out. Disputes are in fact an excellent way to approach the study of a community.
- Disputes are cultural constructs, not concrete entities. The relationships within which grievances emerge, the concerned audiences, the things people quarrel over, the way disputes are handled, the course of

the dispute, and so on acquire their meaning within cultural contexts and in relation to the values and beliefs of members of the society.

- There is some skepticism about the possibility of settling, let alone resolving, disputes in any definitive sense; hence the preference for the neutral term *processing*. Disputes tend to drag on, sometimes going underground for an extended period only to reemerge much later.
- Litigation in particular rarely settles a dispute. Contention is not pathological but an inevitable dimension of social life.
- Third parties, including the various moderators, interested parties, and audiences, are viewed not as neutral observers but as agents that crucially affect the definition of a dispute and the behavior of the disputants. They do so by encouraging, discouraging, supporting, opposing, validating, and disconfirming disputants' claims.
- There is characteristic interest in the ways in which disputes are handled in communities throughout the world, Western and non-Western, industrial and preindustrial alike. The United States is not considered to be paradigmatic and, indeed, disputing behavior in a New England town, a Midwestern ranching community, a Los Angeles courtroom, or a culturally diverse inner city is observed to be as distinctive as that of any Third World village.
- Finally, the "anthropology of law" approach makes careful use of field research and observational methods, while shunning judgmental or ethnocentric attitudes together with the tendency to prescribe or proselytize.

Apology in the Disputing Process

Looking at a dispute as a process enables apology to be located within a dynamic framework, best viewed not as a hard and fast set of stages but as an overlapping series of unfolding perceptions and subjective experiences (Miller and Sarat, 1980–81). A dispute is not a given but starts out as a grievance. One source of grievance is a perception of injury or wrongdoing blamed on someone else. Felstiner and his colleagues call this a "perceived injurious experience." This is transformed into a grievance when it is "attributed to the fault of another individual or social entity." For there to be grievance "the injured person must feel wronged and believe that something might be done in response to the injury" (Felstiner, Abel, and Sarat, 1980–81). Another source of grievance is the belief of an individual, group, or organization that it is entitled to a resource being withheld by someone else. The next stage occurs with the demand for remedy directed at the agency believed responsible for the injury or deprivation. The final stage in the emergence of a dispute occurs when the claim is rejected in whole or in part. Once a dispute has emerged it follows another transformational trajectory through various remedial (or aggravating) stages of the disputing process (Mather and Yngvesson, 1980–81).

During the course of a dispute, there are three stages at which apology might be appropriate. First, there is the earliest stage, when a grievance is first brought to the attention of the supposed offending party. At this point a voluntary and unsolicited apology may dispose of the grudge before third parties become involved and claims escalate. Second, there is an intermediate stage after the aggrieved party has gone public and put certain claims for redress on the table. Among those claims may be the demand for an apology. Apology is now no longer simply a matter for the disputants alone. Because of the presence of an audience it is bound to be more difficult, raising issues of face. Moreover, the demand for an apology may itself be perceived as an aggressive act. Finally, apology could again become relevant at a later stage as one among various remedies mandated by a court or arbitrator.

At all three stages of the disputing process, apology aims to curtail or alleviate the emotional distress of the plaintiff. It provides psychic satisfaction for nonmaterial injury. Consisting of a verbal formula or a ceremonial act, it is as though apology symbolically wipes the slate clean of the original "sin," restoring the relationship to the situation existing before the injury. Apology cannot solve material grievances—deprivation, discrimination, oppression— but it can address the hard feelings that are present in most disputes. Where the source of grievance is a blow to honor or pride, sense of neglect, deep embarrassment, lingering resentment at a historical wrong, painful memory, or grudge at a real or imagined humiliation, then the remedy has to be psychic in whole or in part: "While there are some injuries that cannot be repaired just by saying you are sorry, there are others that can only be repaired by an apology" (Tavuchis, 1991:487).

Apology across Cultures

The dispute-processing approach alerts us to the fact that disputes are cultural constructs and the mechanisms used to handle them acquire their meaning and use within cultural contexts. There is no single, universally valid paradigm of apology. In English "apology" is a performative utterance, usually the simple articulation of such words as "I apologize" or "I'm sorry." As we shall see, in other cultures the nonverbal, ceremonial dimension of apologizing may be equally or more important. The right body language, decorum, and dress may be as significant as the correct form of words.

From a comparative perspective, apology and its functional equivalents differ in exact meaning, choreography, and purpose across cultures. Among the distinct functions that can be observed are the following:

- In the Japanese *harmony* model, apology is an instrument of social integration and is connected with the high priority assigned to harmonious social relations.
- In the Chinese *hierarchy* model, apology involves rigorous self-criticism and public confession of dereliction. It proclaims the delinquent's subjugation to authority, conceived as the guardian and personification of moral order.
- In the Arab *sulha* model, apology is an integral part of the ceremonial reconciliation of contending, rival clans, and is intended to curtail the destructive blood feud.
- In the Anglo-Saxon *individualist* model, apology has contrapuntal meanings, evoking at one level associations of religious and communal "reconciliation," while at another level conceived in formalistic terms as an acknowledgment of guilt and legal liability.

The classic account of Japanese dispute resolution depicts it as intended to maintain harmonious social relationships within groups. Deference to the transcendent worth of harmony and reconciliation lends apology and forgiveness a key role (Kawashima, 1969). Wagatsuma and Rosett note that "a basic assumption in Japanese society seems to be that apology is an integral part of every resolution of conflict." A "meaningful apology" contains several elements: acknowledgment that a wrongful, injurious act occurred and will not happen again; and that the respondent was at fault, will compensate the injured party, and "intends to work for good relations in the future" (1986: 469–470). Significance is attached to the script and choreography of the apology, and the requirements of protocol must be meticulously observed (1986: 462). When an apology is forthcoming, a dispute is less likely to be brought to court. Conversely, a failure to apologize and offer token compensation increases the chances of a lawsuit (Haley, 1986). A detailed study of automobile accidents confirms the role of "sincere apology" (sincerity mandating compensation and a display of concern and contrition) in managing and disposing of disputes (Tanase, 1990). A noteworthy aspect of Japanese apology, very different from the Anglo-Saxon legal model, is the discontinuity of responsibility and remorse: "Apology means less an admission of guilt than an expression of a continuing commitment to live by the given social order" (1990: fn. 37). Compensation is not computed on the basis of negligence, notoriously hard to establish, but on that of damage to the injured party. Emphasis is placed on the general good rather than on justice.

Like Japan, China assigns considerable weight to the ceremonial dimension of apology. Anecdotal evidence suggests that apologies "are complicated matters in Chinese culture, weighty acts that are rarely offered or accepted, which must be delivered just so, with the proper gravity." Unlike Japan, China does not use apology as a normal, everyday instrument of conciliation. "To Chinese apologies require a great loss of face, and face is not something spent down lightly." Chinese people express surprise at the ease with which Westerners say "sorry"; to them, apology can never be an offhand, casual sort of statement, mere lip service (*New York Times*, April 7, 2001). As a formal, public enactment, apology requires two painful elements: a contrite confession of wrongdoing and a display of humility that may shade into humiliation.

The confession enacts self-examination, admission of transgression, repentance, and the promise of reform. Private self-indictment has a long literary history, though a public acknowledgment of sin is more recent. The liturgy and ritual of a "Confucian confessional" has been traced back to the early sixteenth century and associated with monastic discipline and moral training (Wu, 1979).

Besides the confession, the public apology also requires accompanying rites of contrition and supplication. The repentant sinner finds himself at the center of attention, acknowledging his dereliction by hanging his head in shame. The importance of deferential behavior, involving the acknowledgment of inferior rank, emphasizes the vulnerability of the penitent, who seeks to avoid retribution by placing the recipient of the apology in the role of benevolent superior (Hickson, 1986). Apologies by public officials reported in the Chinese media strikingly exemplify the theatrical dimension of confession in the Chinese system and the continuing relevance of the Confucian notion that the legitimate ruler is not just the prop of cosmic order but also a paragon of moral virtue (Foreign Broadcast Information Service, 1995; *New York Times*, April 7, 2001).

In the Arab world apology entails acknowledgment of error and elicits shame and embarrassment. Inhibitions on its performance resemble those noted in Chinese culture. At the level of the individual, admitting to being wrong and eating humble pie can never be easy. However, apology and forgiveness are Muslim virtues, and to beg pardon for injury may be the right and proper course of action. Thus to apologize can be translated by *tatyeeb el-khater*, to clear one's conscience, emphasizing the moral dimension of the act. To settle a personal grievance, to clear the air, it may be enough to make a propitiatory statement. But it may be more appropriate to restore good relations by paying a visit to the aggrieved party in his or her home, a symbolic display of respect in Arab society, thereby graphically enacting supplication and contrition.

At the collective level, apology is part and parcel of the public custom of *musalaha*, reconciliation, by which a communal dispute between clans within the village is ritually terminated. It is not a separate or sufficient remedy in its own right but acquires significance within the wider context of a restoration and rehabilitation of social relationships. The reconciling families line up facing each other, then shake hands, exchange greetings, and utter words of apology and forgiveness. One family may then visit the other family's home and drink bitter coffee. Finally, the parties break bread together and partake of a common meal. Apology and reconciliation play an essential role in a society where a dispute between clans can trigger an escalating tit-for-tat feud, seriously disrupting the life of the community (Irani, 1999).

Apology in English-speaking culture is embedded in a Christian ethic of reconciliation. Apology solicits forgiveness and thereby creates the conditions for reconciliation, meaning both an end to conflict and an end to estrangement. Pankhurst rightly observes that reconciliation as a paramount goal of conflict resolution entails "forgiveness of former enemies—often with explicit reference to Christian values" (1998: 5). In the parable of the Prodigal Son (Luke 15:11–32), the father forgives his returning son even before the prodigal can get his prepared apology out of his mouth. Forgiveness, the gift of an all-merciful Father-God, becomes a cardinal virtue: "If thy brother trespass against thee, rebuke him; and if he repent, forgive him. And if he trespass against thee seven times in a day, and seven times in a day turn again to thee, saying, I repent; thou shalt forgive him" (Luke 17:3–4).

In English-speaking societies today there is often inconsistency of ideals and practice and the apology-forgiveness-reconciliation paradigm plays a secondary role in dispute settlement compared to Japan. At the everyday level, however, apology is a significant element in an ethic of civility intended to prevent friction, thereby nipping potential minor sources of grievance in the bud. Involuntary contact and unintended discourtesy call forth apology. People from adjacency cultures, where close contact and noise are accepted, are perplexed to observe inconsequential intrusions such as bumping into people or calling the wrong phone number elicit exaggerated expressions of regret and sorrow. Since people who are bumped into also say "sorry" this shows that the word is a marker indicating that contact was accidental, important in a culture that maintains harmony by respecting privacy and personal space. "Sorry" is also used in minor but tricky social situations to disarm interlocutors. On the same principle, apologies that do not entail admission of liability are extravagantly dispensed by public service bodies. "Thames Water apologises for any inconvenience caused while roadworks are under way" or "Virgin Trains apologises for delays because of leaves on the line" are transparent public relations devices intended to divert customer annoyance.

Where apologies are called for to disarm genuine grievance they tend to be given neither spontaneously, willingly, nor wholeheartedly (Tannen, 1996). Ironically, sincere apology is often precisely the remedy that people who have suffered at someone else's hands and through no fault of their own really want. It is only apology, with or without compensation, that gives victims of an offense the comfort of public recognition of what they have been through alongside public censure of the offender.

In the original Greek an *apologia* was a speech in defense, and English speakers continue to see no contradiction between apology and a parade of self-righteous excuses effectively minimizing personal responsibility for wrongful action. In everyday life apology certainly goes along with explanation and justification. The legal consequences of apology are also often feared because in Common Law an apology is admissible as evidence (Shuman, 2000). Insurance companies warn against apologizing after an accident lest this imply an admission of liability. This is ironic given the casual way that apologies are dispensed for minor intrusions into personal space. If accidentally touching someone requires apology, should not accidentally smashing into their car? Some legal authorities dispute the claim that an apology necessarily implies liability and hence possible damages. An expression of sorrow at someone's suffering does not imply guilt unless criminal negligence or responsibility is specifically admitted. Judges and juries have consistently found that apology does not *ipso facto* entail liability where there is no evidence of this (Rehm and Beatty, 1996).

Emphasis on apology as a device for dispute avoidance rather than a mechanism of dispute settlement may reflect the fact that Western societies have largely replaced an ethic of community with an ethic of personal autonomy. Disputes rarely arise over questions of honor, a characteristic feature of group-oriented cultures, such as those of the Middle East and the English-speaking world until the beginning of the nineteenth century. Demonstrably, pardon is now only begged as an archaism and duels are no longer fought. Societies of mobile individuals, enjoying civil rights under law, have less resort to extralegal forms of compensation to restore a good name. Conversely, redress for grievance is interpreted in legal terms of rights and obligations. Reparation for libel and slander has to be pursued through the courts and is notoriously hard to obtain. Apology can be issued impersonally through one's lawyer.

Three Concepts of Diplomatic Apology

Three types of diplomatic apology of diminishing intensity and consequence can be distinguished:

1. An expression of contrition and wish to make amends for a profound historical injustice. This kind of apology, reflecting confession of guilt and a desire for reconciliation in the ethical sense, most closely resembles apology at a personal level. It is as rare as it is momentous. Onerous cross-cultural issues arise.

2. A formal apology or expression of regret for a breach of international law, meant to restore relations to a normal footing. This type of apology is a very common diplomatic instrument and entails acknowledgment of legal liability and usually payment of damages. It helps clear up an awkward interruption in an ongoing relationship. Legal forms and conventions help overcome cultural differences.

3. A diplomatic "nonapology" does not acknowledge legal liability and is a classic compromise form of words suggesting regret but not contrition. It is intended to extract the parties from a situation in which the accused vigorously rebuts the accuser's accusation of responsibility. Both sides can claim that honor is satisfied and normal relations can resume. Cross-cultural misunderstanding is common.

Apology as Moral Restitution

According to Tavuchis, collectivities "are incapable, on the whole, of acknowledging regret and expressing remorse" (1991: 43). For how can a notional entity, a government or a state, apologize or forgive? Notwithstanding this philosophical problem, the representatives of collectivities do in fact sometimes act as though the expression of regret and remorse for historical wrongs is an intelligible act. The United States and Canada have officially apologized for interning citizens of Japanese ancestry in World War II. Australia, Canada, New Zealand, and the United States have also offered forms of apology and material compensation to indigenous peoples, victims of historical injustice and discrimination. Agents acting on behalf of the descendants of supposed offenders have apologized to those deemed to be the descendants of victims. Apology in these cases is a symbolic act intended to promote domestic reconciliation between groups within one nation in the Christian tradition.

Apology for historical injustice at the international level is rare and invariably contentious. Considerations of public opinion and national honor make it extraordinarily difficult for governments to admit guilt for past crimes. Apology in such highly sensitive matters is resisted as placing the nation in a humiliating posture of supplication or subordination, whatever the rights or wrongs of the case. Leaders are deeply reluctant to acknowledge national error and thereby undermine patriotic myths of national virtue and infallibility. There is great unease at the policy implications of acknowledging historical injustice, since apology may imply recognition of contested rights. Apologies for past atrocities also risk opening up cans of worms. If you begin investigating sordid episodes from a nation's past, it is argued, where will it all end? The government of the Republic of Turkey refuses to acknowledge that massacres of Armenians carried out by the Ottoman authorities in 1915 ever took place. President Chirac has rejected calls for a formal apology over France's use of torture during the Algerian war of independence, despite French generals having admitted orally and in writing that it was widely practiced (BBC, 2000). Iraq steadfastly refuses to apologize for its 1990 invasion of Kuwait though such an apology would pave the way for the restoration of Iraqi legitimacy within the Arab League and put an end to its isolation. The problem is not one of money, since Iraq's international ostracism costs it billions of dollars a year anyway. Were Saddam Hussein to apologize and agree to pay appropriate compensation, the effect would be solely to his and his country's benefit and enemies' consternation.

Analysis of cases where deep historical antagonism has been overcome suggests that apology is not a necessary condition for the normalization of relations between states. A fabric of relationships may emerge over an extended period, interspersed by symbolic and other gestures, such as financial reparation. Whether full "reconciliation" in the Christian sense is ever attainable is a philosophical question. In 1951, West German Chancellor Konrad Adenauer agreed to enter negotiations for the payment of reparations to Jewish survivors of the Nazi death camps. In his historic declaration to the Bundestag he acknowledged that "in the name of the German people terrible crimes were committed" but did not apologize, arguing that the majority of Germans were not complicit (Auerbach, this volume). Following many years of close German-Israeli cooperation, Chancellor Willy Brandt enacted symbolic contrition, though avoiding an explicit statement of apology. At the Warsaw Ghetto Memorial in 1970 he fell on his knees. In 1972, on a visit to Yad Vashem, the Jerusalem Holocaust Museum, he read Psalm 103, verses 8–16, referring to God's mercy and expiation of sin, and hinting at historical reconciliation (Brandt, 1978). Brandt admitted that these acts of contrition were as much addressed to Germans as to Jews (Fallaci, 1976: 219). Certainly there was no explicit request for forgiveness, and had there been it is doubtful that Jewish representatives could ever have extended it.

Japan has long found it painfully difficult to apologize clearly and unambiguously for war crimes. The main reason is that the Japanese historical version of the events of the 1930s and 1940s is genuinely different from that of its former enemies. It sees its policies in Asia as well intentioned and itself as a victim of Western aggression, not an aggressor. Apologies were absent from the 1965 treaty of normalization with Korea. After 14 years of tortured negotiations the most that Japan would concede was that it was "truly regretful" and "deeply reflecting" on the "unfortunate period." *Hansei*, the word used for remorse or reflection, does not imply moral guilt. Under prolonged international pressure, Japan has inched forward over the years in adopting a somewhat more explicit vocabulary of recognition and responsibility. By 1990 the word *owabi*, a way of expressing regret and self-reproach, was being used in contacts with South Korea (Field, 1995). A step forward, the term was still felt by Japan's neighbors to be too polite and elegant to match the war crimes actually committed. The truly tough word *shazai*, meaning "deep apology" and containing the Chinese character *zai*, meaning "crime," is avoided like the plague. Moreover, an apology in one forum tends to be retracted or qualified in another. In 1995, Japanese Prime Minister Tomiichi Murayama offered *owabi* in a statement read to the world's press for wartime atrocities. But he then made a speech before Japanese veterans omitting all references to aggression and colonial rule and reverting to the exculpatory word *hansei* (*Daily Telegraph*, August 16, 1995). His *owabi* statement was later clarified as a personal apology and repudiated by other members of the Japanese cabinet. In 1998, Prime Minister Ryutaro Hashimoto offered *owabi* to the people who suffered in the Second World War. A Japanese spokesman then said this merely repeated Murayama's previous personal apology. To the bitter resentment of British war veterans, compensation was not offered, the Japanese government declining to supplement the token damages agreed on by Japan in the 1951 peace treaty. On the eve of his visit to London in May 1998, the Japanese Emperor offered only "sympathy" (BBC, 1998). Nevertheless, though ex-servicemen were dissatisfied, the fact of the visit demonstrated that at both the working and ceremonial levels Japanese-British diplomatic relations were excellent. Here again, normalization of the relationship over a long period had preceded apology.

Apology for Acknowledged Injury

A second type of apology or regret acknowledges responsibility for a particular illegal act committed within the context of an ongoing international relationship. Indemnity is often but not always paid. In these cases apology is a calculated diplomatic and legal instrument of remedy intended to clear up hard feelings and provide satisfaction for nonmaterial damage to the national honor. The terms of the apology are likely to be negotiated at the professional level with due regard to relevant precedents, and the various admissions and regrets carefully calibrated. Apology here is useful for removing misunderstanding in an expeditious way and restoring harmonious relations. There is no doubt that diplomatic apologies are formal instruments of statecraft conforming to international practice. Nevertheless, understanding of the meaning of apology is influenced by local paradigms of dispute processing and not just generic international legal practice.

Cases of apology for a breach of international law go far back into diplomatic history. A typical case occurred in 1924. Robert W. Imbrie, the acting U.S. consul general in Teheran, was brutally killed by a mob while the police and army stood by. The murder occurred against the background of a struggle between the Shi'ite religious establishment and the government of the secular republic. U.S. investment in oil exploration and railway projects in Persia were placed in jeopardy. From a legal point of view the facts of the case were reasonably clear: a representative of a friendly power entitled under international law to enjoy the protection of the host government had been murdered, and a remedy was in order. The U.S. government insisted on "full reparation" and this claim was not contested. To redress the situation the Persian government expressed its "deepest regrets" for the incident, agreed to pay $110,000 for the return of the body to the United States, and paid indemnity of $60,000 (Whiteman, 1937). This effectively disposed of the incident.

What happens when an apology is not forthcoming in good time is exemplified by the case of the *Rainbow Warrior*, a Greenpeace ship sunk by French agents in Auckland harbor, New Zealand, in July 1985, with the death of one of the crew. The vessel was on a voyage protesting against French nuclear testing in the Pacific, something that had long been deeply resented by the New Zealand government and public. The agents were caught, tried, and sentenced to ten years imprisonment by a New Zealand court. Under the threat of French sanctions against New Zealand products, New Zealand agreed to an arrangement negotiated through the good offices of the United Nations to release the agents into French custody in return for $7 million in compensation and a guarantee that they would be confined to a French Pacific base for three years. The French government then violated the agreement by repatriating its agents to Metropolitan France after only a year. New Zealand protested to the United Nations, which set up an arbitration panel. In May 1990, the panel reported that "substantial violations" of the 1986 accord had occurred and suggested that France contribute $2 million to a joint fund to foster "closer relations between citizens of the two countries" ("Rainbow Warrior," 1990). The affair was finally settled in April 1991 when the French prime minister visited New Zealand, agreed to set up the "friendship fund," and at last, six years after the events, apologized for the sinking of the *Rainbow Warrior*, accepting blame and recognizing past wrongdoing (*Le Monde*, April 30, 1991).

Comparison of successful and unsuccessful apologies makes clear the importance of a preexisting relationship and cross-cultural literacy. In the *Greeneville* affair with Japan, the United States apologized adroitly to a friendly power in conformity with local protocol. In the case of the Chinese embassy bombing, a culturally ungrammatical apology failed to convince an anyway skeptical rival.

On February 9, 2001, the U.S. nuclear submarine *Greeneville* collided with a Japanese fishing trawler off Hawaii with the loss of nine lives. Almost immediately, apologies were forthcoming from U.S. dignitaries including the president, two cabinet members, top military officers, and the U.S. ambassador to Japan. Nevertheless, Japanese opinion remained upset because Japanese custom called for a personal, public apology by the responsible officer. A letter of "sincere regret" released on February 25 by the commander of the submarine, Scott D. Waddle, through his lawyer was rejected as belated, impersonal, and insincere (*Washington Post*, February 27, 2001). Admiral William J. Fallon, vice-chief of U.S. naval operations, was then dispatched to Japan as a special envoy of the president. At a personal meeting with the families of the victims, Fallon bowed deferentially, displayed contrition, and clasped the hands of survivors. At the same time, Commander Waddle (who could not yet visit Japan because of the naval investigation) sent unconditional personal letters of apology to the bereaved families against the advice of his lawyer. Family members were quoted as saying that "they were touched by Adm. Fallon's sincerity and accepted the apology offered by Waddle" (*Washington Post*, March 2, 2001).

The successful disposal of the *Greeneville* affair contrasts with the diplomatic mishandling of the bombing of the Chinese embassy in Belgrade by a U.S. B-2 bomber on the night of May 7, 1999, during the Kosovo campaign. Four Chinese citizens were killed and 20 injured. Chinese reaction to the embassy bombing was to call for an "open and official" apology, a thorough investigation with publication of findings, and the punishment of those responsible. Two days after the incident, on May 9, President Clinton reportedly offered his deep regret at the attack in a private letter to the Chinese president.

The following day Clinton said, "I apologize, I regret this," in public remarks made at the opening of a conference in Washington. On May 14, according to the White House spokesman, he telephoned Beijing and "expressed his sincere regrets and condolences to President Jiang and the Chinese people concerning the tragic accident of last week. The President expressed his desire that we move beyond this tragic accident in our relationship" (New York Times, May 15, 1999).

Although the exact content of the May 9 letter is unknown, a private communication rather than an "open and official" apology was not acceptable. The two subsequent apologies also left the Chinese feeling dissatisfied. The May 10 public apology was said to have outraged Chinese feeling in lacking the decorum appropriate in such a grave matter. President Clinton was filmed outdoors in a casual setting, wearing a polo shirt. His words were personal and spontaneous. Chinese television editors were said to have commented that "it was not really an apology at all" (New York Times, January 4, 2001). Also jarring was U.S. impatience to "move beyond" the bombing, seeming to minimize the significance of the tragedy. Less than one week after the bombing there was unconcealed irritation in Washington at continuing protests and demonstrations in Beijing. It was increasingly felt that the Chinese government was behaving unreasonably, that Chinese public outrage was being deliberately whipped up, and that doubts cast on the U.S.-NATO explanation of a targeting error were not in good faith. All this seriously mistook the depth of Chinese anger and overestimated the plausibility of accounts that placed the blame on a technical failure in equipment vaunted for its infallible precision.

An end of sorts to the affair came with the dispatch in June of a high-ranking U.S. delegation of officials headed by Under Secretary of State Thomas Pickering. He brought a letter from President Clinton offering to pay compensation to the families of the victims and a preliminary detailed account of the series of errors that had resulted in the bombing (New York Times, June 17, 1999). In announcing the compensation of $4.5 million, the U.S. government emphasized that the payment was entirely voluntary and did not represent an acknowledgment of legal liability. No formal apology was forthcoming (Keesing's, 1999).

Nonapology

A nonapology looks superficially like an apology and contains expressions of regret and sorrow. But it is not meant to acknowledge deliberate wrongdoing or responsibility for a specific misdemeanor. Indeed it involves a painstaking attempt to avoid acceptance of legal liability. It usually concerns a dispute in which the parties fundamentally disagree in their interpretation of the injury or, indeed, whether a blameworthy offense occurred at all. All that they really agree on is the existence of a grievance. The alleged offender feels obliged to concede a propitiatory form of words, not as an admission of wrongdoing but to conciliate the aggrieved party. The professed victim may have some kind of hold over the so-called offender. In the circumstances, discussion of the dispute modulates into a classic diplomatic negotiation over a form of words acceptable to both sides. The word *apology* or its equivalent, implying guilt, is strongly resisted, but carefully chosen expressions of regret and sorrow, implying sympathy at the human level but not responsibility, may be forthcoming. A satisfactory outcome leaves the parties' honor intact, is defensible before concerned publics, and allows normal interaction to be resumed as soon as possible.

In April 1980, the British television company ATV decided to go ahead with screening the documentary film *Death of a Princess* dealing with the episode of a Saudi princess executed for adultery. When news of the forthcoming documentary came out, the Saudi authorities were deeply angered and embarrassed at what they perceived to be an intrusion into their internal affairs casting the Saudi royal family as well as Islam in an unfavorable light. They blamed the British government for not doing enough to stop the broadcast and presented it as the culmination of a series of attacks on Saudi Arabia in the British media in reaction to Saudi opposition to the peace treaty between Egypt and Israel (*The London Times*, May 2, 1980). To signal displeasure the British ambassador was asked to leave Jedda, contracts were canceled, and a visit by the Saudi king to Britain was called off.

From the beginning, the British government was placed in a tricky situation, since it did not control ATV and could not appear to question the right of free expression. Nor had it done anything wrong. A classic diplomatic damage control operation was called for. Just before the broadcast the foreign secretary, Lord Carrington, sent a message to King Khaled stressing "that the British Government would regret it deeply if our close relations with the Kingdom were damaged by an event for which neither Government was responsible" (Hansard Society, 1980). Further nonapologetic regrets followed, but since the Foreign Office explicitly denied that there had been an "apology" the Saudi government remained unappeased (*The London Times*, April 10, 11, 1980).

The turning point in the crisis came with a much more forthcoming speech by Lord Carrington on May 22 and a fulsome nonapology. The foreign secretary now said that he was "very sorry" for the "understandable offence" that the film had caused to the Saudi royal family and other Saudis and Muslims everywhere. He, too, had "found it deeply offensive" but could not ban it by law. He was also "distressed by charges" that Britain was anti-Muslim, which was far from the truth. He added: "We shall be doing all we can to bring about a reconciliation with Saudi Arabia. We may need to ask them to be more understanding about our way of life. We shall certainly need to be more understanding about theirs." In answer to a question Lord Carrington denied that the Saudi government had requested an apology and characterized his statement as "what Her Majesty's Government think" (*The London Times*, May 23, 1980).

Some weeks later Douglas Hurd, minister of state at the Foreign and Commonwealth Office, visited Jedda. Relations were restored to a normal footing and agreement reached on the return of the British ambassador thanks to an ingenious conciliatory device: a joint Anglo-Saudi committee for cultural cooperation was to be set up. This would be a forum for consultation and cooperation (and by implication a means of avoiding future mishaps) and a token of British respect for Saudi culture. On August 26, the foreign secretary visited Saudi Arabia to set the seal on the agreement. Although no official apology had been made, the nonapologies, the two visits by senior British officials, and the consultative agreement cleared the air and achieved the reconciliation—*sulha*. An apology by any other name would have smelled as sweet.

Conclusion

Apology is not a panacea for resolving conflict and achieving historical reconciliation in international relations. One should beware of tempting but misleading comparisons between personal and diplomatic apology. There are various reasons why this is so:

- Apology and reconciliation can never mean the same thing for states as for individuals. Only individuals can feel contrition and express sincere regret for wrongdoing. States are legal abstractions, not ethical persons. Apologies by states draw on the metaphor of personal repentance and ethical language but are motivated by considerations of expediency and reason of state. Besides, the people doing the apologizing are simply officials acting in a fiduciary capacity.
- In the Christian tradition, reconciliation is the final link in a chain that runs from contrition via apology and forgiveness to absolution. But very different models exist. In the Japanese case, which strongly em-

phasizes apology, contrition need not be contingent on liability. In the achievement of social harmony it is the public display of sincerity (conforming to certain ceremonial features), rather than inward repentance, that is crucial. In the rigidly hierarchical Chinese system, apology is not a central virtue but an instrument of social discipline. In the Arab world, with its stress on group honor, apology is seen as a stylized aspect of peacemaking at the ceremonial level. In other contexts it tends to be perceived as humiliating supplication.

- At an interpersonal level reconciliation is the completion of a process of healing following which a relationship is restored and the penitent readmitted to the community. It is unclear what this might mean in an international context. Japan and West Germany were quickly accepted as allies by the West in the 1950s because they were indispensable as trading partners and needed as assets in the Cold War, not because anyone believed that they had undergone a profound change of heart. Normalization, based on interests, not ethics, was achieved fairly rapidly, with some exceptions (such as Poland and Korea). Only later, when normalization was a well-established and accomplished fact, were apologies offered.

- Apology arouses powerful inhibitions for political reasons. Domestic audiences are rarely keen on propitiating foreigners. They are more likely to believe in "my country right or wrong" and resent their leaders' bending of the knee. We tend to forget just how unpopular Willy Brandt's Warsaw Ghetto gesture was at the time. The international normative implications of apology also loom large. Admission of fault implies tacit recognition of the rules or norms understood to have been infringed in the first place. If you apologize for crossing a notional line, you thereby accept the legitimacy of that line. Saddam Hussein will not apologize for his 1990 invasion of Kuwait because he continues to claim that it is Iraq's nineteenth province.

As a routine instrument of diplomatic dispute processing, though, apology is demonstrably extremely useful. From the few examples presented, it is clear that diplomatic apology can make a significant contribution, by itself or in tandem with other expedients, in curtailing grievance and getting a disrupted relationship back on track. However, "reconciliation" may be a rather elevated term for what sometimes simply comes down to a resumption of normal business relations. The fact that we can couple apology with nonapology, the latter a mere form of words paying lip service to regret but carefully skirting responsibility, indicates that we are not talking here of an instrument of true contrition and reconciliation in any meaningful ethical sense, but simply a pragmatic diplomatic expedient.

ACKNOWLEDGMENTS   Much of the research and writing of this paper were carried out at Nuffield College, Oxford, in the summer of 2001. I am grateful to Andrew Hurrell and the Warden of the college for inviting me. Thanks, too, to Jumana Abu Zayyad and Yoshiko Wada for their assistance.

9

Ritual and the Politics of Reconciliation

Marc Howard Ross

If you ask most political scientists and international relations scholars what role reconciliation should play in peace processes, you are apt to receive a dazed look and perhaps an uneasy silence as well. The reason for this reaction is that political scientists think about peacemaking among large collective entities and see reconciliation as concerning personal relations or religious experiences for individuals and small face-to-face groups.

Peacemaking, from their perspective, is about developing new patterns of behavior built on institutions and practices that reward the parties for desirable behavior and punish them for unwanted actions. Nowhere in this perspective does reconciliation play a role. The argument that institutions and incentives are what matter the most is made explicitly in the works dealing with post-World War II European integration (for example, Deutsch et al., 1957; Haas, 1964; Lindberg and Sheingold, 1970). The founders of the European Community were unequivocal about wanting to construct functional linkages between the economies of the major European countries such that the rewards for cooperation and the costs of conflict would continue to grow. Building an integrated Europe meant emphasizing future benefits while making an implicit comparison with the high costs of past conflict. That is not to say there were no overt efforts at reconciliation in postwar Europe. There were, especially between France and Germany, although they are generally viewed as far less significant than institution building in accounting for Europe's integration and subsequent lack of violent conflict.

Recently, some have suggested that reconciliation may be especially important following domestic, as opposed to international, conflict. It is one thing, the argument goes, for former enemies to reestablish trade and diplomatic relations, but reconciliation is much more crucial if enemies must learn to live as neighbors. Although the distinction between international and domestic conflict is a good deal less precise than is often implied, there is no doubt that building institutions and practices so that former enemies can live more or less harmoniously in the same society is daunting indeed.

Political scientists inquiring into reconciliation seek answers to questions such as

1. What is meant by reconciliation and who is to be reconciled?
2. Is reconciliation necessary for peacemaking or peace building?
3. If reconciliation makes a difference, what does it look like? How do we know it when we see it?
4. What are the techniques and mechanisms by which reconciliation works?

In this chapter, I discuss each of these questions and then emphasize the importance of acknowledgment through symbolic and ritual action for deescalating and redefining long-term ethnic conflicts. Such acknowledgment may be especially important in situations where explicit verbal apology, forgiveness, and reparations—central features of reconciliation in some situations—may not be possible or even desirable. My main emphasis here is on the use of symbol and ritual in intergroup reconciliation, though a more extensive analysis might examine the question as part of a two-part game between the leaders and the public in each community as well as between the two societies.[1] Of particular interest would be the interaction between the two levels in regard to the constraints that within-group politics places on intergroup behavior.

My approach to reconciliation here builds on my prior work examining cross-cultural differences in the incidence and management of conflict as well as the role of culture as a flashpoint of conflict around issues such as Loyalist parades in Northern Ireland or Muslim headscarves in French schools (Ross, 1993a, 1993b, 2001). A core hypothesis in my work is that settling ethnic conflicts is not simply a matter of finding a clever, interest-based constitutional formula or a way to split a limited pie. To develop both institutions and practices that help peoples at odds live together, solutions must also address basic threats to identity and the intense sense of victimization expressed in cultural, and not just political, acts.

This distinction between interest and identity approaches to conflict is useful in examining reconciliation. It is seen in Gardner-Feldman's (1999) differentiation between moral and instrumental reconciliation and in Bar-Tal's discussion of the different dynamics of reconciliation in intrastate and interstate conflicts. In the former, Bar-Tal points out, there will be more emphasis on reconstructing past acts of injustice "in order to foster social healing" (2000: 356), whereas interstate reconciliation is more concerned with building new relationships through institutions and practices that address the parties' interests.

Although the language of interest and identity approaches and the actions that follow from each are often quite different, I argue that effective conflict management needs to address both competing interests and incompatible identities (Ross, 1993a). The distinction between the two is analytic, and for people involved in conflict the two are often merged. For example, although claims to land clearly have a material basis, they are often especially important to a group because of the symbolic significance of such claims.

This means that the analytically meaningful distinction between moral and instrumental reconciliation should not obscure the fact that in practice reconciliation must include both, although the mix in particular cases will vary. Gardner-Feldman (1999) compares German-Israeli with German-French reconciliation and observes that whereas the former focuses on moral concerns, the latter has been more instrumental. Rarely, however, is reconciliation just one or the other. The interrelationship between the two is crucial in cases of reconciliation where the goal is not just to connect former adversaries emotionally but to build institutions and practices to meet their instrumental needs as well.

Finally, I am interested in how in intense conflicts, culture is a powerful vehicle for expressing social and political differences, and in how the tensions and anger that conflicts unleash mobilize communities on sectarian lines. As a result, cultural expressions such as parades, religious sites and practices, public art and monuments (as well as their destruction), holidays, archeological findings and their public presentation, modes of dress, or language use can easily become emotionally charged and politically divisive (Ross, 2001). But such expressions can also be powerful vehicles for narrowing differences between opponents At the same time that all groups are ready to define external enemies, all cultural traditions also contain core images of peace, which can then be adapted to deescalation and reconciliation (Gopin, 2000). The concepts of psychocultural interpretations and psychocultural dramas help us examine conflicts that invoke core cultural images and group identity and to consider reconciliation as acknowledgment through symbolic expression and ritual, which, like culture, has been relatively neglected by political scientists (Ross, 1997, 2001).[2]

What Is Meant by Reconciliation and Who Is to Be Reconciled?

Reconciliation involves changing the relationship between parties in conflict both instrumentally and emotionally in a more positive direction so that each can more easily envision a joint future. Reconciliation is not one thing (Kriesberg, 1998a) and is best viewed as a continuum, meaning that there can be degrees of reconciliation rather than just its presence or absence; furthermore, there are strong and weak versions of reconciliation.[3] The strong version involves a total transformation in the relationship between former opponents; in the weak version there is sufficient change so that interactions between the groups are increasingly constructive and violence comes to an end.

One issue that arises when discussing ethnic conflict in general, and reconciliation in particular, is the naming of groups in ways that imply they are unified actors when most often that is far from the case. For example, in Northern Ireland, Israel-Palestine, and Sri Lanka there are severe within-group differences that have significant bearing on between-group behaviors. On some occasions, in fact, it is easier to build cross-group coalitions than within-group ones. Often, however, within-group dynamics limit and even dictate between-group actions. When maintaining support from one's own group is problematic, intergroup actions will often be hostile and aggressive. This is clearly seen in the electoral arena where, in polarized polities, political parties are generally organized on ethnic lines and few people vote for parties associated with another group (Horowitz, 1985). As a result, intragroup competition determines who represents the group in intergroup situations in ways that can significantly constrain intergroup peacemaking and reconciliation, including the symbolic gestures that leaders, and even ordinary people, in one group can make toward an opposing group.

Goals of Reconciliation

There are several ways to think about the goals of reconciliation. One framework emphasizes the role of reconciliation in different stages of a conflict. During the peacemaking (or preagreement) stage, partial reconciliation can be critical in getting the parties to the negotiating table and persuading them that there are people on the other side worth talking to and things worth talking about with them (Kelman, 1978, 1987; Rothman, 1992). Much of the field of conflict resolution is focused on creating the conditions under which formal agreements between disputants can be negotiated and reached (Ross, 2000b). The argument is that without significant reconciliation, long-term enemies will never get to the table. During the peacemaking phase, the reconciliation process emphasizes identity and recognition as prerequisites for instrumental action. Presettlement reconciliation begins the transformation of an enemy into a future neighbor by helping the parties imagine that coexistence is possible and by creating images of the benefits of such coexistence. Often this process is difficult because in polarized societies, many people have trouble imagining the details of day-to-day existence without the familiar threats and fears. Indeed such fears, periodically reinforced through actual events, play a dominant role in group memory and limit the capacity to offer symbolic gestures of reconciliation lest they be viewed as signs of weakness and lack of resolve.

During the peace-building, or postsettlement, phase the task of reconciliation is more ambitious, addressing further questions associated with the institutions and practices to be established. Even though formal agreements have been reached between the leaders of conflicting groups, their full implementation requires significant changes in public attitudes and behaviors. Such restorative steps, which clearly will vary across contexts, are emotionally critical for building future functional cooperation. At this phase reconciliation is multifaceted, engaging both political elites and the mass public, and involves a wide range of specific actions—as evidenced by the diverse goals that truth commissions tend to address (Minow, 1998: 88).[4]

Reconciliation can vary depending on who is to be reconciled and on the vision of peace that the parties hold. In intrastate conflicts, groups can have very different goals ranging from integration as in South Africa, pluralism as in Northern Ireland, to separation as in Sri Lanka and Israel-Palestine.[5] Each of these is associated with different patterns of reconciliation. Integration probably makes the most strenuous demands on the behavioral and interpersonal level. In contrast, where pluralism is a goal, what is required are institutions and practices that preserve high autonomy for groups in many domains (for example, religion, education, leisure) alongside cooperation in other areas such as government and the economy. Separation is most easily understood in both geographical and political terms but rarely means that groups will cease interaction entirely. The two most common forms that separation takes are independent statehood (for example, Israel-Palestine) and regional autonomy within an existing state (for example, Catalonia in Spain; Quebec in Canada). Here reconciliation requires joint recognition and the development of mechanisms for intergovernmental interactions.

Discussions of reconciliation in Central and Latin America emphasize its importance as a prerequisite for democratic regimes that arise after years or even decades of civil war and military rule (Kaye, 1997; Hayner, 1999). From this perspective, reconciliation has two main components: (partial) truth telling to acknowledge past injustice, and acceptance of both democratic rules and procedures and the political representatives of former opponents. Postsettlement governments in a number of countries (for example, Argentina, Chile, El Salvador, Guatemala, Honduras) have struggled with the issues of truth telling about the past, justice, amnesty, and the creation of new participatory institutions in which power sharing or power alternation is possible without a return to civil war. Reconciliation increases group interdependence (though this can take many different forms) and requires building a basis for democratic institutions and (sometimes) for addressing social inequities at the root of the earlier conflict.

Is Reconciliation Necessary for Peacemaking or Peacebuilding?

It would be hard to argue that peacemaking following either domestic or international conflicts requires formal reconciliation processes, since in the past there have been many civil and interstate wars that have ended without reconciliation in which the former enemies have been able to live peacefully for some time thereafter.[6] One explanation for this is that until the nineteenth century the separation between state and society was sufficiently great so that ethnic and state identities were not particularly relevant to the politics of states. In addition, many wars end with a victor and a vanquished party, and for strategic reasons the latter accepts its status.

International Conflict and Reconciliation Processes

Because of differences between civil and interstate conflicts, it is plausible that there may be differences in the dynamics of reconciliation in each situation. In interstate wars even if there is not a clear winner and loser, treaties or cease-fires that end wars often do little more than "restore normal relations" between the states. Even when these events are accompanied by apologies or admissions of guilt, such as the German admission of responsibility for World War I in the Treaty of Versailles or the United States' 1968 apology that its ship the *Pueblo* had violated North Korean waters, the process often only involves leaders who are seen as acting out of instrumental concerns or weakness.

In the international arena, the most sustained reconciliation efforts in recent decades have been between Germany and Japan and their former enemies in the aftermath of World War II. Japan has issued statements to South Korea, the United States, to China, and to the "comfort women." However, in some cases the expressions of regret fell short of the full apologies that were sought or were only individual statements by leaders.[7] There have been sustained German reconciliation efforts with France, Poland, Israel, and the Czech Republic, and payments of reparations to victims or their survivors in other parts of Europe as well (Handl, 1997; Kopstein, 1997; Dodds, 1999; Gardner-Feldman, 1999).

Although German-French and German-Israeli reconciliation has been significant in recent decades, it is not clear that either provides a model that is easy to generalize to other interstate, let alone intrastate, conflicts. For one thing, the nearly universal condemnation of the Nazi regime removes much of the difficulty associated with deciding who were the perpetrators and who were the victims. Second, although the postwar German government has chosen to acknowledge German responsibility for the war, the German officials who have done so do not see themselves as the natural heirs of the earlier regime. Third, the incentives for German reconciliation efforts were strong; without such efforts, Germany's acceptance into the international system as well as support for its economy would have been problematic. Some Germans certainly were highly motivated for moral reasons as well to seek reconciliation with peoples who had suffered under the Nazis—as when, in 1970, Chancellor Willy Brandt fell to his knees at the site of the Warsaw Ghetto and expressed Germany's guilt, sorrow, and responsibility for the Holocaust.

The particular conditions and incentives at work in the cases of postwar German reconciliation are, however, too often missing in intrastate (and even other international) conflicts to make this model relevant in many settings. Reconciliation is, in fact, difficult to achieve, as is evident from the story of Czech-German reconciliation during the 1990s. On the one hand, Czechs blamed Germany for their suffering during the war; on the other, because ethnic Germans were expelled from part of Czechoslovakia, the Sudetenland, at the end of the war, this is one of the few cases where Germans saw themselves as victims and demanded apology and reparations. Czech President Havel addressed the issue in 1990, saying it was appropriate that Czechoslovakia set the record straight with its neighbors. Yet despite a strong desire on both sides to put the matter to rest, the issue dragged on for seven years before the two governments issued a joint declaration that was then endorsed by both parliaments. Even though the refugees had been vigorously and successfully integrated into German society, they (and their descendants) very much wanted a statement that past injustice had been done and that as expelled persons they had a right to return and a right to property that had been expropriated in 1945. The Czechs for their part, while willing to say that the expulsions had been wrong, wanted the Germans to take responsibility for the upheaval in the region that produced the action. They also knew that few of the expellees would want to return, and the Czechs were totally unwilling to restore property after 50 years. In the end, Czech desire to be admitted to European organizations, and Chancellor Kohl's desire to end the matter, led to negotiations that produced a final document despite much difference and even bitterness over the wording (Handl, 1997; Kopstein, 1997).

Although initially many expected this case to be a relatively easy one in which to achieve reconciliation, in the end it turned out to be awkward and conflictual. More important, there is little sense that the outcome had much significant impact on the people in either country. Reconciliation, in this case, eased the situation for officials in both governments but hardly produced a major shift in the German-Czech relationship. What this case does offer is the example of joint responsibility.[8] Yet the brief declaration that took years to achieve also showed that efforts to address problematic issues explicitly can sometimes stir up as many problems as they settle. If reconciliation was so difficult in the Czech-German case, we need to recognize that it will be far more difficult in situations where the perceived injustices are more recent, more severe, and where the will to address them is weaker.

What Does a Political Reconciliation Process Look Like? What Does It Require?

Reconciliation can be examined as both a process and product. A process analysis emphasizes how reconciliation unfolds; analysis of the product considers how the parties and their relationship change as a result of the process. But what elements of reconciliation should we view as the core of the process, and can we identify the outcome that reconciliation achieves when it is successful?

In a very personal account of reconciliation in which he describes a number of his own experiences, Lederach (1999) identifies four main features of reconciliation: truth, mercy, justice, and peace. In his view, each of the four is needed for reconciliation, yet there are different ways to combine them. He argues that although reconciliation must address the past, present, and future, this can be done in different ways and in different sequences. Although it is easiest to think in terms of a past-present-future sequence, he shows how in some situations where past trauma is too great, reconciliation is more likely to succeed if it begins either with the present or the future. By addressing the immediate needs of people in a postconflict situation (1999:71–75), or by starting with a vision of building a future that is far more positive than either the immediate past or the present (1999:75–77), the reconciliation process has a greater chance to succeed.

Long and Brecke (2000) offer a very different emphasis in their recent analysis of reconciliation following civil violence.[9] They argue that the chances for domestic peace increase significantly where there are "reconciliation events" that involve:

> (1) direct physical contact or proximity between opponents, usually senior representatives of the respective factions; (2) a public ceremony accompanied by substantial publicity or media attention that relays the event to a wider national society; and (3) ritualistic or symbolic behavior that indicates the parties consider the dispute resolved and that more amicable relations are expected to follow. (2000: 2)

Their analysis of cases from Latin America (they promise a future analysis of African cases) leads them to conclude that reconciliation is most successful when it entails truth telling that acknowledges past abuses by all parties. However, they also conclude that the process almost always needs to be partial because of intragroup constraints on the expression of reconciliation gestures and fears about the backlash effects of an unfettered process. The need for both justice and amnesty means that full justice is never meted out through punishment and reparations, although acknowledgment can significantly help victims of violence and the redefinition of social groups and institutions can help prevent future violence. Long and Brecke assert that their evidence supports what they call the "forgiveness hypothesis," by which forgiveness is a mechanism for changing shame and anger into empathy and a desire for affiliation. They also emphasize the symbolic acknowledgment of past injustice, most often through rendering elaborate accounts of a small number of cases, even when full judicial accountability is not possible.

Apology and Forgiveness

In some religious traditions, reconciliation requires that perpetrators apologize for past harm done and the decision about whether to grant forgiveness is left to victims. Apology contains the admission that past actions were wrong or unjust, and is a way in which groups take responsibility for the past. In some cases apology is a one-way process, but in many conflicts it must be mutual to be effective. Marty argues that in the Christian tradition "forgiveness always leads to reconciliation, and reconciliation results from mutual experiences of forgiveness. They cannot, finally be separated" (1998: 11).[10] Lederach, in describing his personal approach to reconciliation, also emphasizes that forgiveness is a critical element. Minow and other observers of the Truth and Reconciliation Commission process in South Africa discuss how the need to grant forgiveness can be empowering to victims, who ultimately can choose whether or not to forgive perpetrators of violence and other crimes (Minow, 1998).

Apology, which was uncommon in politics until recently, has suddenly become central to the dynamics of conflict resolution at many levels. Political leaders, groups, states, and even international organizations are asked to apologize and their response is taken as a measure of their sincerity and future intentions. At the same time, apologies are relatively easy to offer and frequently there is debate about whether they are sincere. As a result, apologizers are often asked to demonstrate their sincerity with actions such as reparations payments (Dodds, 1999).

A significant political problem can be deciding who, if anyone, can apologize for the actions of people who are no longer in power or are now dead. But that is not always an issue. For example, many Jews have had little trouble accepting statements from recent popes about the church's earlier stances on the role of Jews in Jesus' death or the role of the church during World War II. A more complicated situation arises when there is not only a change of leaders but also of regime. Can current German leaders apologize for the atrocities of the Nazi regime, or can current Russian leaders address the crimes of the Soviet era?

Similarly, there can be confusion about forgiveness. Who can ask for it, and who can grant it? What does it mean that cultures and religious traditions differ in how they view forgiveness (Dorff, 1998; Marty, 1998)? To what extent are apology and forgiveness substitutes for formal justice mechanisms; and are they appropriate in situations where formal justice also is brought to bear?

Apology and forgiveness can be powerful symbolic statements. What is of real significance is who is able to make these statements, particularly when those making them are not necessarily the same people who were either the original perpetrators or victims. Can (and should) white Americans today offer a meaningful apology to African Americans for slavery? What should it entail? Perhaps the most appropriate focus would be on the benefits of white privilege, which still accrue in American society. Could Willy Brandt, himself a victim of Nazi persecution, apologize on behalf of the German people? Can the children of Nazis apologize to the children of Holocaust survivors for the deeds of a previous generation? And can an apology be accepted that involves forgiving the children without forgiving the Nazi perpetrators themselves?

Apology and forgiveness can be difficult steps for groups that may, in many ways, be prepared to settle their conflict but find themselves unable or unwilling to apologize or forgive. To my knowledge, none of the major actors in the Israeli-Palestinian or Northern Irish conflicts has publicly expressed a willingness to apologize (though they certainly would accept one from the other side) or forgive. But many have made clear that they want to develop new institutional arrangements to end the long-term pattern of violent conflict.

Reparations

Reparations are payments to compensate victims for their suffering that are often taken to indicate that an apology is sincere. At the same time that victims often demand reparations, the actual amount of reparations is rarely seen as full compensation for the suffering (let alone the material losses) that victims or their survivors have endured. Yet reparations, like apology, take on an important symbolic and emotional meaning.

Even though apology and reparations seem warranted when there is broad consensus that past actions were wrong, they rarely are offered quickly. During World War II, the United States seized the property of Japanese Americans living on the West Coast and placed them in internment camps for most of the war even though there was no evidence of a security threat. (It is interesting that residents of Hawaii of Japanese origin, a larger but more integrated group than those on the mainland, were never detained.) At first the U.S. government defended its actions (which were supported by a 1943 Supreme Court decision). Over the years, however, there was an increasing consensus that the government had overreacted and had denied the Japanese Americans their basic rights.[11] By the 1970s there was an organized movement seeking an apology and reparations, both of which were finally granted in 1989 (Espiritu, 1992; Takezawa, 1995).

Apologies (and perhaps reparations) are most likely to occur in situations where there is clearly a perpetrator and a victim and a clear consensus that the perpetrator's actions were wrong, as in the case of the Japanese Americans. In the cases of the Nazi regime or South Africa under Apartheid, the widespread agreement about the evils committed has resulted in apologies being offered (though in the South African case only from some of Apartheid's architects and implementers). Apology can be even slower than in the Japanese American case; two striking examples are British Prime Minister Tony Blair's apology to Ireland for the British failure to distribute food to it during the potato famine of the 1840s, a fact that historians have widely accepted for some time, and the pope's recent apology for the Crusaders' sacking of Constantinople in the thirteenth century.

Thus, even when there is a clear perpetrator and victim, apology and reparations often do not follow quickly (if at all). In most long-term ethnic conflicts, however, steps toward reconciliation involving explicit apology, forgiveness, and reparations are rare. More common are cases in which both groups see themselves as victims of past injustices that are not necessarily fully redressed by recent goodwill gestures or even apology. Certainly this is the case with Protestants and Catholics in Northern Ireland, Palestinians and Jews in the Middle East, and Tamils and Sinhalese in Sri Lanka. It applies as well to black-white relations in the United States (Myers, 2000).

Acknowledgment

Apologies and reparations are one way to signal a readiness to launch a new relationship, but fortunately not the only way since instances where apology occurs and reparations are paid are rare. When all parties emphasize their vulnerability and see themselves as victims, apology is not imaginable either politically or psychologically. A possible alternative, however, is acknowledgment. It involves recognizing that a group or individuals have suffered past injustices while remaining ambiguous about one's own connection to those actions. To be effective acknowledgment must offer sincere, powerful symbolic gestures to victims that can help restore (or build) bonds. What needs to be acknowledged varies, of course, across situations, but at the most general level acknowledgment works by recognizing the existence of a group and the emotional significance of its narrative of past injustices.

Let us, then, imagine three different white responses to an African American's account of slavery:

1. "Don't blame me, my ancestors didn't get here until 1905."
2. "It must be terrible to think about the pain and suffering your ancestors experienced while living as someone else's property."
3. "Slavery is awful to imagine. What's worse is that there is still a legacy today. There is no doubt that even since slavery was ended, my ancestors and I have benefited from white privilege even though my family didn't come to this country until 1905."

The first response is a defensive nonstarter; it is inflammatory since the responder shows no empathy whatsoever. I imagine that in Israel the equivalent occurs when Palestinians tell Jews not to blame them for the Holocaust ("We don't want to suffer because of something that was done to you") or when Jews tell Palestinians that their loss of homes and olive groves in 1948 would have been avoided if they had accepted the 1947 Partition Plan.

The second and third responses are different because they offer an emotional connection. In neither case does the responder apologize for slavery in the sense of taking responsibility for it, but the statements do perhaps speak to the need for recognition and acknowledgment. The second response does so by identifying with the recounter's feelings; in the third response this is also accompanied by an acknowledgment of the modern legacy of slavery and the admission that the responder has probably benefited from it, at least unintentionally. Statements of this sort can open the door to dialogue and possible remediation, such as affirmative action programs.

Acknowledgment can take many forms, but its significance lies in the emotional linkage it establishes between individuals or groups. Acknowledgment has an important symbolic component. It may take a verbal form, as in President Lyndon Johnson's 1965 speech on civil rights in which he said, "We shall overcome," a clear sign that he, a white Southerner, identified fully with the civil rights movement's major goals. Or the words that are uttered may be far less significant than the action that accompanies them, such as Tony Blair's January 2001 meeting with the Catholic family of a man killed three and a half years years earlier by a Protestant mob in Portadown, the site of the most bitter conflicts over Loyalist parades in the region.

Mechanisms of Reconciliation

There are two questions to ask about the mechanisms underlying reconciliation. First, if reconciliation works, how does it work? Second, is reconciliation between individuals and small face-to-face groups similar or different from reconciliation between large social groups or countries? I explicitly address the first here while the second remains in the background, although the similarity across the levels is implicit here and in the spate of writings on this issue in recent years.

The most general explanation for how reconciliation works focuses on emotional and cognitive reordering, which enables the development of a new relationship between former enemies. Bar-Tal (2000b) calls this a shift from a conflictive ethos to a peace ethos. This changed worldview can be understood in terms of a variety of specific mechanisms. They include the psychodynamic processes of grief and mourning (Volkan, 1988; Kelman, 1991); the use of apology, forgiveness, and reparations (Minow, 1998); the development of a more inclusive vision of the society to which one is emotionally connected (Ross, 2001); the rehumanization of former opponents; acknowledgment and recognition; and incentives that reward cooperation.[12]

Lederach's (1999) three sequences—(1) past, present, future; (2) present, future, past; and (3) future, present, past—are strategies for promoting reconciliation and for increasing the likelihood that its four key elements (truth, mercy, justice, and peace) are included in the process. In addition, his approach emphasizes the importance of narratives (storytelling) in reconciliation. This theme is echoed in Minow's and other discussions of truth telling as a mechanism for validating past trauma and healing deep psychological wounds. The stress on validation and acknowledgment not only addresses the experience of individuals but also is significant because it resonates with the traumas that many have experienced. The accounts of the work of various truth commissions suggest that their effectiveness is not in their capacity to compile a complete and accurate historical record, but in the fact that the cases they hear (in some cases a small, well-selected sample) resonate so widely among the population.[13] Identification with the individual victims and victims' sense of being members of a community of victims are central elements of this dynamic.

Truth and reconciliation matter because they validate the emotional core of individual and group memory in settings where the absence of validation was a central fact of social existence. What is addressed is the deep fear that opponents are engaged in efforts not only to threaten a group physically but also to deny their past. How else can we understand the Serb effort to bulldoze mosques and immediately pave the ground with parking lots as soon as they captured Bosnian villages, or the deliberate Serb actions to destroy culturally significant objects and manuscripts at the National Library in Sarajevo during the war (Sells, 1996)? Or Golda Meir's widely publicized comments that there was no such thing as a Palestinian? Or the rage that Holocaust deniers evoke? Or the use of archeological evidence to assert one's national claims and deny those of an opponent (Abu el-Haj, 1999; Benvenisti, 2000)? In each of these situations not only is the core of a group's narrative challenged, but their "known" experience is destroyed or denied.

Understanding the power of a group's narratives requires that we examine the symbolic and ritual dimensions of reconciliation. Because of the political complexity surrounding the use of apology and reparations, acknowledgment may be an especially useful mechanism for achieving at least partial reconciliation, and ritual and symbolic action can be crucial in the dynamics of acknowledgment.

Reconciliation as Ritual and Symbolic Action: Sacred Sites and Cultural Performance

Symbolic and ritual action can be helpful in reconciliation processes for a number of reasons: (1) when direct apology is difficult, symbolic action can be easier for former enemies to express; (2) when words are sometimes seen as easy to utter, symbolic actions can be viewed as more sincere; and (3) whereas verbal apologies are more cognitive, symbolic actions are often more affective. My argument is not that symbolic actions are more important than verbal ones but rather that because the two work differently, they can both contribute to reconciliation processes.[14]

Symbolic actions are behaviors whose significance lies less in the actions themselves than in the meanings individuals and groups ascribe to them. For example, a handshake between two older men is a commonplace occurrence. However, when PLO Chairman Yasir Arafat and Israeli Prime Minister Yitzak Rabin shook hands on the White House lawn in 1993, Israelis, Palestinians, and many others ascribed great emotional significance to this simple gesture. Symbolic action takes many forms, and its importance lies in the capacity of symbols and rituals to variously provoke arousal or reassurance in observers (Edelman, 1964). Symbols work by evoking narratives about the past to make sense of the present (Buckley, 1998: 9).

When we examine long-term ethnic conflicts, it is evident that almost any difference between groups can serve as a symbolic focal point for conflict. Many conflicts today involve issues of language use in government, schools, road signs, and even in offices and stores (Laitin, 1989, 1998; Levine, 1991). Music and public art such as murals or sculptures are statements of group identity and are easily transformed into sources of conflict (Jarman, 1997).[15] Cultural performances such as parades or religious ceremonies can be among the most powerful expressions of group identity and can produce some of the strongest reactions from groups locked in conflict (Jarman, 1997; Bryan, 1998, 2000). The Taliban's destruction of ancient Buddhist statues in Afghanistan and the conflict over antiquities in Jerusalem's Old City show that present fears infuse the past and its objects with significance.

Sacred Sites

Almost all groups have places that are sacred to them. These places mark key events in a group's past and are often associated with emotionally charged victories or defeats, miracles, and the exploits of ancient heroes (Levinson,

1998). Often, though not always, these places will be associated with past battles. Sacred places are treasured and protected (Linenthal, 1993). So are religious sites that have been purified and sanctified. Sacred places often are particularly valuable because they contain holy relics that link a group's past to its present and future (Benvenisti, 2000).[16]

When I was in Sri Lanka in 1994, I visited the ancient city at Anuradhapura. This is an important Buddhist pilgrimage center that features beautiful buildings, thousands of monks in flowing saffron robes, as well as ordinary people. It is also the site of a sacred Bohdi-tree, which is guarded day and night. It grew from a sapling from the tree under which the Buddha gained Enlightenment in 528 B.C., and was brought from India in the third century. The mood is tranquil. A few years earlier a group of Tamil Tigers attacked Anuradhapura, firing automatic weapons that killed 180 people and wounded hundreds more. On my visit there I was told about the attack, but instead of focusing on the dead and wounded my host emphasized, "They tried to destroy our tree." Destruction of the tree would for him have been a far deadlier assault on Sinhalese Buddhists than the murderous one that took place.

Sacred places involve a number of contradictions. On the one hand, they represent strength and continuity; on the other, the need to safeguard them suggests that they also connote potential weakness and vulnerability. Catholic (and other) holy places need to be consecrated, but they can also be desecrated and this can threaten the foundations of a group's existence.[17] If sacred sites are corrupted, their special significance is in jeopardy unless they are ritually repurified. Sometimes groups are expelled from their sacred sites, and this highlights their vulnerability in ways that all can see. Possession and control over its sacred sites signifies a group's strength and well-being, but sometimes it is believed these must be validated by recapturing lost sites as Christians did during the Crusades when they sought to liberate the land of Jesus' birth from "the infidels." Finally, there is a radical contrast between, on the one hand, the importance of concrete, material ownership (for some, sovereignty) and control over sacred sites and the relics they contain and, on the other, the very emotional, spiritual, and nonmaterial significance of sacred places that transcends their physical significance.

Cultural Expression Through Public Performance: Loyalist Parades in Northern Ireland

Contentious Loyalist parades in Northern Ireland are a case that illustrates the role of ritual action in ethnic conflict and reconciliation.[18] These parades become a focus of yearly psychocultural dramas in areas such as South Belfast and Portadown. Each side bases its position on competing rights—freedom of speech ("The right to walk the King's highway") versus the right to be free from intimidation (not unlike competing definitions of Ariel Sharon's September 2000 visit to the Temple Mount/Noble Sanctuary). In the context of a polarized society such as Northern Ireland or Israel, there is no effective jural solution to such a conflict, since neither side views the judiciary or administration as sufficiently legitimate to rule in the matter. Thus, in Northern Ireland since 1995 parade disputes have resulted in violence. Yet whereas the Orange Order parades in Portadown lead to annual confrontations, some parade disputes, such as those in Londonderry/Derry, have moved toward settlement through ritual and symbolic redefinition from exclusive to inclusive cultural events.

Throughout the "marching season" in Northern Ireland, Protestant men in dark suits and bowler hats assemble at local lodges, attend church services, and hold parades, celebrating past victories, such as the Battle of the Boyne in 1690 when William of Orange's Protestant forces defeated the army of the Catholic King James II, and commemorating losses, such as the many deaths of soldiers in the Battle of the Somme in World War 1. Protestant accounts of the parades and the occasions they mark emphasize their solemn, religious nature (Lucy and McClure, 1997). Banners celebrate key events in Protestant history, especially those of the Williamite period such as the Battle of the Boyne, and represent important religious themes, symbols, and persons. Bands accompany the marchers playing familiar music, and at major parades important politicians address the crowd (Bryan, 1998, 2000; Jarman, 1997). Catholics, however, are often angry when the marchers parade through their neighborhoods. They resent what they regard as the parades' narrow, sectarian nature. They are also upset about what they see as a stress on Protestant triumphalism and domination, the aggressive music of the "blood and thunder" (or "kick the pope") bands that often flaunt paramilitary symbols, and the anti-Catholic lyrics of many of the songs.[19]

In recent years Loyal Order parades in South Belfast and Portadown have provoked intense conflict and violence, and competing definitions of group rights have produced standoffs. In Londonderry/Derry, however, contestation over the Apprentice Boys of Derry parades has been mitigated by redefinition. The Catholic-dominated City Council, various third parties, and cross-community dialogue have played important roles in a process lasting several years and still continuing (Kelly and Nan, 1998; Ross, 2001). This process has led to changes in the structure of the celebration, including agreements about the time of day and the number of marchers on the historic city walls, the parade organization and routes, the music played, and control over the bands that accompany the march. Today the Derry summer parade is recast as part of a larger nine-day cultural festival, a more inclusive event that has helped reduce Catholic-Protestant tension in the city. Certainly some of the changes result from the sides' acknowledging each other's most basic concerns, though pragmatic self-interest plays a part as well.

Whereas the parades in Portadown and South Belfast are a yearly ritual of polarization, the more inclusive cultural festival in Derry has become a tool for deescalation. Even more significant in terms of identity is the gradual expansion of the celebration into a cultural festival focusing on the city's history. Each year the festival, partially financed through municipal funds, has broadened to include such features as an exhibition at city hall, a talk by a Catholic historian, contests involving Protestant and Catholic schoolchildren, a bluegrass festival, and a street fair. Although there are still plenty of tensions and unresolved issues surrounding the Apprentice Boys' parades, the lines of cleavage in the city have been blurred and the deep threats to, or attacks on, group identity associated with the marches have diminished in many ways.

Psychocultural dramas reveal important fault lines in relations between ethnic groups. They can highlight both the specific interests around which ethnic conflicts are waged and the deeper identity dynamics at work that often make it so hard to settle these conflicts (see, for example, Northrup, 1989). Turner's (1957) idea that effective redress requires the performance of public ritual is fully consistent with what psychoculturally oriented theorists such as Kelman, Montville, and Volkan propose. By mobilizing deeply held cultural understandings, ritual action emphasizes what groups in conflict have in common and provides reassurance that future relationships will be less threatening than past ones. Ritual, therefore, is an important mechanism for redefining ethnic conflict away from incompatible differences and threatened identities to agreed-upon relations, or to separation as the best solution.

Different outcomes such as continued intense polarization in Portadown and ritual redefinition in Derry show how parade disputes are really about the deeper identities each community feels are at stake. This also accords with Turner's (1957) observation that ritual redefinition is often necessary when there is no clear way to choose between competing rights. Attending to cultural expression and ritual action is not a substitute for politics and negotiations but can be a valuable supplement to them.

Rituals as Mechanisms of Acknowledgment and Reconciliation

I began with the observation that political scientists have given scant, if any, attention to reconciliation in analyzing the termination of interstate conflicts. I then asked whether reconcilation, even if it is not necessary, can facilitate peacemaking or peacebuilding. The evidence for or against reconciliation in large-group and interstate conflicts is thin. Here I have marshaled some theory and anecdotal evidence that reconciliation helps groups redefine their relationships in more constructive directions. Finally, I maintained that if reconciliation is understood to include explicit apology, forgiveness, and reparations, it will probably be extremely difficult to implement in either intrastate or interstate politics; instead, it may be more widely relevant if it is defined in terms of acknowledgment, which involves symbolic and ritual acts that help reorient how groups perceive each other.

Acknowledgment and reconciliation can perhaps help in implementing agreements through the development of inclusive rituals that link different communities or the redefinition of older rituals so that they are no longer highly threatening and exclusive. This is not easy where group identity and group celebrations are often defined in opposition to another community.[20] However, legitimating divergent identities in ways that are non- (or less) threatening is an important part of the reconciliation process.[21]

Most commonly we think about the divisive role that symbolic and ritual action plays in ethnic conflict. There is no doubt that ethnic entrepreneurs, political leaders interested in short-term gains, and even sincere patriots at times mobilize support through emotionally charged symbolic appeals. Although it is easy to berate figures such as Ariel Sharon for further polarizing Jews and Palestinians with his visit to the Temple Mount/Noble Sanctuary in September 2000, or Slobodan Milosevic for his constant invocation of the Serb defeat in the battle of Kosovo in 1389 to mobilize support throughout the 1990s, the more central question concerns not leaders' motives but why followers respond as they do. It is obvious what the "sellers" hope to gain; but what explains the "buyers"? The answer seems to lie in the dynamics of social identity, in which they see their fate as intimately tied to that of the group. When the group prospers, so do they; when it suffers, so does their self-esteem (Tajfel, 1981; Brown, 1986). Recent psychodynamically informed theorizing gives a similar answer, suggesting that leaders play on followers' need for attachment and their vulnerability to claims that the symbols of their identity are at risk (Volkan, 1988, 1997; Ross 1995).

A Small and a Large Caution

Two cautions about the politics of reconciliation relate to the fact that reconciliation can be part of peacemaking and peacebuilding but is not a substitute for them. Since at the core of ethnic conflicts lie real differences in interests and identities, peace processes must address both of these as broadly as possible and reconciliation cannot do the whole job itself.

My first caution is to note that there may be significant costs to reconciliation events that might actually inhibit rather than advance peace processes. Since reconciliation is difficult, not all former enemies may be ready for it even if they have signed an agreement ending overt hostilities. Insisting on reconciliation before the parties themselves are ready for it may exacerbate delicate situations and remove the sense that parties have chosen to move toward each other, an essential element in reconciliation.

A more serious warning is that the need, and timing, for reconciliation are often not the same for all parties. Not surprisingly, in most conflicts the dynamics are different in each community. However, when one party reaches out to the other and feels rebuffed, anger and even rage can be released. In situations of great inequality in power and economic resources, for example, a central question for the weaker party—and sometimes a key test of the stronger party's desire for reconciliation—is the latter's willingness to redistribute resources. In both South Africa and Israel-Palestine, and to some extent in black-white relations in the United States, for the weaker parties moral reconciliation is much more connected to questions of inequality than for the stronger one, reminding us that different parties' needs are often not reciprocal.

The Need for Inclusive (New and Transformed) Symbols and Rituals

All too common are divisive, exclusive rituals that pit one group against another. In terms of reconciliation, the symbols and rituals of interest are those of a very different character that help previously separated groups feel less threatened.

Consider the following images: Anwar Sadat addressing the Knesset; Nelson Mandela donning a Springbok jersey; the Rabin-Arafat handshake; pictures of Sinn Fein's Gerry Adams and unionist leader David Trimble talking and then shaking hands; Mandela and F. W. de Klerk holding hands while seated side-by-side during a presidential debate; President Bill Clinton reviewing Vietnamese troops in Hanoi; Willy Brandt on his knees in Auschwitz; King Hussein of Jordan on his knees with the families of Israeli children killed by a deranged Jordanian soldier; black and white Americans holding hands in the Selma to Montgomery march. Each of these is a powerful image of intergroup connectedness, of reaching out and acceptance. By themselves these are not complete reconciliation events, but they are significant components of them. What these images communicate is both acknowledgment of a past and the image of a different future. They establish, or strengthen, a link between previously divided people.

When single actions such as these are generalized and regularized, when events once exclusively associated with one group are transformed, or when new behaviors are institutionalized as more inclusive events that involve participants from different communities, rituals can serve as instruments for reconciliation. This is seen, for instance, in the changed relations between religious communities. Since the 1960s Catholics have participated in ecumenical services with other Christian denominations including the Orthodox, and Pope John Paul II recently became the first pope to attend an Orthodox mass or to visit a mosque. In addition, in some places different denominations have been willing to share the same buildings.[22] In some venues such as certain American college campuses, different religious communities (Catholic, Protestant, Jewish, Muslim, and Hindu) use the same building for their religious services. At times temples in Sri Lanka have been places of worship for both Hindus and Buddhists (Tambiah, 1986); certain sites in India have been sacred to both Hindus and Muslims (van der Veer, 1994); in the Middle East there have been sites such as the Cave of Jeremiah near Haifa that members of many faiths regard as sacred and use for prayer.

Holidays

Many groups have exclusive marked days. One sign of a highly divided society is the absence of holidays and other rituals that are commemorated across groups. In Northern Ireland the anniversary of the Battle of the Somme, in which so many British soldiers died in 1916, is a solemn occasion for Protestants, even though the soldiers killed included a large number of Catholics as well as Protestants from Ireland. Republicans, however, view fighting and dying in this battle as support for the British and have been unwilling to mark their own losses in a way that would communicate a link with Protestants. Another example from Northern Ireland is that for years St. Patrick's Day has been celebrated exclusively by Catholics even though there is no religious reason that Protestants could not mark the day as well. In recent years there have been efforts to invite Protestants to march in the St. Patrick's Day parades in Dublin, Belfast, and elsewhere. Although some have done so, Republicans' aggressive displaying of the Irish Tricolour has so far hindered the parades' effectiveness for building cross-community bridges.[23]

It should not be surprising that there are few shared symbols and rituals across groups in divided societies. Following the American Civil War, Memorial Day emerged as a solemn occasion to pay tribute to those who had died in battle. In the North, however, the soldiers who were remembered were exclusively northern soldiers who had died to save the Union (Warner, 1959); in the former Confederate states, the fallen who were honored were Southerners. There was no acknowledgment that both sides had suffered severe loses. Similarly, Civil War statues and other memorials in the United States almost never are to soldiers of both sides, though on the battlefield at Gettysburg there are memorials to both in close proximity (Linenthal, 1993).[24] What does exist in the United States, however, are other holidays and memorials that bring together those from the former Union and the former Confederacy, such as Veterans Day, July 4, and Thanksgiving. Of course, the passage of time and geographic mobility within the country have considerably mitigated the divisions of the mid-nineteenth century.

In polarized settings, holidays marking glories of one group are often experienced as sharply humiliating for another.[25] For example, Israel's Independence Day is called *al-nakba* (the catastrophe) by Palestinians. In Europe, the French have on occasion rebuffed the Germans when they have made overtures to hold joint ceremonies on Armistice Day, November 11, or on the anniversary of the D-Day invasion.

Invented or redefined holidays can be important to one or several groups. If they are to serve as rituals for reconciliation, it is crucial that these holidays not be exclusive. Kwanza is an invented festival for African Americans that celebrates their African heritage. However, just like Martin Luther King Day, now a national holiday, its recognition of black experiences and roots is not hostile to whites and does not discourage white involvement and participation. Indeed, on Martin Luther King Day many communities hold intergroup services and community service activities in which blacks and whites participate.

Language

A last domain for symbolic and ritual action to explore is that of language, which is perhaps the most common area of cultural conflict. Language serves as both an obvious marker of group differences and a focal point for bitter ethnic conflict when groups make demands that their language be the state's official language or have a privileged status in the public domain. Language is also one of the easiest ways to associate the state with a particular group. In Quebec, conflict between francophones and anglophones has raised important questions of economic power and political control. Similarly in Catalonia, language is the basis on which demands for regional and cultural autonomy are justified. In many Third World countries and recently independent states in Eastern and Central Europe, language rights are seen as essential to issues of group recognition (Laitin, 1998). Sometimes a sign of reconciliation between groups is increasing bilingualism, or regional autonomy in language policy.

It is not hard to find psychocultural dramas that develop around language issues. In Quebec, following the Parti Quebeqois's victory in 1976 and the passage of Law 101, angolophones emigrated from the region and many of those who stayed protested new restrictions on the use of English in offices and education as well as the prohibition of English street and business signs (Levine, 1991). The result was a series of protracted negotiations among the Canadian provinces and continued threats of Quebec's secession, still continuing today. It is interesting that in this conflict, just when the federal government accepted the notion of Canada as a bilingual state, Quebequers asserted the need for a monolingual region.

In Central and Eastern Europe, bitter conflicts over language policy since 1990 in Slovakia, Estonia, Moldova, and elsewhere have unleashed violence at times and pitted hard-core nationalists against regional minorities in newly independent states. In Slovakia, the conflict focused on Hungarian-speakers in the southern part of the country and demands that they show their loyalty by learning Slovak and removing public signs in Hungarian. Although the ethnic tension seems to have eased following the 1998 elections, the conflict has not been settled. Similarly, Estonia and Moldova are two newly independent states with large Russian minorities. In Estonia the conflict has centered on the question of citizenship; Estonians passed legislation that granted citizenship to Russian-speakers only if they passed an examination in the Estonian language, which many long-time Russian residents of Estonia had never bothered to learn.

Despite the intensity of some language disputes, a number of countries have found ways to settle them or at least keep them nonviolent. In Canada, for example, despite all the strident rhetoric of oppression and the strong support for secession, language conflict has not been violent. Similarly, Spain since Franco's death has granted regional autonomy to Catalonia and other regions, allowing them to set their own language policies, thereby avoiding confrontations between minorities and the state. India is another interesting, and complicated, case. In the 1950s there were widespread language riots in many parts of the country. Since that time, however, the situation has calmed as linguistic and political boundaries have come into better alignment; each Indian state now has three official languages—Hindi, English, and the language of the largest linguistic group in that state.

Finally, I wish to make clear that cultural differences are not what causes ethnic conflicts. People battle over real interests and identities. Culture, however, is often mobilized in ethnic struggles. Because of its ambiguous and emotionally charged nature, culture can serve as a vehicle for peacemaking and peacebuilding as well as escalation and division. To put ethnic conflicts on a more constructive course, cultural acts and expressions are needed as part of intergroup reconciliation. I have tried to suggest how this might be fostered through ritual and symbolic action as an aspect of the broader process of redefining group relationships in long-term conflicts.

NOTES

1. I am grateful to Yaacov Bar-Siman-Tov for this suggestion.

2. Psychocultural interpretations are the worldviews found in the rich, image-laden accounts of people locked in conflict. Interpretations are contained in the stories groups tell; they reveal key fears and hopes, assumptions about how social and political relations are organized, and views about the possibilities for political action. Psychocultural dramas (an extension of Turner's [1957, 1974] concept of the social drama) are conflicts between groups over competing, and apparently irresolvable, claims that engage the central elements of each group's historical experience and identity and invoke suspicions and fears of the opponent. They are polarizing events involving nonnegotiable cultural claims, threats, or rights that become important because of their connections to core metaphors that are central to a group's identity. Psychocultural dramas may never be fully resolved, but they can be settled for a time when the conflict is redefined away from incompatible principles to the symbolic and ritual domain where disputants can emphasize shared concerns and superordinate goals. Intense psychocultural dramas are found in all long-term ethnic conflicts, and their development and escalation reveal the central role of culture and identity in ethnic conflict.

3. This is consistent with my emphasis (Ross, 1998, 2000a) on peacemaking and peacebuilding as a series of steps, which emphasizes that instead of asking whether things are perfect, we should ask if they are good enough.

4. The twelve include overlapping aspirations for truth commissions that Minow lists: overcoming communal and official denial of past atrocities and gaining public acknowledgment; obtaining facts so as to satisfy victims' need to know; building a public record for history; forging the basis for a democratic public order that respects and enforces human rights; promoting reconciliation across social divisions; restoring dignity to victims; punishing, excluding, and shaming offenders; and building an in-

ternational order to try and prevent and also to respond to aggression, torture, and atrocities (1998: 88).

5. Although I suggest that specific goals are associated with particular situations, this does not mean that these goals are those of all people and groups in these countries. Instead, I am referring to what I understand to be the dominant pattern in each of these long-term conflict situations.

6. Reconciliation at the interstate level as it is now discussed is a relatively recent phenomenon. Given the view of states as strategic actors (at least since the Treaty of Westphalia), the need to address moral or identity issues through a process such as reconciliation was not apparent. At the intrastate level as well, losers of civil wars were expected to accept their vanquished status and to benefit from the institutional benefits the state offered.

7. For example, Dodds reports that the mayor of Honolulu invited Japanese officials to a ceremony to mark the fiftieth anniversary of the attack on Pearl Harbor on the condition that they apologize for the war. The Japanese refused, claiming that "the entire world is responsible for the war" (Dodds, 1999: 36). In December 1991 the Japanese foreign minister expressed "deep remorse" for the wartime suffering that followed Japan's attack on Pearl Harbor; yet a few days later the Japanese parliament considered apologizing for the attack but did not do so in the end.

8. The declaration recognized past injustices that both countries had committed. The Germans admitted responsibility for the Munich Agreement in 1938 and for the expulsion of people from the border regions; the Czechs expressed regret for the suffering and wrongs caused by the expulsion and forced resettlement of the Sudeten Germans (Handl, 1997: 157). It was also agreed not to burden each side with political and legal questions from the past, and a fund was created for projects of mutual interest.

9. For a discussion of some of the problems and ambiguities in studying reconciliation with large quantitative data, see Brecke and Long (1999).

10. Dorff (1998) discusses some important differences between the Christian and Jewish approaches to forgiveness.

11. Not all were citizens; only those born in the United States were citizens, since U.S. law at the time prohibited the naturalization of all but white immigrants.

12. It is often implicitly assumed that one begins by changing attitudes and that behavior change then follows. This is particularly important in what Gardner-Feldman (1999) calls moral recognition. However, instrumental-pragmatic reconciliation probably works differently. Here, behaviors are changed and it is hoped that new beliefs will follow. One example of such a dynamic is found in Phase 3 of the Robber's Case experiment, in which superordinate goals are used to produce cooperation among the two groups. Following several positive experiences of working together, the researchers found that the groups came to view each other more favorably (Sherif et al., 1988). In the case of European integration, many assumed that once the benefits of economic cooperation were visible, political integration would proceed and national identities would weaken. Events in Europe in the 1990s, however, suggest important limits to that assumption.

13. The South African TRC is probably the most ambitious effort to date. It heard thousands of cases and reported widespread requests from victims to hear their stories. We can only make sense of this as reflecting a deep need for validation of the suffering during the Apartheid years. For a more complete discussion of Truth and Reconciliation processes, see Avruch and Vejarano (n.d.).

14. Symbolic and ritual actions are most often associated with group identity, but sometimes they are also relevant to interests as well. In addition, many interests often have an important symbolic component. Consider the appointment of a minority person to a major political post or cabinet position. Although the person may well provide significant material benefits to his or her community, there will be symbolic benefits as well.

15. In Northern Ireland, wall murals have been used extensively over the past 20 years to express both Catholic and Protestant identities. So have monuments and public buildings. For the most part the symbols and images associated with each community are very distinct, although there are some symbols and a few places or events that are found in the imagery of both communities. For example, see the symbols discussed and displayed at http://cain.ulst.ac.uk/images/symbols/crosstrad.htm.

16. Monuments and war memorials often are the focus of intense emotions (Levinson, 1998). One fascinating case is the United States' Vietnam memorial in Washington, which was a source of intense conflict when it was first proposed and now helps to bring together people who were strongly at odds in the past (Wagner-Pacifici and Schwartz, 1991).

17. Recently Member of Knesset Shaul Yaholom (National Religious Party) called for the arrest of members of the Muslim Waqf who were "desecrating antiquities at the [Temple Mount] in an effort to wipe out the traces of the Jewish nation from its most sacred site" (Ha'aretz, January 22, 2001).

18. Jarman (1997) reports that there are over 3,000 parades in Northern Ireland each year—most of them by Loyalists (Protestants expressing their loyalty to the Crown) during the "marching season" from June to August. The vast majority of parades are not contentious, often because they involve Protestants marching through Protestant communities. Contentious parades have, however, been the focus of intense political controversy in recent years, and a Parades Commission now has the authority to decide whether or not a parade can take place along a particular route, who will participate in it, the music that will be played, and at what time it will occur. Often these issues are negotiated at the local level and are not presented to the Parades Commission for decision (Ross, 2001).

19. For further discussion of symbols and rituals of identity in Northern Ireland, see Bryson and McCartney (1994) and Buckley (1998).

20. An interesting question concerns the changing content and significance of group rituals, holidays, and festivals as a function of intergroup relations and a group's political needs (Cohen, 1969, 1993).

21. Reconciliation is not about ending group differences or assimilating members of one group into the other; only in certain situations can integration of this sort be sought.

22. The case of the Church of the Holy Sepulcher in Jerusalem shows, however, that sharing is not necessarily associated with goodwill and trust.

23. Recently I learned of a more local effort to create cross-community linkage around St. Patrick's Day. In Derry in 2000, the Apprentice Boys of Derry, the loyal order whose parade and cultural festival were described above, decided to host a St. Patrick's Day and invited a number of Catholics, who told me that the event was highly successful.

24. In recent years there have been intense disputes over flying the Confederate flag in southern states and the inclusion of it in some state flags. See Forman (2000), as well as a more general treatment of the symbolic power of the American flag in Marvin and Ingle (1999).

25. Volkan's term, "the chosen trauma," is particularly apt (Volkan, 1997).

10

Social-Cognitive Mechanisms in Reconciliation

Ifat Maoz

Over the past decade or so, the term *reconciliation* has gained prominence in academic literature on international and interethnic conflicts and their management (Bar-Tal, 2000b). In this literature, however, the term tends to be fuzzy, its meaning largely determined by the context in which it appears (Wittgenstein, 1953/1968). Reconciliation is discussed from religious, historical (Minow, 1998; Bargal and Sivan, this volume), political, cultural, and cross-cultural perspectives (Ahluwalia, 2000; Cohen, this volume), as well as from psychological perspectives including emotional, psychodynamic, and cognitive ones (Ross, 1995, this volume; Bar-On, 1997, 1999; Kriesberg, 1998a, this volume; Lederach, 1998; Bar-Tal, 2000b; Bar-Tal and Bennink, this volume). Furthermore, reconciliation is studied both at the microlevel of individual and interpersonal processes (Azar, Mullet, and Vinsonneau, 1999) and at the macro level of ethnic groups, nations, and states (Kriesberg, 1998a; Lederach, 1998; Bar-Tal, 2000b; Bar-Siman-Tov, this volume).

Since the term *reconciliation* is so widely and diversely defined, before dealing with the topic one needs to clarify in what sense one is using it (Kriesberg, 1998a; Bar-Tal, 2000b). A working definition of this term that will be used in this study is as follows: *Reconciliation is a cluster of cognitive and emotional processes through which individuals, groups, societies, and states come to accept relationships of cooperation, concession, and peace in situations of former conflict* (for related definitions and discussions of this term, see Kriesberg, 1998a, this volume; Lederach, 1998; Saunders, 1999; Bar-Tal, 2000b; Bar-Tal and Bennink, this volume; Bar-Siman-Tov, this volume). Reconciliation, in other words, comprises psychological processes and the forming of relationships that must accompany political and structural processes in the transition from conflict to peace (Lederach, 1998; Kelman, 1999a, this volume; Saunders, 1999; Bar-Tal, 2000b; Bar-Tal and Bennink, this volume; Bar-Siman-Tov, this volume).

Such a definition of reconciliation still leaves two questions to be addressed:

1. To what psychological processes does the term actually refer?
2. What conditions are necessary for this psychological transition from conflict to peace to occur (Kriesberg, 1998a)?

Descriptions of the psychological processes involved in reconciliation point to emotional, spiritual, and psychodynamic components of forgiveness; a reaching beyond past grievances; and an acknowledgment or taking of responsibility for harm done to the other in the past (Lederach, 1998; Minow, 1998; Azar et al., 1999; Staub, 2000). Other descriptions focus on more cognitive aspects such as belief and attitude change as well as increased readiness for cooperation, peaceful relations, and concession making (Kelman, 1999a; Mi'ari, 1999; Bar-Tal, 2000b; I. Maoz, 2000b; Bar-Siman-Tov, this volume). The necessary conditions for reconciliation include forgiving, taking responsibility for harms done and making reparations for them (Lederach, 1998; Azar et al., 1999; Minow, 1998; Staub, 2000), and changing the allocation of resources to one that the involved parties will perceive as socially just (Kriesberg, 1998a).

However, there are also more minimalistic formulations of reconciliation, according to which it consists of an increased readiness for cooperation or peaceful relations with the other side, without explicitly requiring deeper emotional transformations or a structural change in the status quo (Bar-Tal, 2000b; I. Maoz, 2000b; Bar-Siman-Tov, this volume). Here I will use a minimalistic definition of reconciliation as a readiness for transition to a more peaceful relationship based on cooperation. In more formalistic terms of game theory, I will regard reconciliation as a psychological willingness for transition from conflictual interaction defined as Defect-Defect to a more cooperative relationship of Cooperation-Cooperation.

Within the range of psychological processes involved in reconciliation, I will focus here on psychological-cognitive aspects. Specifically, this refers to the way in which our subjective construal of the sociopolitical reality affects our readiness for a peaceful relationship with our former opponent.

Whereas spiritual, emotional, and psychodynamic aspects of reconciliation (as well as cultural, religious, and historical ones) have been the subject of considerable theorizing and research (M. Ross, 1993a, 1995, this volume; Bar-On, 1997, 1999; Minow, 1998; Azar et al., 1999; Bargal and Sivan, this volume), there has been little explicit study of cognitive aspects such as the beliefs, attitudes, cognitions, and schemas involved in this transformative process. An outstanding exception is the recent work by Bar-Tal (2000b; Bar-Tal and Bennink, this volume), which investigates societal beliefs, national conflictive ethos, and transformations in these constructs in the evolvement of an ethos of peace. Whereas Bar-Tal deals with transformations in the contents of societal beliefs and national ethos, I focus here on more generalized and formal constructs, that is, mechanisms of subjective construal of social and political information that operate on the level of individuals in conflict and in the transition from conflict to cooperation.

People in conflict hold sets of preconceptions, schemas, assumptions, and categories that affect how they process and understand information related to conflict and its management. I will maintain here that the way in which people subjectively construe events, actions, and behaviors related to conflict and to the transition from conflict to peace can significantly influence their tendency to form a cooperative relationship of reconciliation. (For a related discussion of the crucial role that interpretive frameworks play in conflict situations, see M. Ross, 1995.)

Accordingly, this chapter has two main objectives:

1. To map major cognitive biases and subjective construals of information in conflict situations that can serve as barriers to reconciliation
2. To present cognitive "debiasing" techniques that may help overcome these barriers and shift toward frames that are more conducive to forming a relationship of cooperation and reconciliation.

Cognitive Biases and Subjective Construal between Groups in Conflict as Barriers to Reconciliation

Research on social information processing has documented cognitive, perceptual, and motivational biases that systematically distort our judgments and inferences. By the mid-twentieth century, classic texts in social psychology already emphasized that in interpreting social stimuli people tend to go "beyond the information given" (Bruner, 1957), and that our responses to our social

environment are significantly determined by our subjective perception of i
(Lewin, 1935).

Biases in perception of social or political information have been found t
play an important role in intergroup conflict. Our perception of events, behav
iors, and information in conflict situations is affected both by our previou
experiences, beliefs, and conceptions and by our current hopes, fears, an
needs (L. Ross and Ward, 1996).

Studies of biased construal of information in conflict have generall
stressed the possible contribution of these biases to perpetuating conflict sit
uations. In a sense, these studies elaborate Sadat's famous words about psy
chological barriers that exist between sides in conflict:

> Yet there remains another wall. This wall constitutes a psychological
> barrier between us, a barrier of suspicion . . . of rejection . . . of fear
> . . . of deception . . . a barrier of distorted interpretation of every
> event and statement. Today, through my visit to you, I ask why don't
> we stretch out our hands with faith and sincerity so that together we
> might destroy this barrier? (statement by Egyptian President Anwar
> al-Sadat before the Israeli Knesset, Jerusalem, November 29, 1977)

The phrase "barrier of distorted interpretation of every event and state
ment" has been thoroughly elaborated by researchers on cognitive
psychological dimensions of conflict and its management. This has yielde
definitions and demonstrations of several phenomena of subjective construa
of information that are characteristic of groups in conflict (Bar-Tal and Geva
1986; M. Ross, 1995; L. Ross and Ward, 1996; L. Ross, 2000). Generall
cognitive biases that have been documented between sides in conflict fall int
two broad categories:

1. *Solution-centered biases*. These biases involve the sides' ability to reach
negotiated solution to the dispute between them, and can be generally define
as constituting perceptual barriers to their reaching a mutually acceptabl
agreement. This category includes biases in negotiations such as *optimisti
overconfidence*, the tendency of sides to overrate their chances to survive an
attain their objectives even without continuing the negotiations or arriving a
an agreement with the other side (Neale and Northcraft, 1991; Mnookin an
L. Ross, 1995); and the effect of *framing*, the way in which negotiators fram
their outcomes as gains or losses, which biases negotiators' perceptions an
influences their inclination to arrive at an agreement with the other sid
(Kahneman and Tversky, 1979; Bazerman, 1983). This category also include
biases in evaluation of concessions in conflict, such as the *reactive devaluatio
bias*, which refers to sides' tendency to devalue concessions proposed by th

other side because of the very fact that they have been offered by the opponent (L. Ross, 1995; I. Maoz, 1997).

2. *Relationship-centered biases.* These biases involve the way the sides perceive and relate to each other, and can be generally defined as constituting barriers to the sides perceiving and relating to each other and to each other's positions and actions in a more positive and less unidimensional way. This category includes the following biases in intergroup and conflict situations that will be surveyed here: negative images of the opponent (Silverstein, 1989; Volkan, 1998b), and the ingroup favorability bias (Crabb, 1989).

Although the above two categories are not completely mutually exclusive, and certainly are not independent of each other (that is, one can think of ways in which negative mutual perceptions can also hinder reaching an integrative solution in a conflict [Keltner and Robinson, 1993; Kriesberg, 1998a]), the differentiation between solution-centered biases and relationship-centered ones[1] is useful in terms of defining the main thrust of the different biases, and thus their relevance to reconciliation.

Of these two categories of bias, the one that is more directly relevant to the sides' ability to build a relationship of reconciliation and cooperation is the second, which focuses on how the sides perceive and relate to each other. Although the relationship-centered biases constitute a barrier to conflict resolution, they also constitute, perhaps more importantly, a barrier to reconciliation.[2] Perceiving the other side in a negative, unidimensional way prevents developing more complex and multidimensional, less dichotomous perceptions of both self and other, which is defined as a fundamental requirement for reconciliation (Bar-Tal and Bennink, this volume; Kelman, this volume; Kriesberg, this volume; see also Saunders, 1999).

Recent studies of reconciliation and peace-building have noted that negative images, stereotypes, and prejudice against the other side, which characterize populations in conflict, are strongly resilient and tend to persist among these populations even after formal peace agreements have been reached (Bar-On, 1997, 1999; Rothstein, 1999a; Bar-Tal, 2000b; Bar-Tal and Bennink, this volume; I. Maoz, 2000a, 2000b). Such relationship-centered biases of groups in conflict, when they linger on and accompany the transition to peacemaking and building, can form a major barrier to reconciliation.

We turn now to two types of relationship-centered bias and how they may act as barriers to reconciliation.

Negative Perceptions and Images of Opponents

A basic cognitive bias that operates between groups in conflict and is often sustained in phases of reconciliation is that of negative representations and images of opponents (Bar-On, 1999; Bar-Tal, 2000b). The opponents are perceived as having evil intentions, low morality, and inferior traits (Bar-Tal, 1990). Such perceptions may be manifested, specifically, in the phenomenon of the diabolical image of the opponent (White, 1984) and in the mirror-image phenomenon, where one side's negative images of its opponent reflect, in a mirror image, similar negative images that its opponent has of it.

This phenomenon was first defined in the context of intergroup relations by Bronfenbrenner (1961), in a study dealing with Soviet-American perceptions of each other during the 1960s. The mirror-image phenomenon has also been demonstrated in other conflicts, such as the Arab-Israeli conflict (Haque and Lawson, 1980). Studies have found that each of the sides tends to attribute positive traits to itself and to see itself as moral, fair, and peace-seeking, while attributing negative traits to the opponent and seeing it as immoral, unfair, and aggressive.

In addition to the negative image of the opponent, studies of relations between opposing national and social groups have found consistent biases of negative evaluation of behavior ascribed to the opponent that were manifested in perceptions, judgments, and patterns of attribution (Silverstein, 1989; Silverstein and Flamenbaum, 1989; Hirshberg, 1993).

Studies of U.S.-Soviet relations also found consistent biases involving the use of a double standard, where American students evaluated the same actions as more negative when they were attributed to the Soviets and as less negative when they were attributed to the United States (Oskamp, 1965).

Similar biases were found in the arena of Arab-Israeli relations. In a series of studies by Heradstveit (1974), he interviewed members of the political elites of the two sides to the conflict (members of the Israeli elite and of the Egyptian, Lebanese, and Syrian elites). He found that the sides had a greater tendency to mention and emphasize hostile and extreme behavior of their opponents, on the one hand, with indications of extreme intentions that were low in credibility taken as indicators of the opponent's belligerent intentions in general. On the other hand, the sides belittled the value of positive indications and moderate actions of their opponents, expressing lack of trust in the "real moderacy" of their intentions.

In addition, the respondents showed characteristic self-serving attributional bias in using two different norms of attribution, one toward themselves and one toward their opponents. Whereas they tended to explain their own friendly and moderate behavior in terms of internal traits and their aggressive behavior in terms of external factors, they used an opposite norm of attribution for their opponents. Moderate or friendly behavior of the latter was perceived as imposed on them by the situation and, thus, as temporary and not reflecting their real inclinations, whereas their hostile behavior was attributed to internal, and therefore stable, factors (Heradstveit, 1974).

A similar bias was found in studies by Rosenberg and Wolfsfeld (1977), where Israeli Jews tended to attribute successes and moral acts of their own side to internal factors, while tending to attribute *im*moral acts of Arabs to internal factors. The Arabs, for their part, tended to attribute failures of Israeli Jews to internal factors.

The Ingroup Favorability Bias

Such distortions of perception and attribution are also characterized in the research literature as manifesting the ingroup favorability bias, with identical behaviors of the ingroup and outgroup being perceived, judged, and given explanations that favor the ingroup.

Evidence of ingroup bias was also found in studies focusing on violent or aggressive behavior. Studies in the context of the Arab-Israeli conflict found a tendency to evaluate given violent or aggressive behavior as more grave and less justified when it was attributed to the adversary than when it was attributed to one's own side (Crabb, 1989).

Other studies found attributions that favor the ingroup. Aggressive behavior of a member of an adversary group was attributed to personality factors, whereas aggressive behavior of a member of one's own group was attributed to situational factors (Duncan, 1976).

A relationship of reconciliation requires a complex view of both self and other, in which each side perceives and relates both to the positive and negative aspects of its own as well as the other side's characteristics and behavior (Bar-On, 1999; this volume). The tendency to favor one's own group, which persistently appears in intergroup situations, can sustain and strengthen dichotomous, mutual perceptions of "I am good and you are bad" (Volkan, 1998b; I. Maoz, 2000a), and thus constitutes a fundamental barrier to building a more complex relationship of mutual acknowledgment of identity that is essential to reconciliation (Bar-On, this volume; Kelman, this volume).

We have reviewed perceptual biases and distortions that are characteristic of groups in conflict and that act as a barrier to developing more conciliatory relations. Two major principles or "frames of conflict" (Bar-Tal and Geva, 1986) can be seen as underlying these cognitive biases. The first is the ingroup favorability bias—that is, the tendency to see the ingroup or "my" side in a conflict in a more favorable light than the outgroup. The second is the incompatibility bias (Thompson and Hastie, 1990; Rubin, Pruitt, and Kim, 1994): the construal or framing of the relations between the sides as a situation of win-lose, where the sides' interests, motivations, and claims are totally opposed to each other.

These two frames of conflict are deeply ingrained. They are often transmitted to members of a society from a young age by socialization, and are widely propagated through mechanisms such as the mass media and school textbooks (Bar-Tal, 1990, 2000b, 2001; Bar-Tal and Bennink, this volume). Thus they endure and retain their impact on sides' perceptions, views, and behaviors in phases of peacemaking and peacebuilding, constituting barriers to reconciliation (Bar-On, 1997, 1999; Kelman, 1999a; Rothstein, 1999a; Bar-Tal, 2000b; Bar-Tal and Bennink, this volume).

Now that we have identified ways in which relationship-centered biases and frames of conflict that underlie them pose barriers to reconciliation, the question is how our subjective cognitive construals can help overcome these barriers and promote frames of reconciliation.

Promoting Frames of Reconciliation

Research in political cognition and political communication has demonstrated the power of framing—the manipulation of how events, processes, and issues are presented. Such research has also shown how the political manipulation of meanings, images, and labels can lead to differential framing of conflict situations (L. Ross and Ward, 1996). In recent times such political manipulation, aimed at inducing support or opposition to certain policies, has increasingly been conducted via the media (L. Ross and Ward, 1996; Wolfsfeld, 1997a, 1997b). Thus, depending on the views and interests represented through the media, the same people can be called terrorists or freedom fighters and the same acts can be referred to as murder or self-defense, "violent riots" or "peaceful Intifada," "restrained response" or "the injuring of dozens of civilians." Such manipulation of labels can be effective in influencing political attitudes and behavior (Cohen and Wolfsfeld, 1995; L. Ross and Ward, 1996; Wolfsfeld, 1997b).

Most discussions of manipulative framing by political stakeholders and by the media emphasize the use of meanings and images that ignite and perpetuate conflict and misunderstanding. However, events, processes, and issues can be also framed in a way that encourages cooperation and reconciliation. I turn now to three major frames that studies have shown to promote cooperation and reconciliation.

1. Replacing the Win-Lose Frame with a Win-Win One

The first and most basic cognitive technique involves situational manipulations that replace the typical conflict frame of win-lose with a win-win frame. An especially impressive study in this vein was conducted within the paradigm of the well-known Prisoner's Dilemma game (L. Ross and Ward, 1996).

Participants in this experimental laboratory study were explained the nature of the Prisoner's Dilemma game and its payoff matrix, and were asked to play it. At this phase a simple framing manipulation was introduced. In explaining the nature of the game, the experimenter gave it two different labels: in one experiment (to half of the participants) he labeled it the "Wall Street game"; in the second, the "Community Game." The two experimental conditions were identical in every other respect.

The results showed that the construal manipulation dramatically affected the participants' choice of strategy in the game. When it was labeled the Wall Street game, only about a third of the players chose to cooperate on the first trial, whereas over two-thirds cooperated on the first trial when it was called the Community Game. The effect of the framing manipulation here was dramatic, influencing both players' perceptions of the situation they were in and their strategic choices for style of interaction (L. Ross and Ward, 1996).

People who live in actual situations of intractable conflict (Kriesberg, 1998b; Bar-Tal, 2000b), however, may have deeply ingrained frames of win-lose or zero-sum. In such cases, attempts to impose via the mass media, political discourse, or dialogue such frames such as "cooperation," "reconciliation," or "the new Middle East" may meet resistance and rejection when these notions actually contradict the life experience, knowledge, and emotions of the target audience. For example, long-term commitments to being victims in a conflict (Bar-Tal, 2001; Bar-On, this volume) cannot be changed by a simple manipulation of frames.

Thus, to be more relevant to overcoming barriers to reconciliation, techniques should presumably focus more substantially on *existing* negative perceptions the sides have of each other and of the relationship between them, and on changing these perceptions toward ones more conducive to reconciliation. We will now look at two such techniques.

2. Mutual Disclosure of the Sides' Views

A more ambitious attempt at changing subjective construals of conflict situations and promoting frames of cooperation and reconciliation was made in studies of an interesting bias of parties to a conflict, the false polarization bias. These studies used the technique of mutual disclosure of the sides' ideological views.

Our ingroup or egocentric bias tends to make it difficult for us to relate to the other side's perspective (L. Ross and Ward, 1996). If we think our side is better than the other side, we also tend to see our own views as more objective and less biased than the other side's. Thus, an interesting derivative of the ingroup bias (as well as of the incompatibility bias) is the false polarization bias, where each side regards its own views as moderate and realistic and the other side's as extreme and diametrically opposed (Keltner and Robinson, 1993; L. Ross, 2000).

This bias was documented in a series of studies (described in Keltner and Robinson, 1993) that examined parties' views in disputes over several ideological issues such as abortion, the death penalty, and multicultural education. Parties both presented their own views of issues and assessed the views of "typical" or "average" members of the opposing side. Two kinds of misperception emerged. First, even though disagreement was limited to certain issues within the controversial topic, the sides assumed that their differences permeated all aspects of the question. Second, the sides were found to attribute ideological extremism and bias to the opponents, who in reality (based on data collected from each side) were usually more moderate than such judgments indicated. Thus, in ideological, value-based disputes, sides believe that their differences encompass entire belief systems and fundamental values, and are firmly convinced that only their own views are based on reason and evidence (Bar-Tal and Geva, 1986; L. Ross and Ward, 1996).

The false polarization bias, like other kinds of subjective construal in conflict, acts as a potent barrier to reconciliation, and can do so in two major ways (Keltner and Robinson, 1993). First, sides that assume their opponents are extremist are less likely to understand the opponent's actual views—an understanding that is important in enabling a transition to a more cooperative relationship of reconciliation (Keltner and Robinson, 1993; also see the chapters by Bar-Tal and Bennink, Kelman, and Kriesberg, this volume). Second, false polarization can also be expected to increase mutual recrimination, mistrust, and hostility and thus prevent shifting to reconciliation.

How can our cognitions and perceptions of each other in conflict be moderated so as to counteract the false polarization effect and enable a shift to understanding and cooperation? The mutual disclosure of each side's views is one way to alter the conflict frame of polarization.

Keltner and Robinson (1993) assumed that if sides were brought to disclose their actual ideological views to each other, this would help them become more aware of possible areas of agreement and less inclined to attribute extremism and bias to each other. In a series of experimental studies, negotiators with strong ideological differences disclosed to each other both their actual views and their beliefs about the other side's views (see the next subsection) before attempting to reach agreement on crucial issues. It was found that opposing sides that had made these disclosures reached more substantial agreement with each other. But perhaps even more important in terms of reaching reconciliation, they attributed less extremism and felt less antagonistic other toward each other than sides that had not made such disclosures.

The disclosure-of-views technique, however, can be less effective in real-life interactions, in which additional social factors related to the intergroup situation may come into play (L. Ross, 2000). During discussions between groups in conflict, participants who hold more complex or ambivalent views of the situation may be reticent to speak. This, in turn, may perpetuate misperceptions such as the false polarization bias (L. Ross, 2000). Alternately, participants, when addressing the other side, may mainly seek to defend their own side's position rather than exposing doubts or complexities in their beliefs that may make them seem weaker. Such dynamics work against a mutual disclosure of views that might counteract false polarization, and may indeed reinforce mutual assumptions of extremism and intractability (L. Ross, 2000).

Following this reasoning, a second and more sophisticated cognitive technique of counteracting false polarization has been developed.

3. Mutual Disclosure of Beliefs about the Other Side's Views

In a series of studies by Puccio and L. Ross (cited in L. Ross, 2000), the researchers compared two possible techniques of counteracting the false polarization bias. In one experimental condition, participants from each group expressed and defended their own side's views on the issue in dispute. In the second condition, participants from each side had to tell each other what they considered to be the *other side's* best arguments; the researchers assumed that this would lead the parties to reveal complexities and uncertainties in their views that they might normally conceal. Thus, the researchers predicted that via this technique the sides would gain more accurate presentations of each other's views.

The results confirmed these predictions. Whereas participants who expressed their own side's positions showed the expected false polarization effect of overestimating the scope of disagreement, participants who expressed the other side's positions only slightly overestimated this. Furthermore, the sides perceived each other as less extreme after each had articulated and even acknowledged the arguments of the other, so that they changed their attitudes and related to each other in a way more conducive to the process of reconciliation.

Conclusion

This chapter presented relationship-centered biases; defined two major cognitive frames that underlie them and guide the processing of social and political information in situations of conflict, namely, the ingroup favorability bias and the incompatibility bias; and described how these biases and frames may act as barriers to reconciliation.

Next, it discussed three ways in which subjective construals can be used to counteract these biases and frames and thereby to promote frames that support reconciliation: (1) framing or labeling an interactive situation as one of cooperation rather than conflict; (2) having sides disclose their actual views to each other; and (3) having sides disclose their beliefs about each other's views.

The consideration of these debiasing techniques leads us to the connection between approaches to reconciliation such as the present one, which focus on cognitive factors and subjective construals, and "deeper" and more holistic approaches that relate to psychodynamic and identity-construction aspects of reconciliation. Of the three above-mentioned techniques for counteracting conflict frames, the second and third can be viewed as methods of helping opposing sides develop more complex representations of each other (Kelman, 1998c, 1999a, this volume).

Identity constructions of sides in a conflict tend to be monolithic and dichotomic, with one's own side construed as good and just and the other as evil and unjust (Bar-Tal, 1990; Lederach, 1998; Volkan, 1998b; Bar-On, 1999). Thus, mutual disclosure of views and of beliefs about the other side's views can bring the sides to more complex representations of each other and of the relationship between them (Bar-Tal, 2000b; Bar-Tal and Bennink, this volume). Both the more "mechanistic," social-cognitive approaches and more holistic approaches (M. Ross, 1995; Bar-On, 1997, 1999) regard such complexity of mutual perceptions as a necessary factor in the transition to reconciliation.

ACKNOWLEDGMENTS   The preparation of this chapter was supported by a grant from the Leonard Davis Institute of the Hebrew University of Jerusalem and by a grant from the Israel Foundation Trustees (1998–2000). Correspondence about this chapter should be directed to Ifat Maoz, Department of Communication and Journalism, Hebrew University of Jerusalem, Mt. Scopus, Jerusalem, Israel; e-mail: msifat@ pluto.mscc.huji.ac.il.

NOTES

1. There are interesting similarities between the relationship-solution differentiation suggested here and another differentiation that is prevalent in the social sciences between process and product.

2. In the present context, conflict resolution is defined as reaching a mutually agreed solution at the formal, official level of leaders and policymakers on both sides. Reconciliation concerns a deeper process of change in relationship and perceptions (for a discussion of the change process required in reconciliation, see Bargal and Sivan, this volume) at the grassroots level, encompassing the broader populations on both sides (Bar-Tal and Bennink, this volume). For a comprehensive analytical discussion of the relationship between conflict resolution and reconciliation, see Bar-Siman-Tov, this volume.

II

Will the Parties Conciliate or Refuse? The Triangle of Jews, Germans, and Palestinians

Dan Bar-On

The concept of conciliation[1] represents a modern version of the ancient, prescriptive Judeo-Christian prophecy: *Ve'gar ze'ev im keves* ("And the wolf shall lie down with the lamb"). In our efforts to resolve protracted violent conflicts, however, we need to adjust prescriptive thinking about peaceful coexistence, forgiveness, and conciliation by relating to specific cultural and historical human conditions and social-psychological processes of working through an identity of victimhood.

In this chapter the concepts of forgiveness and conciliation will be discussed from a historically and socially contextualized, psychodynamic standpoint. Two related contexts will be discussed: the German-Jewish situation after the Holocaust, and the Israeli-Palestinian conflict. In neither of these contexts have forgiveness and conciliation gained momentum.

As we shall see, the concept of conciliation involves both conceptual and practical complexities (Bar-Tal, 2000b). The social sciences have borrowed this concept from normative religious discourse, in which there was no need to account for the variety of specific conditions that the social sciences address. In the religious discourse, the ancient prophecy "And the wolf shall lie down with the lamb" sounds like "successful" conciliation. Yet when one applies this normative metaphor to the complex reality of the social sciences, the concept presumably reflects liberal thinking by the "wolves." They are powerful enough and have other sources of food supply; hence, they can give up the idea of hunting the lambs. But what do we know about how the lambs feel about this idea? Would they ever feel safe "lying down" with the wolves? What if the wolves were to suddenly change their minds? What security do the lambs have? Or, alternatively, when the wolves consider lying down with the lambs and falling asleep in their arms, how safe do they feel? Perhaps the lambs are only "wolves in sheep's clothing"; perhaps the wolves internalized something about the "lambs" a long time ago that now leads them to fear them as wolves. Now we are in the domain of the social sciences, having left idealized prophecy, and prescriptive-normative ways of looking at conciliation, behind.

From its historically and socially contextualized, psychodynamic perspective, this chapter will consider the following issues in regard to certain human "wolves" and "lambs":

1. Why are the "lambs" unwilling to conciliate with the "wolves"? Specifically, why were the Jews unwilling to conciliate with the Germans after the Holocaust? Does the cultural and religious gap between Christians (especially Germans) and Jews in regard to conciliation and forgiveness account for this refusal?
2. In light of their own refusal to conciliate with the Germans, why do Israeli Jews expect that the Palestinians will be willing to conciliate with them?

Following the macrolevel analysis, I will present a case study in which the parties in question (Germans, Jews, as well as Palestinians and others) tried to work through the contradictions involved in conciliation. I will also discuss the possible relationships between the micro- and macrolevels.

Jewish and German-Christian Perspectives on Conciliation after the Holocaust

We know of many cases[2] in which German Christians approached Jews sincerely, asking for conciliation and forgiveness over the Holocaust. Jews who were approached, however, felt offended by this request (Wiesenthal, 1997; Bar-On, 2000), and this seemed to reflect, in part, different approaches to forgiveness and conciliation in Christianity and Judaism.

The Holocaust was an earthquake for the Jewish people. It was, after all, the most extreme event of persecution and annihilation ever conducted against any human collective and specifically against them as Jews, a third of the Jewish population perishing in it. Some Jewish thinkers regard this earthquake as part of the Christian anti-Semitic tradition of persecution and humiliation going back centuries (Wiesel, 1995b). The only event comparable in magnitude, but still far from the totality of the Shoah, was the Spanish Inquisition and expulsion that occurred 500 years earlier. During the Inquisition, however, one could escape the Jewish fate by converting to Christianity and even return, if only clandestinely, to Judaism a few generations later (the people who did so being known as Marranos). No such option existed during the Shoah.

One of the first intellectuals to react to the Holocaust as an earthquake was Adorno. As early as 1950, he made the famous statement that after the Holocaust there could be no more poetry. A direct demand, however, of "not to forgive and not to forget" was expressed in Simon Wiesenthal's *The Sunflower* (1997) and in Elie Wiesel's words at the Auschwitz memorial in 1995:[3]

> Although we know that God is merciful, please God, do not have mercy on those who created this place. God of forgiveness—do not forgive the murderers of Jewish children here. Do not forgive the murderers and their accomplices. . . . God, merciful God, do not have mercy on those who had no mercy on Jewish children.

In the Christian tradition, such a plea would be viewed as a provocation. How could a Jewish leader of Wiesel's stature ask God not to forgive when, according to Christian tradition, God forgives all human beings even before they seek repentance (Miller-Fahrenholz, 1996)? Perhaps Wiesel's statement should be seen as manifesting the fact that the Holocaust had opened old wounds between Jews and Christians that had never properly healed. Some Christian leaders asked: Are the Jews exaggerating their plight after the Holocaust as part of their stubborn refusal to conciliate with the Christian world after so many years? Perhaps this attitude among Christians, in turn, was linked to the earlier notion that the Jews should continue to be held accountable for the death of Jesus (Rittner and Roth, 2000). At the same time, Jewish leaders questioned Christian accountability in regard to the Nazis. Specifically, they asked to what extent Pope Pius XII, during the Nazi regime, knew about the extermination of the Jews and why he did not act against it—in sharp contrast to the Church's action against the Nazis' euthanasia program for German non-Jews. Had the Church, these Jewish leaders asked, properly addressed this aspect of its coresponsibility, or was it continuing to send mixed messages? These unanswered questions form an abyss that has been difficult for Jews and Christians to bridge since Auschwitz (Rittner and Roth, 2000).

The idea of bringing Jews and Germans together to try and bridge this abyss was initially rejected by the postwar Jewish religious leadership (Dorff, 1992). Dorff stresses that according to the Jewish tradition, no *primary concil-iation* of the first generation was possible after the war.[4] The perpetrators and survivors of the Holocaust would never be able to honestly confront one an-other, especially since so few people had survived the Nazi extermination cam-paign and since most of the Nazi perpetrators had not assumed responsibility or expressed remorse for their atrocious acts. According to Dorff, however, the descendants of the victims and the victimizers, especially those who had *worked through* the silence and acknowledged the traumatic or atrocious part of their family biography, could test the possibility of a *secondary conciliation*.

Dorff (1992) considers whether, according to Jewish tradition and law, there is a possibility of conciliation or forgiveness between the Catholic Church and the Jews or between Jews and Germans after the Holocaust. Unlike more conservative Jewish leaders, Dorff rejects the notion that this is an act the Gentiles must accomplish by themselves, as well as the idea that the descen-dants of the victims have no right to be part of a conciliation process on behalf of their parents. In this regard, Dorff, as a Jewish religious leader, broke a post-Holocaust taboo. In his view, children of survivors have a right to act on their own, independent of their parents' perspective: "if we see ourselves as part of an extended corporate entity known as the Jewish people, then we, as its present members, do have the right (indeed, the responsibility) to act on behalf of the group—past, present and future—in this issue as in all others" (209).

Dorff asserts that what should determine Jews' willingness to engage in the process of secondary conciliation is the quality of the acts and feelings of the German people and the Church: "specifically, evidence of recognition of the act as a violation, admission of guilt, remorse, efforts to seek forgiveness and steps to insure that the act will not happen again" (208). Feeling the weight of the collective responsibility he has undertaken, Dorff summarizes his ar-gument:

> Shall we forgive? That is a matter the Jewish community must still discuss. It will depend, in large measure, upon continued evidence of a Christian (German) desire to repent. A positive Jewish response to this will probably not take place in one single moment or be uni-versally offered by all Jews. Forgiveness will rather be achieved little by little through joint word and action, just as personal forgiveness usually is. . . . Whether this will happen remains to be seen. . . . at least in a secondary form of forgiveness, it is logically possible for us to do so. (214)

Dorff is more open than other Jewish leaders on the question of working through the Holocaust (Bar-On, 1990). He does not, however, address the question of whether the German people should also work through the past for the sake of their own moral and emotional health (Bar-On, 1990). He also does not say whether the encounter between the two groups of descendants will foster a genuine discourse, necessary to establish a new social bond as part of the moral, emotional, and psychological healing process (Bar-On, 2000). As we know, these are usually conditions for successful conciliation in intractable conflicts (Bar-Tal, 2000b).

It is interesting that although the Jews were not willing to forgive and conciliate with the Germans, they rarely engaged in acts of revenge against Germans after the Holocaust, despite the fantasies that survivors of Nazi camps reported having about perpetrating such acts (Bar-On, 2001). A possible explanation is that the Jews did not want to lower themselves to the Nazi oppressors' level of inhumanity. Refraining from revenge made them feel they were "stronger than Hitler," and the "eye for an eye" option seemed to contravene the Jewish tradition and religion. Another possibility, from a psychodynamic perspective, is that aggression does not vanish but is transformed (Bar-On, 2001). According to this view, some of the unretaliated aggression that the Jews internalized from the Nazis (and from previous persecutions throughout the ages, especially in Europe) may later have been collectively displaced against another group, namely, the Palestinians.

This brings us to the interaction between the German-Jewish unresolved past conflict and the Israeli-Palestinian unresolved present conflict, and, specifically, a contradiction involving the Jews' role in this triangle.

The Holocaust and al-Naqba: Related Historical Events, Difficult to Overcome

It is clear that for Jews, the change of context involved in moving from Europe to the Middle East created a dilemma. Many of them felt culturally closer to their previous enemies (especially the Germans), with whom they were not willing to conciliate (and no longer had any common, current context), than toward their new, Arab Middle Eastern neighbors, with whom they were both sharing and struggling over one land (Segev, 1990). Specifically, many survivors of the Shoah had taken refuge in Israel. Despite the survivors' resistance to conciliating with the Germans in regard to the Holocaust, their descendants (as a collective, not necessarily as individuals) now expected the Palestinians to conciliate with them as part of an Israeli-Palestinian peace agreement. What can explain this seeming contradiction? Is it the perceived difference in the magnitude of violence (the Holocaust as compared to the Palestinian plight) that justifies such a disparity in attitude? Is it a matter of total responsibility (of the Germans for the Holocaust) versus shared responsibility (in the case of al-Naqba, the Palestinian "catastrophe")? Or does it have to do with the power asymmetries between Germans and Jews and between Jews and Palestinians, which do not allow the "lambs" to conciliate with the "wolves" and do not impel the "wolves" to seek conciliation with the "lambs" (thus maintaining the status quo of power asymmetry) (I. Maoz, 2000c, 2000d)? Alternatively, the contradiction in question may manifest an identity attribute of assuming permanent victimhood. That is, it may represent the Jews' self-justification and self-definition as victims of both the Germans and the Arabs, which dominates the construction of their identity (Bar-On, 1998).

In this triangle of Germans, Jews, and Palestinians (Bar-On, 2000), then, the Jewish collective that survived the Holocaust is unwilling to forgive and conciliate with the Germans but expects a different attitude among its Palestinians partners in the current conflict, whereas the Palestinians are unwilling to meet that expectation. Palestinians say that for them to conciliate with the Israeli Jews, the latter must accept the moral responsibility for their part in al-Naqba and the creation of the Palestinian refugee problem in 1948. For Israeli Jews, such recognition represents a loss of the moral basis of their national existence in the Middle East. According to this logic, if they were to accept such responsibility they also would have to accept the Palestinian demand for the refugees' right of return to their land and homes within Israel, which would mean, among other things, a potential influx of millions of refugees into Israel that would make the Jews a minority in their own state. In other words, the Palestinians would both get their own state in the West Bank and Gaza and become the majority within Israel. Israeli Jews perceive this as a nightmare in which the Palestinians strive, in stages, to drive the Jews "into the sea." One way this nightmare is fantasized is that the Jews are forced to give up the homes that were taken over from Palestinians, who had lived in them before 1948, and become refugees again in their own land (Litvak-Hirsch, in preparation).

This construction could account for the fact that a society composed mainly of (Jewish) refugees repressed, for such a long time, the plight of their fellow (Palestinian) refugees, since the Palestinian claim was perceived as a threat to the Jews' independent existence, survival, and morality. In other words, on the one hand, the Israeli Jews could not cope with the implications of the Palestinian demand that past wrongdoing be recognized. On the other hand, they are asking at present for a "final" conciliation with the Palestinians as part of the peace process.

The contradiction between the Jewish expectation of conciliation with the Arabs and their refusal to conciliate with the Germans has a long history, of course. The United Nations recognized Israel as the Jewish state in 1947, shortly after World War II. In a sense, the United Nations accepted a certain responsibility for ensuring that the survivors of the Holocaust would have a national home of their own (Segev, 1990). This decision, however, had very painful consequences for many Palestinians. Not accepting the historical justification, their leaders and the leaders of the Arab states rejected the UN decision. As a result, many Palestinians had to flee their homes or were driven from them during the 1948 and 1967 wars (Morris, 1996, 1999). Over the years, Israeli Jews claimed that they had been prepared to accept the 1947 Partition Plan and that it was the Arabs who had rejected it and declared war on Israel. According to the official Israeli standpoint, the refugee problem was one of the unfortunate outcomes of this Arab refusal. Therefore, Israel did not see itself as morally responsible for creating this problem and was not willing to take sole responsibility for solving it.

Palestinians, however, saw themselves as victims of the constant influx of Jewish immigration to their land, and of Western international support for that influx (fueled by the West's guilt over its inactivity during the Holocaust). Later, they came to regard themselves as victims of Israel as a Jewish state. Overall, they viewed themselves as direct and indirect victims of acts of violence in Europe for which they were not responsible (Bar-On, 2001). They defined the 1948 war as al-Naqba, viewing it as their "own holocaust." In political disputes, they tried to downplay or ignore the Holocaust as being irrelevant, from their perspective, to the Middle East conflict. Only recently has there been some change among their intellectuals in this regard (Sarghie and Bashir, 2000). However, the Palestinians have felt all along that the Jews in general and the Israeli Jews in particular have been using the Holocaust to justify their moral claims to the establishment of Israel and to taking over the Palestinians' homes and land. Thus, according to the Palestinian viewpoint, the Israeli Jews have ignored their plight, which Israel, among others, caused during the 1948 and 1967 wars.

In my own view, now that the Israeli-Palestinian peace process has reached a critical phase, the issues of coresponsibility, forgiveness, and conciliation have become the most crucial. Israeli Jews are now the ones who expect forgiveness and conciliation to take place as part of the top-down peace agreement that will end the "hundred years of conflict." The Palestinians are the ones who resist this, similar to the way the Holocaust survivors resisted earlier German appeals for conciliation after the Nazi era. This is because the Palestinians feel that the Israeli Jews do not acknowledge their own moral responsibility for the plight of the Palestinian refugees (Rouhana, in press).

An interesting argument recently presented by Rouhana (in press) links the Palestinians' resistance to conciliation to the asymmetry of power relations between the parties and the social-justice aspect of the conflict. Rouhana maintains that since the Israelis are the stronger party in the conflict, their narrative about its origins and what constitutes a socially just solution to it has become the ultimate truth for them and the dominant version of the conflict and its solution. The Israeli Jews have not, however, acknowledged their share of responsibility for the injustice inflicted on the Palestinians, especially in 1948. Israeli Jews still "instinctively" view such acknowledgment as a threat to their independent existence, because of the claim of a right of return for the Palestinian refugees. Rouhana suggests that so long as this link between asymmetrical power relations and the dominant Israeli Jewish version of social justice in the conflict prevails, no conciliation process will be possible from the Palestinians' perspective.

More broadly, the asymmetry of power relations is related, in a complex way, to the differences between cultures (Western and non-Western) and between religions (Islam, Judaism, and Christianity). As Irani and Funk (2000) assert:

> Although individuals from non-Western cultures often consider Western assumptions about conflict and conflict resolution provocative, they may also find them difficult to accept and apply in their own circumstances. First of all, non-Western students of conflict resolution are likely to be highly sensitive to the general lack of correspondence between the principles and practices espoused by Western conflict resolution professionals and the actual conduct of Western nation-states (primarily the United States) in the international system. If Western conflict resolution specialists are unable or unwilling to diagnose and critique the actual conflict behaviors of their home countries, their message may not be regarded as credible, particularly in societies that have recently experienced fragmentation and violence. Second, there are genuine cultural barriers to the widespread diffusion of Western assumptions about conflict and conflict resolution in non-Western contexts. (9)

Irani and Funk (2000) suggest that the asymmetrical power relations between a Western society and a non-Western one account for part of the Arabs' resistance to conciliating with the Israeli Jews. They also propose the more traditional Islamic concepts of *sulha* (settlement) and *musalaha* (reconciliation) as ways of helping the Palestinians approach the issues in the conflict. It is interesting that the religious aspects of these concepts in Islam and Judaism are similar, while differing from those of Christianity. In both Islam and Judaism, the rights of the victims, especially the powerless, are a major issue; it is only they who can decide whether to accept requests for forgiveness by the perpetrators. Forgiveness asked from God on days of atonement is not a substitute for such necessary interpersonal processes.

From this standpoint, then, the difficulties in conciliating between Israeli Jews and Palestinians are associated with the current asymmetry of power and the historical dispute over the issues of social justice. This dispute goes back to the origins of the conflict and each side's subsequent justifications for its use of power and violence (Rouhana, in press). A major impediment to creating a genuine dialogue between Israeli Jews and Palestinians is the difficulty of both sides in giving up their construction of themselves as the victim of the other side (Bar-On, 2000).

Sharing Storytelling between Parties in Conflict: Acknowledgment and Working Through

We now turn to a small-group process that can be used in cases where parties are not ready to forgive and conciliate with one another for reasons such as those in the complex situation described above. Specifically, I shall focus on a microsetting of a group process that tried to address and work through the various levels of the conflicts and painful memories among Germans, Jews, Palestinians, and others.

When it began in 1992, the TRT (To Reflect and Trust) group initially brought together descendants of Holocaust survivors from the United States and Israel and descendants of Nazi perpetrators from Germany (Bar-On, 1995b, 2000). The group process that evolved was based on the participants' sharing of personal stories, which helped them work through the abyss between them. What is interesting in the present context, the group rejected the concept of conciliation altogether and instead chose the terms *trust and reflection* to describe the group's work. Moreover, the issue of forgiveness never came up in the group discussions. A possible explanation is that conciliation and forgiveness must be worked through by individuals rather than in interaction with others. Over the generations, the concepts of conciliation and forgiveness have become fraught with deep religious connotations, fostering differences and social exclusion rather than bridging of differences and social inclusion (Irani and Funk, 2000). Therefore, these concepts had to be bypassed rather than addressed in intercultural peacebuilding activities (Bar-On, 1995b).

The First Phase: Developing a Common Emotional and Conceptual Language across the Abyss

After some years of intensive work with descendants of survivors in Israel (Bar-On, 1995a), and after interviewing descendants of Nazi perpetrators in Germany (Bar-On, 1989), a group setting was formed in which both these groups could face one another and initiate an open dialogue. The questions addressed were as follows: Could they face each other genuinely? Could this meeting help each party work through aspects that they could not work through in their separate, "tribal ego" settings? Through such an encounter, would a common agenda emerge that transcended the separate agendas of each side?

Over six years, six encounters occurred between a group of eight descendants of Holocaust perpetrators and a group of five American and four Israeli descendants of Holocaust survivors, as well as a Jewish child-survivor who lived in Germany. The meetings rotated among Germany, Israel, and the United States and usually lasted four to five days. Except for the first encounter, which was devoted to getting acquainted mainly by listening to each other's personal stories, the scheduling was done by the group itself and the content of the meetings continued to focus on those stories, though many issues were intensively discussed.

During this joint effort at working through, a kind of common emotional and conceptual language developed, beyond the separate "languages" that characterized the participants' original communities. This development also created a dilemma for the two groups of descendants, who had to struggle with the question: Shall we become an isolated sect, since the communities we belong to cannot yet cope with our mutual experience, or will we have to give up our common experience so as to remain active members of our communities? Significantly, the groups chose to go in neither of these directions, and instead were willing to pay the price of maintaining the tension between these options, with support from the group, while hoping that their communities would gradually move closer to each other. This may account for the fact that the TRT process is a slow and intense one.

Let us look at how the process unfolded.[5] In the beginning, members of both groups shared their own experiences—that is, how they traced the aftereffects of the Holocaust within their own lives. For some this was a daily struggle that was accompanied by sleeplessness, fears, and uncontrollable re-actions. Often these phenomena were associated with the silence, repression, or other difficult reactions of their parents. In many cases, acknowledgment of a personal relationship to the Holocaust was accompanied by a strong feeling of estrangement, both internal (from oneself) and external (from one's social surroundings). Generally it took many years to clarify and comprehend how these aspects of estrangement were associated with one's personal relationship to the Holocaust.

The Jewish members of the group suffered, first of all, from physical uprootedness, their parents having immigrated to the United States or Israel after the Holocaust. This was usually accompanied by psychological uproot-edness, associated with the fact that their parents could not overcome the loss of so many family members and had difficulty integrating themselves into the new society. The German members of the group shared this feeling of psy-chological uprootedness, but for other reasons: they felt that because of the atrocities committed by their parents, their roots had become corrupted and untenable. Thus, like the descendants of the survivors, they felt a need to develop new roots.

Struggling with the feelings of estrangement and uprootedness brought up the question: Can I allow myself to live my own life, neither dependent nor counterdependent to that of my parents? This was, indeed, a major issue for members of both groups. Whereas for the Jewish descendants separation from their parents was more difficult (the latter tending to lean on them emotionally in the late stages of their lives), the descendants of perpetrators tended to counterreact and distance themselves from their Nazi parents, thereby suffer-ing an emotional void (Berger and Berger, 2001). This problem became more severe over time, especially when the parents aged and the objective need to care for them became a daily reality.

Members of both groups struggled daily with dreams of death, bearing names of dead people (especially among the descendants of survivors), and fantasies of sacrificing themselves for a human cause (especially among the descendants of perpetrators). As one member of the group put it: "We talk about our feelings, emotions, and ideas, but they all concern the dead people who are in the back of our minds." Perhaps not by coincidence, some members of the group belonged to the helping professions; they may have been trying to give a special meaning to their lives under the shadow of death.

Members of the group could, quite easily, establish an open dialogue with the victim in themselves. This was easy for both descendants of Jewish victims and descendants of Nazi victimizers. But it was much more difficult for both groups to identify and enter into an open dialogue with the victimizer within themselves and to let the two "figures" talk with each other. Eventually it became clear that we all have this potential role within ourselves, the "wolf" under the "sheep's" clothing, and that only by openly acknowledging and entering into a dialogue with it can its uncontrolled potential be reduced in future, unexpected situations. After this realization, a new issue was defined: once we accept and let go of these two roles of victim and victimizer within ourselves— what is left? Who are we if not defined through these roles? This in fact suggested the beginning of a new process of identity construction that was not based on a negation of the other (Bar-On, 1999).

The issues associated with identity construction brought up the question, Who suffered more? This was a new issue that involved the scaling of suffering, heroism, and power. In the group context, it became evident that we all tend to create a subjective scale of suffering. Perhaps, when extreme suffering causes us to feel helpless, scaling it gives us a sense of control. One cannot grasp the experiences of parents during the Holocaust, but scaling helps one live with this fact. Something similar happened when the topics of heroism or power were discussed: it is much more difficult to relate to the experiences of the other as just being *different*, not more or less. Thus, an issue emerged for the group: how to maintain the legitimacy of grasping the difference without scaling it, which in itself creates unnecessary pain and humiliation for others.

It was significant that members of the group developed feelings of mutual trust and respect, suggesting a new symmetry between parties in the dialogue. However, this by no means erased the asymmetry that people felt regarding their parents, that is, between being victimizers and victims. The symmetry and asymmetry were difficult to maintain simultaneously, but it was important to seek a way to navigate between them. Such navigating was associated with the relationship between the past and the present.

Through the group experience, it became clear that the outcome of the process was not to forget or be done with the past, but to find new ways to *live with it*, perhaps ways that were more conscious but also less threatening and self-destructive. In working through such massive trauma one does not end it or let go of it; the Holocaust will always be there, will always be a presence. However, its negative impact on the lives of both descendants of Holocaust survivors and descendants of Nazi perpetrators can be reduced through such conscious working-through processes, by groups as well as individuals. In a sense these issues were the group's main "product," which could be presented as its way of working through forgiveness and conciliation rather than talking about them.

The Second Phase: Bringing in Practitioners from Current Conflicts

In 1998, the group decided to invite practitioners who work with victims and victimizers in current conflicts (South Africa, Northern Ireland, and Palestinians and Israelis) and test whether the TRT group process was relevant to their settings. As in the former process, the larger TRT encounters (1998–2000) involved storytelling that fostered trust, reflection, and the inclusion of the other, rather than explicit discussions on conciliation and forgiveness.

The question that remained open was, To what extent may one generalize from the TRT group process to other, current situations in which conciliation efforts are occurring between populations during or after conflict? It was clear that each conflict setting had its own "biography" that had to be carefully studied and taken into account. Still, we assumed that such dialogue between members of the opposing sides could be a step toward reaching the deeper issues that political, legal, or financial measures, or even time alone, may be inadequate to address. The TRT experience also suggested that the process of conciliation is intergenerational, and cannot be culminated, at least in the case of severe conflicts, in the life span of a single generation.

It is still too early to summarize this experience.[6] There are, however, some first signs of the process being applied to the current conflicts. For example, in Northern Ireland, TRT members initiated a seminar based on the TRT model (Hetherington et al., 2000), which included British bereaved relatives of British soldiers and British ex-combatants, together with Protestant and Catholic representatives who had actively participated in the "troubles," including ex-prisoners from both sides. Another example is the establishment of PRIME (Peace Research Institute in the Middle East) by Israeli and Palestinian TRT members (Adwan and Bar-On, 2001a, 2001b). In addition, a Jewish-Palestinian student group was initiated at Ben-Gurion University in 2000–01 that was based on collecting family stories going back two generations; the facilitators were Fatma Kassem and the author, who drew on their experience with the TRT group. However, more time will be needed to evaluate the results.

Conciliation and Forgiveness between the Micro and Macro Levels

When and why do people refuse to conciliate? As we saw, when Germans, as part of their Christian tradition, asked Jews for forgiveness and conciliation after the Holocaust, the Jews refused, reflecting their own religion and tradition (Dorff, 1992).[7] The issue of willingness became even more complicated when we asked why the Israeli Jews expect the Palestinians to conciliate with them when they themselves have not agreed to do so with the Germans. According to an explanation focusing on asymmetric power relations and social justice, the more powerful party, the Israeli Jews, seek to maintain their social-justice perspective about the origin of the conflict; whereas the Palestinians are not willing to conciliate with the Israeli Jews so long as their own perspective on the injustice done to them, and the Israeli Jewish responsibility for it, is not acknowledged and accepted (Rouhana, in press). Thus, both parties remain committed to their dichotomized constructions of the other side as perpetrators and their own side as victims.

Following this macrolevel analysis, we considered a microsetting of dialogue groups in which different expectations about conciliation among Germans, Jews, Palestinians, and others were addressed and worked through.

The question remains, however, of how the micro-approach can be applied to the macrosocial level. On the one hand, the macro-analysis did not help us work through the deeper processes involved in the refusal to conciliate, at least not in the German-Jewish-Palestinian triangle. On the other hand, the learning achieved in the microsetting cannot easily be translated into macroprocesses. The case study of the TRT group showed that microsettings are important for identifying undercurrents, working through painful emotions, and experimenting with metaphors and verbal expressions that are necessary for understanding the macroprocess. One cannot, however, simply duplicate the TRT process thousands of times. Perhaps the learning achieved in the TRT group can tell us about the symbolic, metaphorical stratum that will have to be addressed on the macrolevel so as to reach successful conciliation. Some attempts on the symbolic level of social justice have been made in other intractable conflicts—for example, the South African Truth and Reconciliation Commission. There, the fact that both parties belonged to the same church had both a symbolic and a practical significance that facilitated the process. For example, it was no coincidence that Desmond Tutu was chosen to chair the Commission. Still, the process required much experimentation and learning in dialogue groups before the macrosetting was designed and put into practice, and even then its success was only partial (Boraine and Levy, 1995). We cannot say for certain whether a similar process could be designed for enhancing an Israeli-Palestinian conciliation process. If such a possibility is explored, the TRT setting could help suggest what sorts of issues should be approached in such a process.

Still, the problem remains: What one can accomplish in microsettings if dialogue groups cannot be directly transferred to the macropolitical level. This may, then, be the challenge of researchers, educators, and practitioners in the coming years: how to translate microsetting results to the macrolevel as part of the effort to conciliate between parties in intractable conflicts (Montville, 2001).

NOTES

1. In this chapter I will use only the term *conciliation* and not *reconciliation*, since the latter assumes that there was an earlier phase of amity between the parties in conflict. This is clearly not the case in some of the intractable conflicts of our time in the Middle East, unless one goes far back to medieval times (Montville, 2001).

2. This chapter is based on the author's extensive research on families of Holocaust survivors (Bar-On, 1995a), his interviews with descendants of Nazi perpetrators (Bar-On, 1989), and his work with the TRT group (see below), made up of descendants from both sides (Bar-On, 1995b, 2000).

3. Although Wiesel includes a slightly different version of this prayer in his memoir, *And the Sea is Never Full* (2000), it is taken from the *New York Times* (January 27, 1995). This version is corroborated by what was reported in the *Washington Post* (January 27, 1995), and also by the excerpt of his speech reprinted in *Maclean's* (February 22, 1995).

4. According to the Talmud, primary forgiveness can occur only between the perpetrator and the victim.

5. A detailed description of the TRT group process can be found elsewhere (Bar-On, 1995b, 2000). The BBC documentary *Children of the Third Reich* (Timewatch, 1993) also tells the story of this group.

6. Three such encounters have been held so far: near Hamburg in August 1998 (Bar-On, 2000), in Bethlehem in October 1999 (Adwan and Bar-On, 2001b), and at Stockton College in New Jersey in July 2000. The next meeting is planned to take place in Northern Ireland in the fall of 2002.

7. In this context one could also ask why the Americans were not willing to conciliate with Bin Laden or the Taliban after the September 11 attack. Conciliation probably requires much more specific conditions than the literature takes into account (Bar-Tal, 2000b).

Bibliography

Aall, P. 1996. "Non-governmental Organizations and Peace Making." In *Managing Global Chaos: Sources of and Responses to International Conflict*, eds. C. A. Crocker, F. O. Hampson, and P. Aall, pp. 433–443. Washington, D.C.: United States Institute of Peace Press.

Abu el-Haj, N. 1999. "Translating Truths: Nationalism, the Practice of Archaeology, and the Remaking of Past and Present in Contemporary Jerusalem." *American Ethnologist* 25(2): 166–188.

Acharya, A. 1998. "Collective Identity and Conflict Management in Southeast Asia." In *Security Communities*, eds. E. Adler and M. Barnett, pp. 198–227. Cambridge: Cambridge University Press.

Ackermann, A. 1994. "Reconciliation as a Peace-Building Process in Post-War Europe: The Franco-German Case." *Peace & Change* 19(3): 229–250.

Adenauer, K. 1966. *Erinnerungen, 1953–1955.* Stuttgart: Deutsche Verlag-Anstalt.

Adler, E., and M. Barnett. 1998a. "Security Communities in Theoretical Perspective." In *Security Communities*, eds. E. Adler and M. Barnett, pp. 3–28. Cambridge: Cambridge University Press.

Adler, E., and M. Barnett. 1998b. "A Framework for the Study of Security Communities." In *Security Communities*, eds. E. Adler and M. Barnett, pp. 29–65. Cambridge: Cambridge University Press.

Adwan, S., and D. Bar-On. 2001a. "Personal Summaries." In *A Study of Palestinian and Israeli Environmental NGOs*, eds. S. Adwan and D. Bar-On, pp. 237–253. Beit Jala, PA: Peace Research Institute in the Middle East (PRIME).

Adwan, S., and D. Bar-On, eds. 2001b. *Victimhood and Beyond.* Beit Jala, PA: Peace Research Institute in the Middle East (PRIME).

Ahluwalia, P. 2000. "Towards (Re)conciliation: The Post-Colonial Economy of Giving." *Social Identities* 6(1): 29–48.

Allport, G. W. 1954. *The Nature of Prejudice*. Cambridge, Mass.: Addison-Wesley.

Amir, Y. 1969. "Contact Hypothesis in Ethnic Relations." *Psychological Bulletin* 71: 319–341.

Anderson, B. 1991. *Imagined Communities: Reflections on the Origin and Spread of Nationalism*. London: Verso.

Arendt, H. 1958. *The Human Condition*. Chicago: University of Chicago Press.

Arian, A. 1999. "Israeli Public Opinion on National Security." *Memorandum* No. 53. Jaffee Center for Strategic Studies, Tel Aviv.

Arnson, C. J., ed. 1999a. *Comparative Peace Processes in Latin America*. Stanford, Calif.: Stanford University Press.

Arnson, C. J. 1999b. "Conclusion: Lessons Learned in Comparative Perspective." In *Comparative Peace Processes in Latin America*, ed. C. J. Arnson, pp. 447–463. Stanford, Calif.: Stanford University Press.

Aron, R. 1996. *Peace and War: A Theory of International Relations*. New York: Doubleday.

Arthur, P. 1999. "The Anglo-Irish Peace Process: Obstacles to Reconciliation." In *After the Peace: Resistance and Reconciliation*, ed. R. L. Rothstein, pp. 85–109. Boulder, Colo.: Lynne Rienner.

Artzi, Y. 1997. "Lo Mevakesh Selicha" (I don't ask for forgiveness). *Ha'aretz* (Israeli daily newspaper, Hebrew), September 29.

Asmal, K., L. Asmal, and R. S. Roberts. 1997. *Reconciliation Through Truth: Reckoning of Apartheid's Criminal Governance*. Capetown: David Phillips.

Auerbach, Y. 1980. "Foreign Policy Decisions and Changing Attitudes." Unpublished doctoral dissertation, the Hebrew University of Jerusalem (Hebrew).

Auerbach, Y. 1991. "Ben-Gurion and Reparations from Germany." In *David Ben-Gurion: Politics and Leadership in Israel*, ed. R. W. Zweig, pp. 274–292. London: Frank Cass.

Averill, J. R., G. Catlin, and K. K. Chon. 1990. *Rules of Hope*. New York: Springer-Verlag.

Avruch, K. 1998. *Culture and Conflict Resolution*. Washington, D.C.: United States Institute of Peace Press.

Avruch, K., and B. Vejarano. n.d. "Truth and Reconciliation Commissions: A Review Essay and Annotated Bibliography." Unpublished manuscript, Institute for Conflict Analysis and Resolution," George Mason University.

Azar, E. E. 1990. *The Management of Protracted Social Conflict*. Hampshire, U.K.: Dartmouth.

Azar, E., E. Mullet, and G. Vinsonneau. 1999. "The Propensity to Forgive: Findings from Lebanon." *Journal of Peace Research* 36(2):169–181.

Azburu, D. 1999. "Peace and Democratization in Guatemala: Two Parallel Processes." In *Comparative Peace Processes in Latin America*, ed. C. J. Arnson, pp. 97–127. Stanford, Calif.: Stanford University Press.

Ball, N. 1996. "The Challenges of Rebuilding War-Torn Societies." In *Managing Global Chaos: Sources of and Responses to International Conflict*, eds. C. A. Crocker,

F. O. Hampson, and P. Aall, pp. 607–622. Washington, D.C.: United States Institute of Peace Press.

Barkan, E. 2000. *The Guilt of Nations: Restitution and Negotiating Historical Injustices.* New York, London: Norton.

Barnes, H. E. 1997. "Theatre for Reconciliation: Desire and South African Students." *Theatre Journal* 49: 41–52.

Barnett, M., and E. Adler. 1998. "Studying Security Communities in Theory, Comparison and History." In *Security Communities*, eds. E. Adler and M. Barnett, pp. 413–441. Cambridge: Cambridge University Press.

Bar-On, D. 1989. *Legacy of Silence: Encounters with Descendants of the Third Reich.* Cambridge: Harvard University Press.

Bar-On, D. 1990. "Children of Perpetrators of the Holocaust: Working Through One's Moral Self." *Psychiatry* 53: 229–245.

Bar-On, D. 1995a. *Fear and Hope.* Cambridge: Harvard University Press.

Bar-On, D. 1995b. "Encounters Between Descendants of Nazi Perpetrators and Descendants of Holocaust Survivors." *Psychiatry* 58(3): 225–245.

Bar-On, D. 1998. "Israeli Society Between the Culture of Death and the Culture of Life." *Israel Studies* 2(2): 88–112.

Bar-On, D. 1999. *The "Others" Within Us: A Sociopsychological Perspective on Changes in Israeli Identity.* Beersheba: Ben-Gurion University with Mossad Bialik (Hebrew).

Bar-On, D., ed. 2000. *Bridging the Gap: Storytelling as a Way to Work Through Political and Collective Hostilities.* Hamburg: Köber-Stiftung.

Bar-On, D. 2001. "Who Counts as a Holocaust Survivor? Who Suffered More? Why Did the Jews Not Take Revenge on the Germans After the War?" *Freie Assoziationen* 4(2): 155–187 (German).

Bar-On, M. 1996. *In Pursuit of Peace: A History of the Israeli Peace Movement.* Washington, D.C.: United States Institute of Peace Press.

Bar-Siman-Tov, Y. 1994. "The Arab-Israeli Conflict: Learning Conflict Resolution." *Journal of Peace Research* 31(1):75–92.

Bar-Siman-Tov, Y. 2000. "Israel-Egypt Peace: Stable Peace?" In *Stable Peace Among Nations*, eds. A. M. Kacowicz, Y. Bar-Siman-Tov, O. Elgstrom and M. Jerneck, pp. 220–238. Boulder, Col.: Rowman and Littlefield.

Bar-Tal, D. 1990. "Causes and Consequences of De-legitimization: Models of Conflict and Ethnocentrism." *Journal of Social Issues* 46(1):65–81.

Bar-Tal, D. 1998. "Societal Beliefs in Times of Intractable Conflict: The Israeli Case." *International Journal of Conflict Management* 9(1):22–50.

Bar-Tal, D. 2000a. *Shared Beliefs in a Society: Social Psychological Analysis.* Thousands Oaks, Calif.: Sage.

Bar-Tal, D. 2000b. "From Intractable Conflict Through Conflict Resolution to Reconciliation: Psychological Analysis." *Political Psychology* 21:351–365.

Bar-Tal, D. 2001. "Why Does Fear Override Hope in Societies Engulfed by Intractable Conflict, as It Does in the Israeli Society?" *Political Psychology* 22:601–627.

Bar-Tal, D. 2003. "Collective Memory of Physical Violence: Its Contribution to the

Culture of Violence." In E. Cairns and M. D. Roe, eds., *Memories in Conflict*, pp. 77–93. London: Macmillan.

Bar-Tal, D. 2002. "The Elusive Nature of Peace Education." In *Peace Education: The Concept Principles and Practice Around the World*, eds. G. Salomon and B. Nevo, pp. 27–36. Mahwah, N.J.: Lawrence Erlbaum.

Bar-Tal, D., and N. Geva. 1986. "A Cognitive Basis of International Conflicts." In *Psychology of Intergroup Relations*, eds. S. Worchel and W. G. Austin, pp. 118–133. Chicago: Nelson-Hall.

Bar-Tal, D., and N. Oren. 2000. "Ethos as an Expression of Identity: Its Chances in Transition from Conflict to Peace in the Israeli Case." *Davis Occasional Papers*, No. 83. Leonard Davis Institute, Jerusalem.

Bar-Tal, D., and Y. Teichman. *Stereotypes and Prejudice in Conflict: The Case of the Perception of Arabs in the Israeli Society*. Cambridge: Cambridge University Press, in preparation.

Barua, P. 1995. "Economic CBMs Between India and Pakistan." In *Crisis Prevention, Confidence Building and Reconciliation in South Asia*, eds. M. Krepon and A. Sevak, pp. 153–169. New York: St. Martin's.

Bass, B. 1985. *Leadership and Performance Beyond Expectations*. New York: Free Press.

Bass, B. 1990. *Bass and Stogdill's Handbook of Leadership: Theory, Research and Managerial Applications*, 3rd ed. New York: Free Press.

Bass, B. 1997. "Does the Transactional-Transformational Leadership Paradigm Transcend Organizational and National Boundaries?" *American Psychologist* 52(3):130–239.

Bass B., and B. Avolio. 1993. "Transformational Leadership: A Response to Critiques." In *Leadership Theory and Research: Perspectives and Directions*, eds., M. Chemers and R. Ayman, pp. 49–88. San Diego, Calif.: Academic Press.

Bazerman, M. H. 1983. "Negotiator Judgement: A Critical Look at the Rationality Assumption." *American Behavioral Scientist* 27:211–228.

Bazerman, M. H., T. Magliozzi, and M. A. Neale. 1985. "The Acquisition of an Integrative Response in a Competitive Market." *Organizational Behavior and Human Performance* 34: 294–313.

Bazerman, M. H., and M. A. Neale. 1995. "The Role of Fairness, Considerations and Relationship in a Judgmental Perspective of Negotiation." In *Barriers to Conflict Resolution*, eds. K. Arrow et al., pp. 87–106. New York: Norton.

Beeman, J. H., and R. Mahony. 1993. "The Institutional Churches and the Process of Reconciliation in Northern Ireland: Recent Progress in Presbyterian-Roman Catholic Relations." In *Northern Ireland and the Politics of Reconciliation*, eds. D. Keogh and M. H. Haltzel, pp. 150–159. Washington, D.C.: Woodrow Wilson Center Press.

Ben-Ari, R., and Y. Amir. 1988. "Cultural Information, Intergroup Contact and Change in Ethnic Attitudes and Relations." In *The Social Psychology of Intergroup Relations: Theory, Research and Applications*, eds. W. Stroebe, A. W. Kruglanski, D. Bar-Tal, and M. Hewstone, pp. 151–166. New York: Springer-Verlag.

Benvenisti, M. 1990. "The Peace Process and Intercommunal Strife." In *The Elusive*

Search for Peace: South Africa, Israel, Northern Ireland, eds. H. Giliomee and J. Gagiano, pp. 117–131. Cape Town: Oxford University Press.

Benvenisti, M. 2000. *Sacred Landscapes: The Buried History of the Holy Land Since 1948.* Berkeley and Los Angeles: University of California Press.

Benvenisti, M. 2001. "Just Waiting for a Sign." *Ha'aretz,* April 27, B1 (Hebrew).

Bercovitch, J., ed. 1995. *Resolving International Conflicts.* Boulder, Col.: Lynne Rienner.

Berger, A., and N. Berger. 2001. *Second Generation Voices.* Syracuse, N.Y.: Syracuse University Press.

Bjerstedt, A. 1988. *Peace Education in Different Countries.* No. 81, Educational Information and Debate. Malmö, Sweden.

Bjerstedt, A., ed. 1993. *Peace Education: Global Perspective.* Malmö, Sweden: Almqvist & Wiksell.

Blumental, T. 2001. *Ha'aretz,* Jan. 30, 2001 (in Hebrew).

Boraine, A., and J. Levy, eds. 1995. *The Healing of a Nation? Justice in Transition.* Cape Town: Institute of Democracy.

Boulding, K. E. 1962. *Conflict and Defense: A General Theory.* New York: Harper & Row.

Boulding, K. 1978. *Stable Peace.* Austin: University of Texas Press.

Brandt, W. 1978. *People and Politics.* London: Collins.

Brecke, P., and W. J. Long. 1999. "War and Reconciliation." *International Interactions* 25(2): 95–117.

Broder, John M. 1999. "Clinton Apologizes for U.S. Support of Guatemalan Rightists." *New York Times,* March 11, A12.

Bronfenbrenner, U. 1961. "The Mirror Image in Soviet-American Relations: A Social Psychologist's Report." *Journal of Social Issues* 17(3): 45–56.

Bronkhorst, D. 1995. *Truth and Reconciliation: Obstacles and Opportunities for Human Rights.* Amsterdam: Amnesty International.

Brown, R. 1986. "Ethnic Conflict." In R. Brown, ed., *Social Psychology,* 2nd ed., pp. 531–634. New York: Free Press.

Brown, R. 1988. *Group Processes: Dynamics within and between Groups.* Oxford: Blackwell.

Bruck, P., and C. Roach. 1993. "Dealing With Reality: The News Media and the Promotion of Peace." In C. Roach, ed., *Communication and Culture in War and Peace.* pp. 71–95. Newbury Park, Calif.: Sage.

Bruner J. S. 1957. "Going Beyond the Information Given. "In H. Gruber, K. R. Hammond, and R. Jesser, eds., *Contemporary Approaches to Cognition,* pp. 41–96. Cambridge: Harvard University Press.

Bryan, D. 1998. "The Right to March: Parading a Loyal Protestant Identity in Northern Ireland." *International Journal on Minority and Group Rights* 4: 373–396. 1998.

Bryan, D. 2000. *Orange Parades: The Politics of Ritual, Tradition and Control.* London: Pluto.

Bryson, L., and C. McCartney. 1994. *Clashing Symbols?: A Report on the Use of Flags, Anthems and Other National Symbols in Northern Ireland.* Antrim: W. & G. Baird.

Buckley, A. D., ed. 1998. *Symbols in Northern Ireland.* Belfast: Institute for Irish Studies.

Burns, J. 1978. *Leadership.* New York: Harper & Row.

Burns, R. J., and R. Aspeslagh, eds. 1996. *Three Decades of Peace Education Around the World.* New York: Garland.

Burton, J. W. 1969. *Conflict and Communication: The Use of Controlled Communication in International Relations.* London: Macmillan.

Burton, J. W. 1987. *Resolving Deep-Rooted Conflict.* Lanham, Md.: University Press of America.

Burton, J. W. 1988. "Conflict Resolution as a Function of Human Needs." In *The Power of Human Needs in World Society,* eds. R. A. Coate and J. A. Rosati, pp. 187–204. Boulder, Colo.: Lynne Rienner.

Burton, J. 1990. *Conflict: Resolution and Prevention.* New York: St. Martin's Press.

Calleja, J. 1994. "Educating for Peace in the Mediterranean: A Strategy for Peace Building." In *Building Peace in the Middle East: Challenges for States and Civil Society,* ed. E. Boulding, pp. 279–285. Boulder, Colo.: Lynne Rienner.

Canas, A., and H. Dada. 1999. "Political Transition and Institutionalization in El Salvador." In *Comparative Peace Processes in Latin America,* ed. C. J. Arnson, pp. 69–95. Stanford, Calif.: Stanford University Press.

Carr, R., and J. P. Fusi. 1979. *Spain: From Dictatorship to Democracy.* London: George Allen & Unwin.

Chadha, N. 1995. "Enemy Images: The Media and Indo-Pakistani Tensions." In *Crisis Prevention, Confidence Building and Reconciliation in South Asia,* eds. M. Krepon and A. Sevak, pp. 171–198. New York: St. Martin's Press.

Charif, H. 1994. "Regional Development and Integration." In *Peace for Lebanon? From War to Reconstruction,* eds. D. Collings, pp. 151–161. Boulder, Colo.: Lynne Rienner.

Chetkow-Yanoov, B. 1986. "Improving Arab-Jewish Relations in Israel: The Role of Voluntary Organizations." *Social Development Issues* 10:58–70.

Chirwa, W. 1997. "Collective Memory and the Process of Reconciliation and Reconstruction." *Development in Practice* 7:479–482.

Cloke, K. 2001. *Dangerously Mediating: The Frontiers of Conflict Resolution.* San Francisco, Calif.: Jossey-Bass.

Cohen, Abner. 1969. *Custom and Politics in Urban Africa.* Berkeley and Los Angeles: University of California Press.

Cohen, Abner. 1993. *Masquerade Politics.* Berkeley and Los Angeles: University of California Press.

Cohen, Akiva, and G. Wolfsfeld, eds. 1995. *Framing the Intifada: People and Media.* Norwood, N.J.: Ablex.

Corm, G. 1994. "The War System: Militia Hegemony and Reestablishment of the State." In *Peace for Lebanon? From War to Reconstruction,* ed. D. Collings, pp. 215–230. Boulder, Colo.: Lynne Rienner.

Corr, E. G. 1995. "Societal Transformation for Peace in El Salvador." *Annals of the American Academy of Political and Social Science* 541:144–156.

Coser, L. A. 1961. "The Termination of Conflict." *Journal of Conflict Resolution* 5: 347–353.

Crabb, P. B. 1989. "When Aggression Seems Justified: Judging Intergroup Conflict from a Distance." *Aggressive Behavior* 15:345–352.

Dadrian, V. 1995. *The History of the Armenian Genocide*. Providence, R.I. and Oxford: Berghahn.

Dahrendorf, R. 1959. *Class and Class Conflict in Industrial Society*. Stanford, Calif.: Stanford University Press.

Darby, J., and R. MacGinty, eds. 2000. *The Management of Peace Processes*. London: Macmillan.

De la Rey, C., and I. Owens. 1998. "Perceptions of Psychological Healing and the Truth and Reconciliation Commission in South Africa." *Peace and Conflict: Journal of Peace Psychology* 4:257–270.

De Soto, A. 1999. "Reflections." In *Comparative Peace Processes in Latin America*, ed. C. J. Arnson, pp. 385–387. Stanford, Calif.: Stanford University Press.

De Vries, N. K., C.K.W. De Dreu, E. Gordijn, and M. Schuurman. 1996. "Majority and Minority Influence: Dual Role Interpretation." In *European Review of Social Psychology*, eds. W. Stroebe and M. Hewstone, vol. 7, pp. 145–172. Chichester, U.K.: Wiley.

Deutsch, K. W., S. A. Burell, R. A. Kann, M. Lee, Jr., M. Lichterman, R. E. Lindgren, F. L. Loewenheim, and R. W. van Wagenen. 1957. *Political Community and the North Atlantic Area: International Organization in the Light of Historical Experience*. Princeton: Princeton University Press.

Deutsch, M. 1973. *The Resolution of Conflict: Constructive and Destructive Processes*. New Haven: Yale University Press.

Deutsch, M. 2000. "Justice and Conflict." In *The Handbook of Conflict Resolution: Theory and Practice*, eds. M. Deutsch and P. T. Coleman, pp. 41–64. San Francisco: Jossey-Bass.

Deutscher I. 1973. *What We Say/What We Do*. Glenview, Ill.: Scott, Foresman.

Divrei Haknesset (Knesset Records). 1952. January 8–9.

Dodds, G. G. 1999. "Political Apologies and Public Discourse." Unpublished paper for the Penn National Commission on Society, Culture and Community. University of Pennsylvania, Philadelphia.

Dorff, E. N. 1992. "Individual and Communal Forgiveness." In *Autonomy and Judaism*, ed. D. Frank, pp. 193–217. Albany: State University of New York Press.

Dorff, Elliot N. 1998. "The Elements of Forgiveness: A Jewish Approach." In *Dimensions of Forgiveness: Psychological Research and Theological Perspectives*, ed. E. L. Worthington, Jr., pp. 28–55. Philadelphia and London: Templeton Foundation Press.

Doyle, W. M. 1983. "Kant, Liberal Legacies and Foreign Affairs." *Philosophy and Public Affairs* 12:205–235.

Duffy, T. 2000. "Peace Education in a Divided Society: Creating a Culture of Peace in Northern Ireland." *Prospects* 30:15–29.

Duncan, B. L. 1976. "Differential Social Perception and Attribution of Intergroup Violence: Testing the Stereotyping of Blacks." *Journal of Personality and Social Psychology* 34:590–598.

Du Toit, P. 2001. *South Africa's Brittle Peace: The Problem of Post-Settlement Violence.* New York: Palgrave.

Edelman, M. 1964. *The Symbolic Uses of Politics.* Urbana: University of Illinois Press.

Elhance, A. P., and M. Ahmar. 1995. "Nonmilitary CBMs." In *Crisis Prevention, Confidence Building and Reconciliation in South Asia,* eds. M. Krepon and A. Sevak, pp. 131–151. New York: St. Martin's.

El-Hoss, S. 1994. "Prospective Change in Lebanon." In *Peace for Lebanon? From War to Reconstruction,* ed. D. Collings, pp. 249–258. Boulder, Col.: Lynne Rienner.

The Encyclopedia of Islam. 1991. Leiden: E. J. Brill, vols. 2, 10, new ed.

Espiritu, L. Y. 1992. *Asian-American Panethnicity: Bridging Institutions and Identities.* Philadelphia: Temple University Press.

Fallaci, O. 1976. *Interview with History.* Boston: Houghton Mifflin.

Feldman, L. G. 1999. "The Principle and Practice of 'Reconciliation' in German Foreign Policy: Relations with France, Ireland, Poland and the Czech Republic." *International Affairs* 75(2): 333–356.

Felstiner, W.L.F. 1974. "Influences of Social Organization on Dispute Processing." *Law and Society Review* 9:63–94.

Felstiner, W.L.F., L. Abel, and A. Sarat. 1980–81. "The Emergence and Transformation of Disputes: Naming, Blaming, Claiming . . . " *Law and Society Review* 15: 631–652.

Festinger, L. A. 1957. *A Theory of Cognitive Dissonance.* Evanston, Ill.: Row, Peterson.

Field, N. 1995. "The Stakes of Apology." *Japan Quarterly* 42.

Fisher, Ronald, ed. 1964. *International Conflict and Behavioral Science.* New York: Basic Books.

Fisher, Ronald J. 1990. *The Social Psychology of Intergroup and International Conflict Resolution.* New York: Springer-Verlag.

Fisher, Roger and W. Ury. 1986. *Getting to Yes.* London: Hutchinson Business.

Forman, J., Jr. 2000. "Driving Dixie Down: Removing the Confederate Flag from Southern State Capitols." In *Confederate Symbols in the Contemporary South,* eds. J. M. Martinez et al., pp. 195–223. Gainesville: University Press of Florida.

French, J., and B. Raven. 1959. "The Bases of Social Power." In *Studies in Social Power,* ed. D. Cartwright, pp. 150–167. Ann Arbor, Mich.: Institute for Social Research.

Frost, Brian. 1998. *Struggling to Forgive.* London: Harper Collins.

Galtung, J. 1980. *The True Worlds: A Transnational Perspective.* New York: Free Press.

Galtung, J. 1996. *Peace by Peaceful Means: Peace and Conflict, Development and Civilization.* London, Thousand Oaks and New Delhi: Sage.

Ganguly, S. 1995. "Mending Fences." In *Crisis Prevention, Confidence Building and Reconciliation in South Asia,* eds. M. Krepon and A. Sevak, pp. 11–24. New York: St. Martin's.

Garcia, C. 1984. "Latin America Traditions and Perspectives." *International Review of Education* 29(3): 369–390.

Gardner-Feldman, L. 1984. *The Special Relationship Between West Germany and Israel.* Boston: Allen & Unwin.

Gardner-Feldman, L. 1999. "The Principle and Practice of 'Reconciliation' in German Foreign Policy: Relations with France, Israel, Poland and Czech Republic." *International Affairs* 75(2): 333–356.

George, A. L. 1992. "From Conflict to Peace: Stages Along the Road." *United States Institute of Peace Journal* 6 (December): 7–9.

Gergen, K. J. 1991. *The Saturated Self.* New York: Basic Books.

Giliomee, H., and J. Gagiano, eds. 1990. *The Elusive Search for Peace: South Africa, Israel, Northern Ireland.* Cape Town: Oxford University Press.

Gleditsch, N. P., and H. Hegre. 1997. "Peace and Democracy." *Journal of Conflict Resolution* 41(2): 283–310,

Goertz, G., and P. F. Diehl. 1993. "Enduring Rivalries: Theoretical Constructs and Empirical Patterns." *International Studies Quarterly* 37: 147–171.

Golan, G., and Z. Kamal. 1999. "Bridging the Abyss: Palestinian-Israeli Dialogue." In *A Public Peace Process,* ed. H. Saunders, pp. 197–220. New York: St. Martin's.

Gonzales, G., and S. Haggard. 1998. "The United States and Mexico: A Pluralistic Security Community." In *Security Communities,* eds. E. Adler and M. Barnett, pp. 295–332. Cambridge: Cambridge University Press, 1998.

Gopin, M. 2000. *Between Eden and Armageddon: The Future of World Religions, Violence and Peacemaking.* Oxford: Oxford University Press.

Gordon, H. 1994. "Working for Peace in the Middle East: The Educational Task." In *Building Peace in the Middle East: Challenges for States and Civil Society,* ed. E. Boulding, pp. 311–317. Boulder, Colo.: Lynne Rienner.

Gulliver, P. H. 1979. *Disputes and Negotiations: A Cross-Cultural Perspective.* New York: Academic Press.

Gurr, T. R. 1970. *Why Men Rebel.* Princeton: Princeton University Press.

Guttman, L. 1968. "A General Non-metric Technique for Finding the Smallest Coordinate Space for a Configuration of Points." *Psychometrika* 33: 469–506.

Haas, E. 1964. *Beyond the Nation-State.* Stanford, Calif.: Stanford University Press.

Hadi, M. A. 2000. *Awakening Sleeping Horses and What Lies Ahead.* Jerusalem: Palestinian Academic Society for the Study of International Affairs.

Haley, J. O. 1986. "Comment: The Implications of Apology." *Law and Society Review* 20.

Hamber, B. 1998. "The Burdens of Truth: An Evaluation of the Psychological Support Services and Initiatives Undertaken by the South African Truth and Reconciliation Commission." *American Imago* 55: 9–28.

Hampton, J. 1988. "Forgiveness, Resentment and Hatred." In *Forgiveness and Mercy,* eds. J. G. Murphy and J. Hampton, Cambridge: Cambridge University Press.

Handl, V. 1997. "Czech-German Declaration on Reconciliation." *German Politics* 6(2): 150–167.

Hansard Society. 1980. *The Parliamentary Debates, House of Lords.* 5th series, 408. London: His Majesty's Stationery Office.

Haque, A., and E. Lawson. 1980. "The Mirror Image in the Context of the Arab-Israeli Conflict." *International Journal of Intercultural Relations* 4: 107–115.

Hardin, R. 1995. *One for All: The Logic of Group Conflict*. Princeton: Princeton University Press.

Harris, I. M. 1988. *Peace Education*. Jefferson, N.C.: McFarland.

Hayes, G. 1998. "We Suffer Our Memories: Thinking About the Past, Healing, and Reconciliation." *American Imago* 55: 29–50.

Hayner, P. B. 1999. "In Pursuit of Justice and Reconciliation: Contributions of Truth Telling." In *Comparative Peace Processes in Latin America*, ed. C. J. Arnson, pp. 363–383. Stanford: Stanford University Press.

Hechter, M. 1975. *Internal Colonialism: The Celtic Fringe in British National Development, 1536–1966*. London: Routledge & Kegan Paul.

Hechter, M. 2000. *Containing Nationalism*. New York: Oxford University Press.

Helman S., and T. Rapoport. 1997. "Woman in Black and the Challenging of the Social Order." *Theory and Criticism*, No. 10, Summer, pp. 175–192. (Hebrew).

Henderson, M. 1996. *The Forgiveness Factor*. London: Grosvenor Books.

Heradstveit, D. 1974. *Arab and Israeli Elite Perceptions*. Norway: Oslo University Press and Humanities Press.

Herf, J. 1997. *Divided Memory*. Cambridge: Harvard University Press.

Hermann, T. 2002. "The Sour Taste of Success: The Israeli Peace Movement 1967–1998." *In Mobilizing for Peace: Conflict Resolution in Northern Ireland, Israel/Palestine, and South Africa*, eds. B. Gidron and S. Katz, pp. 94–129. Oxford: Oxford University Press.

Hetherington, M., E. Deanne, T. Irvine, J. O'Neill, and J. Lindsay. 2000. *Toward Understanding and Healing: An Evaluation Report of the Lusty Bag Residential*. Derry and Londonderry: Derry City Council.

Hewstone, M. 1996. "Contact and Categorization: Social Interventions to Change Inter-Group Relations." In *Stereotype and Stereotyping*, eds. C. N. Macrae, C. Stangor, and M. Hewston, pp. 323–368. New York: Guilford.

Hicks, D. W., ed. 1988. *Education for Peace: Issues, Principles and Practices in the Classroom*. London: Routledge.

Hickson, L. 1986. "The Social Context of Apology in Dispute Settlement: A Cross-Cultural Study." *Ethnology* 25: 283–294.

Hirshberg, M. 1993. "The Self-Perpetuating National Self-Image: Cognitive Biases in Perceptions of International Interventions." *Political Psychology* 14(1): 77–97.

Hogan, R., G. Curphy, and J. Hogan. 1994. "What We Know About Leadership: Effectiveness and Personality." *American Psychologist* 49(6): 493–504.

Holmes, R., and M. C. Cagle. 2000. "The Great Debate: White Support for and Black Opposition to the Confederate Battle Flag." In *Confederate Symbols in the Contemporary South*, eds. J. M. Martinez et al., pp. 281–302. Gainesville: University Press of Florida.

Holsti, K. J. 1966. "Resolving International Conflicts: A Taxonomy of Behavior and Some Figures on Procedures." *Journal of Conflict Resolution* 10: 272–296.

Horowitz, D. L. 1993. "Conflict and the Incentives to Political Accommodation." In *Northern Ireland and the Politics of Reconciliation*, eds. D. Keogh and M. H. Haltzel, pp. 171–188. Washington: Woodrow Wilson Center Press.

Horowitz, D. T. 1985. *Ethnic Groups in Conflict*. Berkeley and Los Angeles: University of California Press.

Hume, J. 1993. "A New Ireland in a New Europe." In *Northern Ireland and the Politics of Reconciliation*, eds. D. Keogh and M. H. Haltzel, pp. 226–233. Washington: Woodrow Wilson Center Press.

Irani, G. E. 1999. "Islamic Mediation Techniques for Middle East Conflicts." *MERIA Journal* 3 (http://www.biu.ac.il/soc/besa/meria/journal/1999/issue2/Jv3n2al .html).

Irani, G. E., and N. C. Funk. 2000. *Rituals of Reconciliation: Arab-Islamic Perspectives*. Washington: United States Institute of Peace Press.

Jamal, A. 2000. "Palestinians in Israeli Peace Discourse." *Journal of Palestine Studies* 30(1): 36–51.

Jarman, N. 1997. *Material Conflicts: Parades and Visual Displays in Northern Ireland*. Oxford and New York: Berg.

Kacowicz, A. M. 1998. *Zones of Peace in the Third World*. Albany: State University of New York Press.

Kacowicz, A. M., and Y. Bar-Siman-Tov. 2000. "Stable Peace: A Conceptual Framework." In *Stable Peace Among Nations*, eds. A. M. Kacowicz, Y. Bar-Siman-Tov, O. Elgstrom, and M. Jerneck, pp. 11–35. Lanham, Md.: Rowman & Littlefield.

Kacowicz, A. M., Y. Bar-Siman-Tov, O. Elgstrom, and M. Jerneck, eds. 2000. *Stable Peace Among Nations*. Lanham, Md.: Rowman & Littlefield.

Kahneman, D., and A. Tversky. 1979. "Prospect Theory: An Analysis of Decision Under Risk." *Econometrica* 47: 263–291.

Kahneman, D., J. L. Knetsch, and R. H. Thaler. 1986. "Fairness as a Constraint on Profit Seeking: Entitlements in the Market." *American Economic Review* 76(4): 728–741.

Katz, D., and R. Kahn. 1978. *The Social Psychology of Organizations*. New York: Wiley.

Kawashima, T. 1969. "Dispute Resolution in Contemporary Japan." In *Law in Japan*, ed. A. T. von Mehren. Cambridge: Harvard University Press.

Kaye, M. 1997. "The Role of Truth Commissions in the Search for Justice, Reconciliation, and Democratization: The Salvadorean and Honduran Cases." *Journal of Latin American Studies* 29:693–716.

Keesing's Record of World Events. (1999). Bethesda, Md.: Keesings Worldwide, LLC.

Kelley, H. H. 1973. "The Process of Causal Attribution." *American Psychologist* 28(2): 107–128.

Kelly, G., and S. A. Nan. 1998. "Mediation in Practice in Northern Ireland." In *Mediation in Practice: A Report of the Art of Mediation Project*, ed. G. Kelly, pp. 50–61. Derry/Londonderry: INCORE.

Kelman, H. C. 1958. "Compliance, Identification, and Internalization: Three Processes of Attitude Change." *Journal of Conflict Resolution* 2:51–60.

Kelman, H. C. 1961. "Processes of Opinion Change." *Public Opinion Quarterly* 25:57–78.

Kelman, H. C. 1969. "Patterns of Personal Involvement in the National System: A Social-Psychological Analysis of Political Legitimacy." In *International Politics and*

Foreign Policy: A Reader in Research and Theory, rev. ed. J. N. Rosenau, pp. 276–288. New York: Free Press.

Kelman, H. C. 1978. "Israelis and Palestinians: Psychological Prerequisites for Mutual Acceptance." *International Security* 3(1): 162–186.

Kelman, H. C. 1979. "An Interactional Approach to Conflict Resolution and its Application to Israeli-Palestinian Relations." *International Interactions* 6(2):99–122.

Kelman, H. C. 1987. "The Political Psychology of the Israeli-Palestinian Conflict: How Can We Overcome the Barriers to a Negotiated Solution?" *Political Psychology* 8: 347–363.

Kelman, H. C. 1991. "Interactive Problem-Solving: The Uses and Limits of a Therapeutic Model for the Resolution of International Conflicts." In *The Psychodynamics of International Relationships*. Vol. 2. *Unofficial Diplomacy at Work*, eds. V. D. Volkan, J. V. Montville, and D. A. Julius, pp. 145–160. Lexington, Mass.: Lexington Books.

Kelman, H. C. 1992. "Informal Mediation by the Scholar/Practitioner." In *Mediation in International Relations*, eds. J. Bercovitch and J. Rubin, pp. 64–96. New York: St. Martin's.

Kelman, H. C. 1996. "The Interactive Problem-Solving Approach." In *Managing Global Chaos: Sources of and Responses to International Conflict*, eds. C. A. Crocker, F. O. Hampson, and P. Aall, pp. 501–519. Washington, D.C.: United States Institute of Peace Press.

Kelman, H. C. 1997a. "Some Determinants of the Oslo Breakthrough." *International Negotiations* 2:183–194.

Kelman, H. C. 1997b. "Social-Psychological Dimensions of International Conflict." In *Peacemaking in International Conflict: Methods and Techniques*, eds. W. Zartman and J. L. Rasmussen, pp. 191–237. Washington, D.C.: United States Institute of Peace Press.

Kelman, H. C. 1998a. "Building a Sustainable Peace: The Limits of Pragmatism in the Israeli-Palestinian Negotiations." *Journal of Palestine Studies* 28(1):36–50.

Kelman, H. C. 1998b. "The Place of Ethnic Identity in the Development of Personal Identity: A Challenge for the Jewish Family." In *Coping with Life and Death: Jewish Families in the Twentieth Century*, ed. P. Y. Medding, pp. 3–26. Oxford: Oxford University Press.

Kelman, H. C. 1998c. "Social-Psychological Contributions to Peacemaking and Peacebuilding in the Middle East." *Applied Psychology* 47(1):5–29.

Kelman, H. C. 1999a. "Transforming the Relationship Between Former Enemies: A Social-Psychological Analysis." In *After the Peace: Resistance and Reconciliation*, ed. R. L. Rothstein, pp. 193–205. Boulder, Colo.: Lynne Rienner.

Kelman, H. C. 1999b. "The Interdependence of Israeli and Palestinian National Identities: The Role of the Other in Existential Conflicts." *Journal of Social Issues* 55(3): 581–600.

Kelman, H. 2000. "The Role of Scholar-Practitioner in International Conflict Resolutions." *International Studies Perspectives* 1(3):273–288.

Kelman, H. C. 2001. "The Role of National Identity in Conflict Resolution: Experiences from Israeli-Palestinian Problem-Solving Workshops." In *Social Identity*,

Intergroup Conflict, and Conflict Reduction, eds. R. D. Ashmore, L. Jussim and D. Wilder, pp. 187–212. Oxford: Oxford University Press.

Kelman, H. C. and V. L. Hamilton. 1989. *Crimes of Obedience: Toward a Social Psychology of Authority and Responsibility.* New Haven: Yale University Press.

Keltner, D., and R. Robinson. 1993. "Imagined Ideological Differences in Conflict Escalation and Resolution." *International Journal of Conflict Management* 4(3): 249–262.

Kerner Commission. 1968. Report of the National Advisory Commission on Civil Disorders. New York: Bantam Books.

Khalaf, S. 1994. "Culture, Collective Memory, and the Restoration of Civility." In *Peace for Lebanon? From War to Reconstruction,* ed. D. Collings, pp. 273–285. Boulder, Colo.: Lynne Rienner.

Klein, D. 1976. "Some Notes on the Dynamics of Resistance to Change: The Defender Role." In *The Planning of Change,* eds. W. G. Bennis, K. Benne, R. Chin, and K. Corey, 3rd ed., pp. 117–124. New York: Holt, Rinehart & Winston.

Kluger, R. 1976. *Simple Justice: The History of Brown v. Board of Education and Black America's Struggle for Equality.* New York: Knopf.

Knox, C., and P. Quirk. 2000. *Peace Building in Northern Ireland, Israel and South Africa: Transition, Transformation and Reconciliation.* London: Macmillan.

Kook, Rabbi A.Y.H. 1994. *Orot Hatshuvah* (The Lights of Repentance). Jerusalem: Rav Kook Institute (Hebrew).

Kopstein, J. S. 1997. "The Politics of National Reconciliation: Memory and Institutions in German-Czech Relations Since 1989." *Nationalism and Ethnic Politics* 3(2):57–78.

Kotzé, H., and P. Du Toit. 1996. "Reconciliation, Reconstruction and Identity Politics in South Africa: A 1994 Survey of Elite Attitudes after Apartheid." *Nationalism and Ethnic Politics* 2:1–17.

Krasner, S., ed. 1983. *International Regimes.* Ithaca: Cornell University Press.

Krepon, M., and A. Sevak, eds. 1995. *Crisis Prevention, Confidence Building and Reconciliation in South Asia.* New York: St. Martin's.

Kriesberg, L. 1992. *International Conflict Resolution: The U.S.-U.S.S.R. and Middle East Cases.* New Haven: Yale University Press.

Kriesberg, L. 1998a. "Coexistence and the Reconciliation of Communal Conflicts." In *The Handbook of Interethnic Coexistence,* ed. E. Weiner, pp. 182–198. New York: Continuum.

Kriesberg, L. 1998b. "Intractable Conflicts." In *The Handbook of Interethnic Coexistence,* ed. E. Weiner, pp. 332–342. New York: Continuum.

Kriesberg, L. 1998c. *Constructive Conflicts: From Escalation to Resolution.* Lanham, Md.: Rowman & Littlefield.

Kriesberg, L. 1999. "Paths to Varieties of Inter-Communal Reconciliation." *In From Conflict Resolution to Peacebuilding,* ed. H. W. Joeng. Fitchburg, Md.: Dartmouth.

Kriesberg, L. 2000. "Negotiating the Partition of Palestine and Evolving Israeli-Palestinian Relations." *Brown Journal of World Affairs* 7 (winter/spring): 63–80.

Kriesberg, L. 2002. "Reconciliation Actions and the Breakdown of Israeli-Palestinian Negotiations, 2000." *Peace and Change* 27(4): 546–571.

Kritz, N. J., ed. 1995. *Transitional Justice*. Washington, D.C.: United States Institute of Peace Press.

Kritz, N. J. 1996. "The Rule of Law in the Postconflict Phase." In *Managing Global Chaos: Sources of and Responses to International Conflict*, eds. C. A. Crocker, F. O. Hampson, and P. Aall, pp. 587–606. Washington D.C.: United States Institute of Peace Press.

Krog, A. 1998. *Country of My Skull*. London: Vintage.

Laitin, D. 1989. "Linguistic Revival: Politics and Culture in Catalonia." *Comparative Studies in Society and History* 31:297–317.

Laitin, D. 1998. *Identity in Formation: The Russian-Speaking Populations in the Near Abroad*. Ithaca and London: Cornell University Press.

Lapidus, G. W. 1992. "From Democratization to Disintegration: The Impact of Perestroika on the National Question." In *From Union to Commonwealth: Nationalism and Separatism in the Soviet Republics*, eds. G. W. Lapidus and V. Zaslavsky, with P. Goldman. Cambridge: Cambridge University Press.

Lederach, J. P. 1995. *Preparing for Peace: Conflict Transformation Across Cultures*. Syracuse: Syracuse University Press.

Lederach, J. P. 1997. *Building Peace: Sustainable Reconciliation in Divided Societies*. Washington, D.C.: United States Institute of Peace Press.

Lederach, J. P. 1998. "Beyond Violence: Building Sustainable Peace." In *The Handbook of Interethnic Coexistence*, ed. E. Weiner, pp. 236–245. New York: Continuum.

Lederach, J. P. 1999. *The Journey Toward Reconciliation*. Scottsdale, Penn.: Herald Press.

Levine, J. M., and E. M. Russo. 1987. "Majority and Minority Influence." In *Review of Personality and Social Psychology: Group Processes*, ed. C. Hendrick, 8:13–54. Newbury Park, Calif.: Sage.

Levine, M. V. 1991. *The Reconquest of Montreal: Language Policy and Social Change in a Bilingual City*. Philadelphia: Temple University Press.

Levinson, S. 1998. *Written in Stone: Public Monuments in Changing Societies*. Durham, N.C.: Duke University Press.

Levy, J. S. 1994. "Learning and Foreign Policy: Sweeping a Conceptual Minefield." *International Organization* 48(2):279–312.

Lewin, K. 1935. *A Dynamic Theory of Personality*. New York: McGraw-Hill.

Lewin, K. 1947. "Frontiers in Group Dynamics: Part II." *Human Relations* 1:143–153.

Liebenberg, I., and A. Zegeye. 1998. "Pathway to Democracy? The Case of the South African Truth and Reconciliation Process." *Social Identities* 4:541–558.

Lindberg, L., and S. Sheingold. 1970. *Regional Integration: Theory and Practice*. Cambridge: Harvard University Press.

Lindgren, R., F. L. Loewenheim, and R. W. van Wagenen. 1957. *Political Community and the North Atlantic Area*. Princeton: Princeton University Press.

Linenthal, E. T. 1993. *Sacred Ground: Americans and Their Battlefields*. Urbana and Chicago: University of Illinois Press.

Lipschutz, R. D. 1998. "Beyond the Neoliberal Peace: From Conflict Resolution to Social Reconciliation." *Social Justice: A Journal of Crime, Conflict and World Order* 25(4): 5–19.

Lipset, M. 1960. *Political Man*. Garden City, N.Y.: Doubleday/Anchor.

Litvak-Hirsch, T. "Who Does This House Belong to? Dilemmas of Israeli Identity Construction." Part of Unpublished Doctoral Dissertation, Ben-Gurion University, Beersheba, in preparation (Hebrew).

Long, W. J., and P. Brecke. 2000. "Civil War and Reconciliation." Paper presented at the Annual Meeting of the International Studies Association, Los Angeles.

Luard, E., ed. 1970. *The International Regulation of Frontier Disputes*. London: Thames & Hudson.

Lucy, G., and E. McClure. 1997. *The Twelfth: What It Means to Me*. Belfast: Ulster Society.

Lustick, I. S. 1997. "Ending Protracted Conflicts: The Oslo Peace Process Between Political Partnership and Legality." *Cornell International Law Journal* 30(3):741–757.

Mailland, R. 1991. *De Gaulle et l'Allemagne: le rêve inachevé*. Paris: Plon.

Makovsky D., and D. Herman. 1999. "MERIA Journalist: Interview with Barak," September 27, *MERIA* (on-line journal : http://www.biu.ac.il/soc/besa/meria/journal/).

Maoz, I. 1997. "The Effect of Bias Mechanisms on Evaluation of Concessions in the Israeli-Palestinian Negotiations." Working Paper No. 10, Jewish-Arab Center, University of Haifa.

Maoz, I. 2000a. "Identities, Identifications, and Evaluation of Concessions in the Israeli-Palestinian Negotiations." *Davis Occasional Papers*, No. 82. Leonard Davis Institute, the Hebrew University of Jerusalem.

Maoz, I. 2000b. "An Experiment in Peace: Processes and Effects in Reconciliation Aimed Workshops of Israeli and Palestinian Youth." *Journal of Peace Research* 37(6).

Maoz, I. 2000c. "Power Relations in Intergroup Encounters: A Case Study of Jewish-Arab Encounters in Israel." *International Journal of Intercultural Relations* 24(4): 259–277.

Maoz, I. 2000d. "Multiple Conflicts and Competing Agendas: A Framework for Conceptualizing Structured Encounters between Groups in Conflict—the Case of a Coexistence Project of Jews and Palestinians in Israel." *Peace and Conflict: Journal of Peace Psychology* 6(2):135–156.

Maoz, M. 1999. "The Oslo Agreements: Toward Arab-Jewish Reconciliation." In *After the Peace: Resistance and Reconciliation*, ed. R. L. Rothstein, pp. 67–84. Boulder, Colo.: Lynne Rienner.

Maoz, Z., and B. M. Russett. 1993. "Normative and Structural Causes of Democratic Peace," 1946–86. *American Political Science Review* 87: 624–638.

Marcus, E. 2000. "Change Processes and Conflict." In *The Handbook of Conflict Resolution: Theory and Practice*, eds. M. Deutsch and P. T. Coleman, pp. 366–381. San Francisco: Jossey-Bass.

Marrow, D. 1999. "Seeking Peace Amid Memories of War: Learning from the Peace

Process in Northern Ireland." In *After the Peace: Resistance and Reconciliation,* ed. R. L. Rothstein, pp. 111–138. Boulder, Colo.: Lynne Rienner.

Marty, M. E. 1998. "The Ethos of Christian Forgiveness." In *Dimensions of Forgiveness: Psychological Research and Theological Perspectives,* ed. E. L. Worthington, Jr., pp. 9–28. Philadelphia and London: Templeton Foundation Press.

Marvin, C., and D. W. Ingle. 1999. *Blood Sacrifice and the Nation: Totem Rituals and the American Flag.* Cambridge: Cambridge University Press.

Mather, L. 1990. "Dispute Processing and a Longitudinal Approach to Trial Courts." *Law and Society Review* 24:357–370.

Mather, L., and B. Yngvesson. 1980–81. "Language, Audience, and the Transformation of Disputes." *Law and Society Review* 15: 775–821.

McGarry, J. 1998. "Political Settlements in Northern Ireland and South Africa." *Political Studies* 46:853–870.

McGarry, J., and B. O'Leary eds. 1993. *The Politics of Ethnic Conflict.* London and New York: Routledge.

Mi'ari, M. 1999. "Attitudes of Palestinians Toward Normalization with Israel." *Journal of Peace Research* 36:339–348.

Miller, B. "The International, Regional and Domestic Sources of Regional Peace." In *Stable Peace Among Nations,* eds. A. M. Kacowicz et al., pp. 55–74. Boulder, Colo.: Rowman and Littlefield, 2000.

Miller, R. E., and A. Sarat. 1980–81. "Grievances, Claims, and Disputes: Assessing the Adversary Culture." *Law and Society Review* 15:525–565.

Miller-Fahrenholz, G. 1996. *The Art of Forgiveness: Theological Reflections on Healing and Reconciliation.* Geneva: WCC Publications.

Minow, M. 1998. *Between Vengeance and Forgiveness: Facing History After Genocide and Mass Violence.* Boston: Beacon Press.

Mitchell, C. R. 1981. *The Structure of International Conflict.* London: Macmillan.

Mitchell, C. 2000. *Gestures of Conciliation: Factors Contributing to Successful Olive Branches.* New York: St. Martin's.

Mnookin, R. and L. Ross. 1995. "Strategic, Psychological, and Institutional Barriers: An Introduction." In *Barriers to the Negotiated Resolution of Conflict,* eds. K. Arrow, R. Mnookin, L. Ross, A. Tversky, and R. Wilson, pp. 2–24. New York: Norton.

Montville, J. V. 1993. "The Healing Function in Political Conflict Resolution." In *Conflict Resolution Theory and Practice: Integration and Application,* eds. D.J.D. Sandole and H. van der Merve, pp. 112–127. Manchester: Manchester University Press.

Montville, J. V. 2001. "Justice and the Burdens of History." Paper presented at the 24th conference of the International Society of Political Psychology, Cuernavaca, Mexico, July 14–18. 2001.

Morris, B. 1996. *Israeli Border Wars, 1949–1956.* Tel Aviv: Am Oved 1996 (Hebrew).

Morris, B. 1999. *Righteous Victims.* New York: Knopf.

Moscovici, S., G. Mugny, and E. Van Avermaet, eds. 1985. *Perspectives on Minority Influence.* Cambridge: Cambridge University Press.

Murakami, T. 1992. *Peace Education in Britain and Japan.* Kyoto: Office of Sociology of Education, Kyoto University of Education.

Murphy, J. G., and J. Hampton. 1988. *Forgiveness and Mercy*. Cambridge: Cambridge University Press.

Murray, M. R., and J. V. Greer. 1999. "The Changing Governance of Rural Development: State-Community Interaction in Northern Ireland." *Policy Studies* 20: 37–50.

Myers, J. 2000. *Afraid of the Dark: What Whites and Blacks Need to Know About Each Other*. Chicago: Lawrence Hill.

Nader, L., and H. F. Todd, eds. 1978. *The Disputing Process: Law in Ten Societies*. New York: Columbia University Press.

Nadler, A. 2001. "Post-Resolution Process: Instrumental and Socio-Emotional Routes to Reconciliation." Paper presented at the Davis Workshop on Reconciliation, Leonard Davis Institute, Hebrew University of Jerusalem, February 7–8.

Nagle, J., and S. Olzak. 1982. "Ethnic Mobilization in New and Old States: An Extension of the Competition Model." *Social Problems* 30:127–143.

Neale, M., and G. Northcraft. 1991. "Behavioral Negotiation Theory." *Research in Organizational Behavior* 13: 147–190.

Northrup, T. A. 1989. "The Dynamic of Identity in Personal and Social Conflict." In *Intractable Conflicts and Their Transformation*, eds. L. Kriesberg, T. A. Northrup, and S. J. Thorson, pp. 55–82. Syracuse, N.Y.: Syracuse University Press.

Norval, A. J. 1998. "Memory, Identity and the (Im)possibility of Reconciliation: The Work of the Truth and Reconciliation Commission in South Africa." *Constellations* 5: 250–265.

Norval, A. J. 1999. "Truth and Reconciliation: The Birth of the Present and the Reworking of History." *Journal of African Studies* 25:499–519.

Nye, J. S., Jr. 1987. "Nuclear Learning." *International Organization* 41(3): 371–402.

Olzak, S. 1992. *The Dynamics of Ethnic Competition and Conflict*. Stanford, Calif.: Stanford University Press.

Oskamp, S. 1965. "Attitudes Toward U.S. and Russian Actions: A Double Standard." *Psychological Reports* 16:43–46.

Owen, M. J. 1994. "How Liberalism Produces Democratic Peace." *International Security* 19:87–125.

Owen, M. J. 1997. *Liberal Peace, Liberal War: American Politics and International Security*. Ithaca, N.Y.: Cornell University Press.

Pankhurst, D. 1998. "All in a Word?: International Currencies in Reconciliation." *Peace Studies News* 19.

Peace Index Survey. http://spirit.tau.ac.il/socant/peaceindex.html.

Peli, P. H. 1974. *On Repentance: From the Oral Discourses of Rabbi Joseph B. Soloveitchik* (Written and ed., P. H. Peli). Jerusalem.: Education Department, World Zionist Organization.

Pettigrew, T. 1998. "Intergroup Contact Theory." *Annual Review of Psychology* 49:65–85.

Phillips, A. L. 1998. "The Politics of Reconciliation in Germany and in Central-East Europe." *German Politics* 7(2):64–85.

Piderit, S. 2000. "Rethinking Resistance and Recognizing Ambivalence: A Multidimensional View of Attitudes toward Organization Change." *Academy of Management Review* 25(4): 783–794.

Powell, C. 1996. *Juan Carlos of Spain*. London: Macmillan.

"Rainbow Warrior," *International Arbitration Report* 5, 1990.

Ram, U. 1993. *Israeli Society: Critical Aspects*. Tel Aviv: Breirot.

Rambam (Maimonides). *Mishneh Torah, Hilchoth Teshuvah* 1(1): 2:9–10.

Raven, B. 1990. "Political Application of the Psychology of Interpersonal Influence and Social Behavior." *Political Psychology* 11(3):493–520.

Raven, B. 1993. "The Bases of Social Power: Origins and Recent Developments." *Journal of Social Issues* 49(4):227–252.

Reardon, B. A. 1988. *Comprehensive Peace Education: Educating for Global Responsibility*. New York: Teachers College Press.

Rehm, P. H., and D. R. Beatty. 1996. "Legal Consequences of Apologizing." *Journal of Dispute Resolution* 7: 115–130.

Rigby, A. 2000. "Forgiving the Past: Paths Towards a Culture of Reconciliation." Paper presented at the IPRA Conference, Tampere, Finland.

Rittner, C., and J. K. Roth. 2000. "Indifference to the Plight of the Jews During the Holocaust." In *The Holocaust and the Christian World: Reflections on the Past and Challenges for the Future*, eds. C. Rittner, S. D. Smith, and I. Steinfeldt, pp. 38–41. London: Kuperard.

Rittner, C., S. D. Smith, and I. Steinfeldt, eds. 2000. *The Holocaust and the Christian World: Reflections on the Past and Challenges for the Future*. London: Kuperard.

Ron, J. 2000. "Savage Restraint: Israel, Palestine and the Dialectics of Legal Repression." *Social Problems* 47(4): 445–472.

Rosenberg, S., and G. Wolfsfeld. 1977. "International Conflict and the Problem of Attribution." *Journal of Conflict Resolution* 21:75–103.

Ross, L. 1995. "Reactive Devaluation in Negotiation and Conflict Resolution." In *Barriers to the Negotiated Resolution of Conflict*, eds. K. Arrow, R. Mnookin, L. Ross, A. Tversky, and R. Wilson, pp. 26–42. New York: Norton.

Ross, L. 2000. "Understanding Misunderstanding: Social Psychological Perspectives." Department of Psychology, Stanford University, Stanford, Calif.

Ross, L., and A. Ward. 1996. "Naive Realism in Everyday Life: Implications for Social Conflict and Misunderstanding." In *Values and Knowledge*, eds. T. Brown, E. Reed, and E. Turiel, pp. 103–135. Hillsdale, N.J.: Erlbaum.

Ross, M. H. 1993a. *The Culture of Conflict: Interpretations and Interests in Comparative Perspective*. New Haven and London: Yale University Press.

Ross, M. H. 1993b. *The Management of Conflict: Interpretations and Interests in Comparative Perspective*. New Haven and London: Yale University Press.

Ross, M. H. 1995. "Psychocultural Interpretation Theory and Peacemaking in Ethnic Conflict." *Political Psychology* 16: 523–544.

Ross, M. H. 1997. "Culture and Identity in Comparative Political Analysis." In *Comparative Politics: Rationality, Culture, and Structure*, eds. M. I. Lichbach and A. S. Zuckerman, pp. 42–80. Cambridge: Cambridge University Press.

Ross, M. H. 1998. "Democracy as Joint Problem Solving: Addressing Interests and Identities in Divided Societies." *Nationalism and Ethnic Politics* 4 (winter): 19–46.

Ross, M. H. 2000a. "Good Enough Isn't So Bad: Success and Failure in Ethnic Conflict Management." *Peace and Conflict: Journal of Peace Psychology* 6: 27–47.

Ross, M. H. 2000b. "Creating the Conditions for Peacemaking: Theories of Practice in Ethnic Conflict Resolution." *Ethnic and Racial Studies* 23(6): 1002–1034.

Ross, M. H. 2001. "Psychocultural Interpretations and Dramas: Identity Dynamics in Ethnic Conflict." *Political Psychology* 22(1): 157–178.

Rotem, T. 2001. "Too Radical for the Co-Existence Industry." *Ha'aretz*, May 24, B5 (Hebrew).

Rothman, J. 1992. *From Confrontation to Cooperation: Resolving Ethnic and Regional Conflict.* Newbury Park, Calif.: Sage Publications.

Rothstein, R. L., ed. 1999a. *After the Peace: Resistance and Reconciliation.* Boulder, Colo.: Lynne Rienner.

Rothstein, R. L. 1999b. "In Fear of Peace: Getting Past Maybe." In *After the Peace: Resistance and Reconciliation,* ed. R. L. Rothstein, pp. 1–25. Boulder, Colo.: Lynne Rienner.

Rothstein, R. L. 1999c. "Fragile Peace and Its Aftermath." In *After the Peace: Resistance and Reconciliation,* ed. R. L. Rothstein, pp. 223–248. Boulder, Colo.: Lynne Rienner.

Rouhana, N. N. 1997. *Palestinian Citizens in an Ethnic Jewish State: Identities in Conflict.* New Haven and London: Yale University Press.

Rouhana, N. N. In press. "Reconciliation in Protracted National Conflict: Identity and Power in the Israeli-Palestinian Case." In *The Social Psychology of Group Identity and Social Conflict: Theory, Application, and Practice,* eds. A. H. Eagly, V. L. Hamilton, and R. M. Baron. Washington, D.C.: American Psychological Association.

Rouhana, N. N., and D. Bar-Tal. 1998. "Psychological Dynamic of Intractable Ethnonational Conflicts: The Israeli-Palestinian Case." *American Psychologist* 53(7):761–770.

Rouhana, N. N., and H. C. Kelman. 1994. "Promoting Joint Thinking in International Conflicts: An Israeli-Palestinian Continuing Workshop." *Journal of Social Issues* 50(1):157–178.

Rubin, J. Z., G. Pruitt, and S. Kim. 1994. *Social Conflict: Escalation, Stalemate, and Settlement.* New York: McGraw-Hill.

Russett, M. B. 1993. *Grasping the Democratic Peace.* Princeton: Princeton University Press.

Russett, M. B., and H. Starr. 1992. *World Politics: The Menu for Choice.* New York: Freeman.

Russett, M. B., and J. R. Oneal. 2001. *Triangulating Peace: Democracy, Interdependence, and International Organization.* Princeton: Princeton University Press.

Ryback, T. W. 1996–97. "Dateline Sudetenland: Hostages to History." *Foreign Policy,* No. 105, 162–178.

Saidi, N. H. 1994. "The Economic Construction of Lebanon: War, Peace, and Modernization." In *Peace for Lebanon? From War to Reconstruction,* ed. D. Collings, pp. 195–212. Boulder, Colo.: Lynne Rienner.

Sambanis, N. 2000. "Partition as a Solution to Ethnic War." *World Politics* 52(4): 437–483.

Sarghie, H., and S. Bashir. 2000. "The Holocaust of the Jews, al-Nakba of the Palestinians." *Ha'aretz*, February 21 (trans. from *Al-Hayat*) (Hebrew and English editions).

Saunders, H., ed. 1999. *A Public Peace Process*. New York: St. Martin's.

Scheff, T. J. 1994. *Bloody Revenge: Emotions, Nationalism, and War*. Boulder, Colo.: Westview Press.

Schnell, I., M. Awerbuch, and Y. Manor. 2000. "Peace Now—Palestinian Dialogue." Unpublished paper.

Segev, T. 1990. *The Seventh Million*. Jerusalem: Keter (Hebrew).

Sells, M. 1996. *The Bridge Betrayed: Religion and Genocide in Bosnia*. Berkeley and Los Angeles: University of California Press.

Sereseres, C. 1996. "The Regional Peacekeeping Role of the Organization of American States: Nicaragua, 1990–1993." In *Managing Global Chaos: Sources of and Responses to International Conflict*, eds. C. A. Crocker, F. O. Hampson, and P. Aall, pp. 531–562. Washington, D.C.: United States Institute of Peace Press.

Shapiro, M. J., and H. R. Alker, eds. 1996. *Challenging Boundaries*. Minneapolis: University of Minnesota Press.

Sharoni, S. 1995. *Gender and the Israeli-Palestinian Conflict*. Syracuse: Syracuse University Press.

Sherif, M., et al. 1988. *The Robbers Cave Experiment: Intergroup Conflict and Cooperation* (with a new introduction by D. T. Campbell). Middletown, Conn.: Wesleyan University Press.

Shinar, F. 1967. *B'Ol Korah Uregashot*. Tel Aviv: Schocken (Hebrew).

Shonholtz, R. 1998. "Conflict Resolution Moves East: How the Emerging Democracies of Central and Eastern Europe Are Facing Interethnic Conflict." In *The Handbook of Interethnic Coexistence*, ed. E. Weiner, pp. 359–368. New York: Continuum.

Shook, E. V., and L. K. K. Kwan. 1991. "Ho'oponopono: Straightening Family Relationships in Hawaii." In *Conflict Resolution: Cross-Cultural Perspectives*, eds. K. Avruch, P. Black, and J. Scimecca. New York: Greenwood Press.

Shriver, D. W., Jr. 1995. *An Ethic for Enemies: Forgiveness in Politics*. New York: Oxford University Press.

Shriver, D. W., Jr. 1998. "Is There Forgiveness in Politics? Germany, Vietnam and America." In *Exploring Forgiveness*, eds. R. D. Enright and J. North, pp. 131–149. Madison: University of Wisconsin Press.

Shriver, D. W., Jr. 1999. "The Long Road to Reconciliation: Some Moral Stepping-Stones." In *After the Peace: Resistance and Reconciliation*, ed. R. L. Rothstein, pp. 207–222. Boulder, Colo.: Lynne Rienner.

Shuman, D. W. 2000. "The Role of Apology in Tort Law." *Judicature* 83: 180–189.

Silverstein, B. 1989. "Enemy Images: The Psychology of U.S. Attitudes and Cognitions Regarding the Soviet Union." *American Psychologist* 44(6): 903–913.

Silverstein, B., and C. Flamenbaum. 1989. "Biases in the Perception and Cognition of Actions of Enemies." *Journal of Social Issues* 45(2): 51–72.

Simpson, G. 1997. "Reconstruction and Reconciliation: Emerging from Transition." *Development in Practice* 7(4):475–478.

Simpson, G. 2000. "Tell No Lies, Claim No Victories: A Brief Evaluation of South Africa's Truth and Reconciliation Commission." *CSVR Papers,* pp. 1–8.

Smith, A. 1991. *National Identity.* Reno, Las Vegas, and London: University of Nevada Press.

Smith C. G., ed. 1971. *Conflict Resolution: Contribution of the Behavioral Sciences.* Notre Dame, Ind.: University of Notre Dame Press.

Smitt, E. W. J. 1943. "Sin and Forgiveness in the Old Testament." Unpublished doctoral dissertation, Drew Theological Seminary.

Spalding, R. J. 1999. "From Low-Intensity War to Low-Intensity Peace: The Nicaraguan Peace Process." In *Comparative Peace Processes in Latin America,* ed. C. J. Arnson, pp. 31–64. Stanford, Calif.: Stanford University Press.

Sparks, A. 1995. *Tomorrow Is Another Country.* New York: Hill and Wang.

Staub, E. 1998. "Breaking the Cycle of Genocidal Violence: Healing and Reconciliation." In *Perspectives on Loss: A Sourcebook,* ed. J. H. Harvey, pp. 231–238. Philadelphia: Brunner/Mazel.

Staub, E. 2000. "Genocide and Mass Killing: Origins, Prevention, Healing and Reconciliation." *Political Psychology* 21:367–382.

Staub, E., and L. Pearlman. 2001. "Healing, Forgiveness and Reconciliation After Genocide and Other Collective Violence." In *Forgiveness and Reconciliation: Religion, Public Policy and Conflict Transformation,* eds. R. G. Helmick and R. L. Peterson. Radnor, Pa.: Templeton Foundation Press.

Stein, J. G. 1994. "Political Learning by Doing: Gorbachev as Uncommitted Thinker and Motivated Leader." *International Organization* 48(2): 155–183.

Steinberg, G. M. 2001. "Conflict Prevention and Mediation in the Jewish Tradition." *Jewish Political Studies Review* 12(1–2):3–21.

Stephenson, C. M. 1999. "Peace Studies: Overview." In *Encyclopedia of Violence, Peace and Conflict,* ed. L. Kurtz, pp. 809–820. San Diego: Academic Press.

Tajfel, H. 1981. *Human Groups and Social Categories.* Cambridge: Cambridge University Press.

Takezawa, Y. I. 1995. *Breaking the Silence: Redress and Japanese American Ethnicity.* Ithaca: Cornell University Press.

Tambiah, S. J. 1986. *Sri Lanka: Ethnic Fratricide and the Dismantling of Democracy.* London: I. B. Tauris.

Tanase, T. 1990. "The Management of Disputes: Automobile Accident Compensation in Japan." *Law and Society Review* 24.

Tannen, D. 1996. "I'm Sorry, I Won't Apologize." *New York Times Magazine,* July 21.

Tavuchis, N. 1991. Mea Culpa: *A Sociology of Apology and Reconciliation.* Stanford, Calif.: Stanford University Press.

Tetlock, P. E. 1991. "Learning in U.S. and Soviet Foreign Policy: In Search of an Elusive Concept." In *Learning in U.S. and Soviet Foreign Policy,* eds. G. W. Breslaver and P. E. Tetlock, pp. 20–61. Boulder, Colo.: Westview Press.

Theissen, G. n.d. "Object of Trust and Hatred: Public Attitudes Towards the Truth and Reconciliation Commission." Transitional Justice Project of the University of the Western Cape and Humboldt University, Johannesburg, n.d.

Thompson, J. L. P. 1990. "Genocide and Social Conflict: A Partial Theory and a Comparison." In *Research in Social Movements, Conflicts and Change*, ed. L. Kriesberg, pp. 245–266. Greenwich, Conn.: JAI Press.

Thompson, L., and R. Hastie. 1990. "Social Perception in Negotiation." *Organizational Behavior and Human Decision Processes* 47: 98–123.

Thompson, M. 1997. "Conflict, Reconstruction and Reconciliation: Reciprocal Lessons for NGOs in Southern Africa and Central Africa." *Development in Practice* 7: 505–509.

Turner, V. 1957. *Schism and Continuity in an African Society: A Study of Ndembu Village Life*. Manchester: Manchester University Press.

Turner, V. 1974. "Social Dramas and Ritual Metaphors." In *Dramas, Fields, and Metaphors: Symbolic Action in Human Society*. pp. 23–59. Ithaca: Cornell University Press.

Tutu, D. 1999. *No Future Without Forgiveness*. New York: Doubleday.

Tutu, D. 2000. "Reconciliation in Post-Apartheid South Africa: Experience of the Truth Commission." In *The Art of Peace: Nobel Peace Laureates Discuss Human Rights, Conflict and Reconciliation*. Ithaca, N.Y.: Snow Lion Publications.

Van der Veer, P. 1994. *Religious Nationalism: Hindus and Muslims in India*. Berkeley and Los Angeles: University of California Press.

Volkan, V. D. 1988. *The Need to Have Enemies and Allies: From Clinical Practice to International Relationships*. New York: Jason Aronson.

Volkan, V. D. 1990. "An Overview of Psychological Concepts Pertinent to Interethnic and/or International Relationships." In *The Psychodynamics of International Relationships*, eds. V. D. Volkan, D. A. Julius, and J. V. Montville, Vol. 1., *Concepts and Theories*, pp. 31–46. Lexington, Mass.: Lexington Books.

Volkan, V. D. 1997. *Bloodlines: From Ethnic Pride to Ethnic Terrorism*. New York: Farrar, Straus & Giroux.

Volkan, V. D. 1998a. "The Tree Model: Psychopolitical Dialogues and the Promotion of Coexistence." In *The Handbook of Interethnic Coexistence*, ed. E. Weiner, pp. 343–358. New York: Continuum.

Volkan, V. D. 1998b. "Ethnicity and Nationalism: A Psychoanalytic Perspective." *Applied Psychology* 47(1): 45–59.

Volpe, M. R. 1998. "Using Town Meetings to Foster Peaceful Coexistence." In *The Handbook of Interethnic Coexistence*, ed. E. Weiner, pp. 382–396. New York: Continuum.

Voutira, E., and S. A. Whishaw Brown. 1995. *Conflict Resolution: A Review of Some Non-governmental Practices—A Cautionary Tale*. Report No. 4. Uppsala, Sweden: Nordic Africa Institute.

Wagatsuma, H., and A. Rosett. 1986. "The Implications of Apology: Law and Culture in Japan and the United States." *Law and Society Review* 20.

Wagner-Pacifici, R., and B. Schwartz. 1991. "The Vietnam Veterans Memorial: Commemorating a Difficult Past." *American Journal of Sociology* 97:376–420.

Wall, J. A., Jr., and R. R. Callister. 1995. "Ho'oponopono: Some Lessons from Hawaiian Mediation." *Negotiation Journal* 11:45–54.

Waltz, K. N. 1979. *Theory of International Politics*. New York: Random House.

Warner, W. L. 1959. "The Symbolic Relations of the Dead and the Living." In *The Living and the Dead*, pp. 248–279. New Haven: Yale University Press.

Watson, G. 1969. "Resistance to Change." In *The Planning of Change*, 2nd ed., eds. W. Bennis, K. Benne, and R. Chin, pp. 488–497. New York: Holt, Rinehart & Winston.

Weick, K., and R. Quinn. 1999. "Organizational Change and Development." *Annual Review of Psychology* 50:361–386.

Weiner, E., ed. 1998. *The Handbook of Interethnic Coexistence*. New York: Continuum.

Weiwen, Z., and G. Deshingkar. 1995. "Improving Sino-Indo Relations." In *Crisis Prevention, Confidence Building and Reconciliation in South Asia*, eds. M. Krepon and A. Sevak, pp. 227–238. New York: St. Martin's.

Wendt, A. 1992. "Anarchy Is What States Make of It: The Social Construction of Power Politics." *International Organization* 46:391–425.

White, R. 1984. *Fearful Warriors: A Psychological Profile of U.S.–Soviet Relations*. New York: Free Press.

Whiteman, M. M. 1937. *Damages in International Law*. Washington, D.C.: U.S. Government Printing Office.

Whittaker, D. J. 1999. *Conflict and Reconciliation in the Contemporary World*. London: Routledge.

Wiesel, E. 1995a. *All Rivers Run to the Sea*. New York: A. A. Knopf.

Wiesel, E. 1995b. "Telling the Tale." In *Against Silence: The Voice and Vision of Elie Wiesel*, ed. I. Abrahamson. New York: Holocaust Library, Vol. 3, I:234.

Wiesel, E. 2000. *And the Sea Is Never Full*. London: Harper Collins.

Wiesenthal, S. 1997. *The Sunflower: On the Possibilities and Limits of Forgiveness*, 2nd ed. New York: Schocken.

Willis, F. R. 1965. *France, Germany, and the New Europe, 1945–1963*. Palo Alto, Calif.: Stanford University Press.

Wilmer, F. 1998. "The Social Construction of Conflict Reconciliation in the Former Yugoslavia." *Social Justice: A Journal of Crime, Conflict and World Order* 25(4): 90–113.

Wittgenstein, L. 1953/1968. *Philosophical Investigations*. New York: Macmillan.

Witztum, D. 1993. "The Image of Germany in Israel: The Role of the Media." In *Normal Relations: The Israel-Germany Relations*, eds. M. Zimmerman and O. Heilbruner, pp. 103–128. Jerusalem: Magnes Press of the Hebrew University (Hebrew).

Wolffsohn, M. 1993. *Eternal Guilt?* New York: Columbia University Press.

Wolfsfeld, G. 1997a. *Media and Political Conflict: News from the Middle East*. Cambridge: Cambridge University Press.

Wolfsfeld, G. 1997b. "Fair Weather Friends: The Varying Role of the News Media in the Arab-Israeli Peace Process." *Political Communication* 14:29–48.

Woodward, S. L. 1999. "Bosnia After Dayton: Transforming a Compromise into a State." In *After the Peace: Resistance and Reconciliation*, ed. R. L. Rothstein, pp. 139–166. Boulder, Colo.: Lynne Rienner.

Worchel, S. 1986. "The Role of Cooperation in Reducing Intergroup Conflict." In *Psychology of Intergroup Relations*, eds., S. Worchel and W. Austin, pp. 288–304. Chicago: Nelson-Hall.

Wu, P. Y. 1979. "Self-Examination and Confession of Sins in Traditional China." *Harvard Journal of Asiatic Studies* 39:5–38.

Yalom, I. 1985. *The Theory and Practice of Group Psychotherapy*. New York: Basic Books.

Yardley, J. 2000. "Panel Recommends Reparations in Long-Ignored Tulsa Race Riot." *New York Times*, February 5.

Yehoshua, A. B. 1998. "Selicha." *Alpayim* 16:178–185 (Hebrew).

Zalaquett, J. 1999. "Truth, Justice, and Reconciliation: Lessons for the International Community." In *Comparative Peace Processes in Latin America*, ed. C. J. Arnson, pp. 341–361. Stanford, Calif.: Stanford University Press.

Zartman, I. W. 1995. *Ripe for Conflict Resolutions and Intervention in Africa*. New York: Oxford University Press.

Zartman, I. W., and J. L. Rasmussen, eds. 1997. *Peacemaking in International Conflict: Methods and Techniques*. Washington, D.C.: United States Institute of Peace Press.

Zimmerman, M. 1993. "The Memory of the War and the Holocaust in Germany: The Place of Israel." In *Normal Relations: The Israel-Germany Relations*, eds. M. Zimmerman and O. Heilbruner, pp. 87–102. Jerusalem: Magnes (Hebrew).

PRESS

Al Ahram, May 3–9, Cairo, Egypt: The Al Ahram Foundation.

BBC News Online, 1998–2000. London, England: BBC. http://www.bbc.co.uk/

Daily Telegraph, August 16, 1995. London, England: Telegraph Group, Ltd. http://www.telegraph.co.uk/

Der Spiegel, May 7, 2001. Hamburg, Germany: Spiegel-Gruppe Presse-Service. http://www.spiegel.de/

Foreign Broadcast Information Service Daily Report, November 19, 1995. China: reporting Zhongguo Tongxun She, January 3, 1995.

Ha'aretz, January 22 and 30, 2001. Jerusalem, Israel: Har'aretz Daily Newspaper, Inc.

London Times, April 10 and 11, 1980; May 2 and 23, 1980. London, England: Times Newspapers Ltd. http://www.timesonline.co.uk/

Le Monde, April 30, 1991. Paris, France: Le Monde.

New York Times, May 15, 1999; June 17, 1999; April 7, 2001; January 4, 2001. New York, New York, U.S.A: The New York Times Company.

Washington Post, February 27, 2001; March 2, 2001. Washington D.C., U.S.A: The Washington Post Co. http://www.washingtonpost.com/

Index

Page numbers in *italics* refer to tables and figures.